ABRAHAM

ABRAHAM

The Story of a Life

Joseph Blenkinsopp

WILLIAM B. EERDMANS PUBLISHING COMPANY

GRAND RAPIDS, MICHIGAN / CAMBRIDGE, U.K.

Published 2015 by
Wm. B. Eerdmans Publishing Co.
2140 Oak Industrial Drive N.E., Grand Rapids, Michigan 49505 /
P.O. Box 163, Cambridge CB3 9PU U.K.

Printed in the United States of America

21 20 19 18 17 16 15   7 6 5 4 3 2 1

Library of Congress Cataloging-in-Publication Data

ISBN 978-0-8028-7287-6

www.eerdmans.com

Contents

v

Contents

CONTENTS

Preface: A Word about Reading

Reading is an art that, like writing, we have to learn. This is especially so with texts that come to us from unfamiliar cultures and ancient times, both of which situations apply to biblical texts. It is no secret that the critical reading of biblical texts, which comes under the rubric of the historical-critical method, has fallen out of favor in large sections of the biblical studies guild, not least among English-language practitioners. Historical-critical readings are indicted on the grounds that they objectify the text, reducing it to a potential source of information or a puzzle to be solved. This approach is also taken to imply that a text has only one correct interpretation, the one intended by the author, or dictated by the circumstances and contingencies in which the text was produced. Yet the historical-critical reading of texts was concerned, no less than any other method, with getting at the meaning of the text, not just identifying its historical referents — individuals, events, social situations, etc. The difference is that it operates on the assumption that the circumstances of the production and reception of the text are important ways of getting at its meaning.

The historical-critical method is located somewhere near one end of a spectrum to which corresponds, at the other end, the idea of the text as a sort of Rorschach ink blot that serves to elicit responses, insights, and emotions that may and often will differ from one reader to the next. On this view, meanings inscribed in texts are as fluid, indeterminate, and perspectival as the cloud to which Hamlet draws the attention of Polonius in *Hamlet,* act 3, scene 2:

> H: Do you see yonder cloud that's almost in shape of a camel?
> P: By th'mass, and 'tis like a camel indeed!

H: Methinks it is like a weasel.
P: It is backt like a weasel.
H: Or like a whale.
P: Very like a whale.

Like all texts, biblical texts are open to a multiplicity of interpretations. But to state this raises at once the question whether there are criteria for demonstrating that some interpretations are better than others, or that this or that interpretation is simply wrong. To state it differently: we may ask whether the text imposes any constraints on the interpreter. We can subscribe, with some reservations, to the "intentional fallacy," that is, we can admit that the intention of the author does not foreclose discussions about meaning; but with biblical texts the issue does not arise since the authors are unavailable and, for the most part, unidentifiable. We may, however, speak in a certain sense of the *intentionality* of the text as manifested or betrayed by the adoption of certain literary conventions. This was the point of studying literary forms in the social contexts that generated them, a study known as form criticism, or the history of forms, or, using the German equivalent, *Formgeschichte.* The idea behind form criticism is that adoption of a specific literary genre, type, or form embodies, especially in ancient texts, an intentionality dictated directly or indirectly by the social situation in which the form had its original location. Even when used in an artificial or ironic fashion, the form or genre *(Gattung)* provides clues to the range of appropriate readings of the text. One would think that neglect of this aspect of the reader's task would not make for good interpretations.

A good reading is always a matter of delicate and precarious balance between text and reader. As Umberto Eco put it, the text is a *macchina pigra* (a lazy machine) needing the cooperation of the reader for the production of meaning. The encounter between text and reader should aim to resemble a successful conversation in which both partners listen and in which there takes place what Hans-Georg Gadamer called a fusion or overlapping of horizons. For this to happen, the reader must respect the otherness of the textual interlocutor, which includes awareness that the text is speaking from a different culture and a different epoch. I would view the historical-critical method, when practiced in a discriminating and imaginative way, as essential for enabling the text to hold up its end of the conversation and to say what it has to say.

It remains true that the historical-critical method is only one of many approaches and perspectives available to the exegete and reader of biblical texts. Some may be surprised to hear that the idea that biblical texts, like all texts, are patient of multiple interpretations is not a discovery of modern or postmodern literary theorists. It was already part of the received wisdom during the patristic period and came to classical expression in the four senses of Scripture of the medieval scholastics: literal, allegorical, moral, anagogical. But it was precisely the tendency of the allegorical method, beloved of the Church Fathers as it was of Philo, to slip into a quite arbitrary mode of interpretation, which led in the medieval period to the promotion of the *sensus litteralis* in Christian exegesis and the *peshat* ("simple," "literal" exposition) in Jewish exegesis.

The words "discursive commentary," of which this book is an example, describe a mode of exposition that, while being basically historical-critical, tries to bear in mind and lead into issues of general theological and human interest that the biblical text itself, and its later elaborations, present for our consideration. It looks for readers who are prepared to make an effort to understand the issues but are in no sense specialists in ancient and especially biblical texts. To that end, I have taken care that the text of the commentary, arranged in ten chapters, is fully intelligible to such readers and purged as far as possible of technical language. The footnotes for the most part document what is said in the text, and are especially for the benefit of biblical specialists and those who feel the need to probe further. Finally, reading the rather long introduction is not a necessary precondition for working through the commentary. It could be read or referred back to at any point where the reader desires further explanation.

I conclude with a brief epilogue setting out my view, as a Christian, on Abraham, drawing on early Christian texts and also on the commentary. Over the past several years, many excellent contributions to interfaith dialogue have taken the figure of Abraham as a starting point for exploring convergences and testing boundaries. I have chosen to take a different approach, but in doing so I of course do not wish to belittle the value of interfaith conversations or, much less, to claim Abraham for one of the three traditions that claim, each in its own way, to be "Abrahamic." Nonetheless, I hope that there may still be some value in a reflection on Abraham as viewed from the perspective of one faith. Kierkegaard's pseudonymous author repeatedly expresses his despair as he tries to come to terms with this great yet obscure figure: "Father Abraham, who can understand you!" I would venture to say that none of the three Abrahamic faiths, not even all of them in conversation, has yet arrived at a full understanding of Abraham. We all have much to learn from one another, and it seemed to me a good idea to return once again to a careful, critical reading of the written record about Abraham and its early commentators.

It remains for me to thank Yale University Press for permission to use a slightly revised version of the section "A Prefatory Word about Reading" in my *Isaiah 40–55: A New Translation with Introduction and Commentary,* AB 19A (New Haven and London: Yale University Press, 2002), 124-26. A very special word of thanks to the patient and generous Mr. Allen Myers of William B. Eerdmans Publishing Company and his colleagues, who have been putting up with me now longer than anyone could reasonably expect. Above all, I am indebted to my beloved wife, to whom I owe more than I can tell.

Abbreviations

AASOR	Annual of the American Schools of Oriental Research
AB	Anchor Bible
ABD	*Anchor Bible Dictionary*. Edited by David Noel Freedman. 6 vols. New York: Doubleday, 1992
Abot R. Nat.	*Abot de Rabbi Nathan*
ADPV	Abhandlungen des Deutschen Palästinavereins
Ag. Ber.	*Aggadat Berešit*
AnBib	Analecta biblica
ANESTP	*The Ancient Near East: Supplementary Texts and Pictures Relating to the Old Testament*. Edited by J. B. Pritchard. Princeton: Princeton University Press, 1969
ANET	*Ancient Near Eastern Texts Relating to the Old Testament*. Edited by James B. Pritchard. 3rd ed. Princeton: Princeton University Press, 1969
Ant.	*Jewish Antiquities*
Apoc. Abr.	*Apocalypse of Abraham*
b.	Babylonian Talmud
b. Avod. Zar.	*b. Avodah Zarah*
b. Ber.	*b. Berakot*
b. B. Mesiʿa	*b. Baba Mesiʿa*
b. Hor.	*b. Horayot*
b. Naz.	*b. Nazir*
b. Ned.	*b. Nedarim*
b. Pes.	*b. Pesahim*
b. Qidd.	*b. Qiddušim*
b. Šabb.	*b. Šabbat*
b. Sanh.	*b. Sanhedrin*
b. Yeb.	*b. Yebamot*

BA	*Biblical Archaeologist*
BASOR	*Bulletin of the American Schools of Oriental Research*
Bib.	*Biblica*
BibOr	Biblica et orientalia
BKAT	Biblischer Kommentar: Altes Testament
BN	*Biblische Notizen*
BZ	*Biblische Zeitschrift*
BZAW	Beihefte zur Zeitschrift für die alttestamentliche Wissenschaft
C. Ap.	*Contra Apion*
CBQ	*Catholic Biblical Quarterly*
DDD	*Dictionary of Deities and Demons in the Bible.* Edited by Karel van der Toorn et al. Leiden: Brill; Grand Rapids: Eerdmans, 1999
DJD	Discoveries in the Judaean Desert. Oxford: Clarendon
EDSS	*Encyclopedia of the Dead Sea Scrolls.* Edited by Lawrence H. Schiffman and James C. VankerKam. 2 vols. Oxford: Oxford University Press, 1993, 2000
Ep. Barn.	*Epistle of Barnabas*
Exp.T.	*Expository Times*
FS	*Festschrift*
Gen. Rab.	*Genesis Rabbah*
HAT	Handbuch zum Alten Testament
HSM	Harvard Semitic Monographs
Hen.	*Henoch*
HUCA	*Hebrew Union College Annual*
IDB	*The Interpreter's Dictionary of the Bible.* Edited by G. A. Buttrick. 4 vols. Nashville: Abingdon, 1962
IDBSup	*Interpreter's Dictionary of the Bible: Supplementary Volume.* Edited by J. Crim. Nashville: Abingdon, 1976
IEJ	*Israel Exploration Journal*
Int.	*Interpretation*
JANESCU	*Journal of the Ancient Near Eastern Society of Columbia University*
JBL	*Journal of Biblical Literature*
JCS	*Journal of Cuneiform Studies*
JJS	*Journal of Jewish Studies*
JSOT	*Journal for the Study of the Old Testament*
JSOTSup	Journal for the Study of the Old Testament: Supplement Series
JSS	*Journal of Semitic Studies*
Jub.	*Book of Jubilees*
KTU	*Die keilalphabetischen Texte aus Ugarit.* Edited by M. Dietrich, O. Loretz, and J. Sanmartín.
LXX	Septuagint
m.	Mishnah

m. Ned.	*m. Nedarim*
m. Qidd.	*m. Qiddušim*
MT	Masoretic Text
NCB	New Century Bible
NEAEHL	*The New Encyclopedia of Archaeological Excavations in the Holy Land.* Edited by E. Stern. 4 vols. Jerusalem: Israel Exploration Society and Carta, 1993
NRSV	New Revised Standard Version
OTL	Old Testament Library
OTP	*Old Testament Pseudepigrapha.* Edited by James H. Charlesworth. 2 vols. Garden City, N.Y.: Doubleday, 1983-1985
OTS	*Oudtestamentische Studiën*
Pirqe R. El.	*Pirqe de Rabbi Eliezer*
Praep. ev.	Eusebius: *Praeparatio evangelica*
Pss. Sol.	*The Psalms of Solomon*
RB	*Revue biblique*
REB	Revised English Version
Sem.	*Semitica*
SJOT	*Scandinavian Journal of Theology*
t.	Tosefta
TDOT	*Theological Dictionary of the Old Testament.* Edited by G. J. Botterweck, H. Ringgren, and H. J. Fabry. 8 vols. Grand Rapids: Eerdmans, 1964-1976
Tg. Neof.	*Targum Neofiti*
Tg. Ps.-J.	*Targum Pseudo-Jonathan*
Tg. Yer.	*Targum Yerushalmi*
TLOT	*Theological Lexicon of the Old Testament.* Edited by E. Jenni, with assistance from C. Westermann. Translated by M. E. Biddle. 3 vols. Peabody, Mass.: Hendrickson, 1994
Transeu	*Transeuphratène*
TZ	*Theologische Zeitschrift*
VT	*Vetus Testamentum*
WMANT	Wissenschaftliche Monographien zum Alten und Neuen Testament
y.	Jerusalem Talmud
y. Šabb.	*y. Šabbat*
ZAW	*Zeitschrift für die alttestamentliche Wissenschaft*
ZTK	*Zeitschrift für Theologie und Kirche*

The Figure of Abraham in the Bible and Beyond

Abraham in the Historical Books

Abraham is a figure from the past known to us exclusively from the Hebrew Bible, and even in the Hebrew Bible he has a relatively low profile
apart from the narrative cycle in Genesis.[1] But it would be imprudent to
conclude from this lack of evidence external to the biblical texts that Abraham is a purely literary creation. Many examples from different parts of
the world and different cultures demonstrate the remarkable durability
of long-dead ancestors and long-past founding events in the collective
memory of societies, however enhanced, refracted, or distorted with the
passage of centuries these memories may be and usually are. On the other
hand, the practice, common in an earlier generation, of arguing from the
realistic presentation of a Middle or Late Bronze Age background (ca.
2000 to ca. 1200 B.C.) to the historicity of Abraham and the other principal
characters in the cycle is equally suspect. Writing in 1949, William Foxwell
Albright claimed that "aside from a few diehards among older scholars,
there is scarcely a single biblical historian who has not been impressed by
the rapid accumulation of data supporting the substantial historicity of
patriarchal tradition."[2] The physical and social background of the land of

---

1. For ease of reading, I have referred to the main character in this work as Abraham
throughout, even though prior to Gen. 17 he is referred to as Abram. I have also referred to
his wife as Sarah throughout, even though prior to Gen. 17 she is referred to as Sarai.

2. William Foxwell Albright, *The Biblical Period from Abraham to Ezra: An Historical
Survey* (New York: Harper and Row, 1949), 2. The relevance of much of this accumulation
of data to the Abraham cycle has since been subjected to serious questioning, notably by
Thomas Thompson, *The Historicity of the Patriarchal Narratives*, BZAW 133 (Berlin: De

Uz in the folktale prologue in Job 1–2 reads much like the Abraham story — feasting, religious practices, large households with many dependents, wealth consisting in flocks, camels, donkeys, and other domestic animals — but Job is without doubt a figure from the legendary past, as is explicitly stated in Ezek. 14:14, 20. Speculation will doubtless continue, but in the absence of external evidence, Abraham's relation to real history will continue to elude us.

With one exception to be considered shortly, there are no narrative traditions about Abraham either in the Pentateuch outside of the Abraham story (Gen. 11:27–25:10) or in the Former Prophets (Joshua to 2 Kings). Throughout the rest of Genesis, after the notice about Abraham's death (25:7-10), we can trace a development leading to the triadic ancestral formula (Abraham, Isaac, Jacob) that became standard and is repeated fairly often in Deuteronomy, occasionally in Exodus-Numbers, and rarely in the Former Prophets, often referred to as the Deuteronomistic History. The evolution of the formula can be traced throughout Genesis: Isaac appeals to the God of Abraham (Gen. 26:23-24), and there are parallels in the Isaac cycle to incidents involving Abraham concerning such things as famines (26:1; cf. 12:10) and access to wells (26:15; cf. 21:25-32). Jacob encounters the God of Abraham and Isaac (28:13; 32:10), and in pronouncing a blessing over Joseph's sons, appeals to the God in whose presence Abraham and Isaac "walked," that is, lived out their lives (48:15-16). Joseph, finally, assures his brothers that the God of Abraham, Isaac, and Jacob will lead them out of Egypt into the Promised Land (50:24). This would therefore be the first use of the triadic and trinominal formula in the biblical record.

Behind the formula, however, especially when spelled out more fully as "the God of Abraham, the God of Isaac, and the God of Jacob," or when identified more explicitly with Yahweh, God of Israel (Exod. 3:6, 15-16;

Gruyter, 1974), and John Van Seters, *Abraham in History and Tradition* (New Haven: Yale University Press, 1975), but a Middle or Late Bronze setting for the physical environment and social customs reflected in the ancestral narratives still has its defenders; see several contributions to A. R. Millard and D. J. Wiseman, eds., *Essays on the Patriarchal Narratives* (Winona Lake, Ind.: Eisenbrauns, 1983); P. Kyle McCarter Jr., "The Historical Abraham," *Int.* 42 (1988): 341-52; A. R. Millard, "Abraham," in *ABD* 1:35-41. From an entirely different direction, Mario Liverani, *Oltre la Bibbia. Storia antica di Israele* (Rome and Bari: Editori Laterza, 2004), 29-30, suggests a possible connection between Abraham and a tribe with the name Raham or Rehem, mentioned on the Beth-shean stele of Seti I (*ANET* 255). Its members may have been known as Banu-Raham (literally "sons of Raham"), and its eponym would therefore have been Abu-Raham (i.e., Abraham).

4:5), some scholars have claimed to discern an early stage of religious development. In a famous essay with the title "The God of the Fathers," Albrecht Alt described a type of religious belief and practice among nomadic tribes like the Palmyrene and Nabatean Arabs according to which each tribe or clan was under the protection and guidance of its own deity whose title bore the name of the founder or head of the group. This practice, he claimed, throws important light on Israelite origins in general and the religious practices of the ancestors in particular.[3] It explains, for example, why the agreement between Laban and Jacob prior to their separation and Jacob's return to Canaan is witnessed to and guaranteed by their respective deities: the God of Nahor for Laban, Nahor's grandson; for Jacob, a deity named "the Fearsome One of Isaac."[4]

The one passage in the historical books in which Abraham is more than a name is the concluding episode in the book of Joshua, the covenant assembly convoked by Joshua at Shechem shortly before his death (Josh. 24:1-28). The historical survey recited by Joshua as prelude to the covenant making (24:2-13) begins not with Jacob, the eponymous ancestor, nor with Abraham, Isaac, and Jacob, but with the more primordial triad Terah, Abraham, and Nahor, described as "your ancestors of old" (24:2). Terah, therefore, is the primordial ancestor, the *Urvater*. Joshua's discourse goes beyond the Genesis narrative with the statement that the Terahite family worshiped other gods while living beyond the Euphrates. It then proceeds to relate how Abraham was led by God to Canaan and given many descendants beginning with Isaac, Jacob, and Esau. The recital is only apparently from the earliest period of Israel's history, however. There is a critical consensus that this *heilsgeschichtlich* (history of salvation) recital of Joshua, together with the account of the covenant of which it is a part, is a supplement to the book appended to the original Deuteronomistic conclusion in the previous chapter. It is therefore of late

---

3. Albrecht Alt, "Der Gott der Väter," first published in 1929, republished in *Kleine Schriften zur Geschichte des Volkes Israel 1* (Munich: C. H. Beck, 1959), 1-78; Eng. *Essays on Old Testament History and Religion* (Oxford: Blackwell, 1966), 1-77.

4. The more common translation of *paḥad yiṣḥāq* is "the Fear of Isaac," but "the Fearsome One" or "the Dreaded One" is more appropriate as a title. In the remote past it may have been attached to a demon that inspired terror; cf. *paḥad lāylâ* ("the Terror of the Night," Ps. 91:5) or *paḥad balêlôt* ("the Terror of the Night-time," Cant. 3:8). The proposal of William Foxwell Albright to translate the title with "the Kinsman of Isaac" is no longer in favor; see his *From the Stone Age to Christianity,* 2nd ed. (Garden City, N.Y.: Doubleday, 1957), 248, and, in general, H.-P. Müller, "פחד pāhad, פחד pahad I and II," in *TDOT* 11:517-26.

date, not far removed from the similar recital in Neh. 9:6-15, in a prayer attributed in the LXX to Ezra.[5]

Within the biblical historical material, therefore, the figure of Abraham and the traditions associated with him represent the latest stage in the formation of the complex narrative about the ancestors in Genesis. Like the mythic history of the archaic period preceding it, the Abraham story deals essentially in matters of genealogy and descent. This makes it easy to accept that the figure of Abraham and his place in the great family drama could have come about by a process of working backward from Jacob, with Isaac, the least developed figure of the three, providing the link in the genealogical chain. The process was enriched by the incorporation of traditions that originally had no connection with Abraham and the historical value of which is not easy to assess. An obvious example is the account of the fate of Sodom and the other associated cities, the tradition about which we know to have been in circulation from the time of the two kingdoms.[6] The distinctive element in the ancestral story is the presence of a deity who, for those who listen to his voice, guides the course of historical events and opens up a future.

Abraham in the Prophetic Books

A survey of the prophetic texts confirms the relatively late development of the Abraham narrative traditions. In all the prophetic writings, preexilic, exilic, and postexilic, whether originating in the north or the south, Jacob is by far the dominant ancestral figure with whom the people of Israel identify. Abraham is named four times in Isaiah (29:22; 41:8; 51:2; 63:16), once in Jeremiah (33:26, in the familiar "Abraham, Isaac, and Jacob"

5. According to Martin Noth, *Das Buch Josua,* 2nd ed., HAT (Tübingen: Mohr Siebeck, 1953), 135-39, Josh. 24 is a late Deuteronomistic creation, indicated, *inter alia,* by the list of nations (v. 11) and the inclusion of the Balaam cycle, as in Deut. 23:5-6. Other indications of Deuteronomism: "the hill country of Seir" (v. 4; cf. Deut. 1:2; 2:1, 5); hornets sent by God to clear the way for the Israelites (v. 12; cf. Deut. 7:20; Exod. 23:28); "towns you did not build, vineyards and olive groves you did not plant," to be occupied (v. 13; cf. Deut. 6:10-11). Van Seters, *Abraham in History and Tradition,* 142-43, notes in addition the Papyrus Sea episode in the account of the exodus (vv. 6-7), which is omitted from the historical surveys in Deut. 6 and 26 but present in later texts (Neh. 9:9; Ps. 136:13-15).

6. Sodom as symbolic of corruption with reference to Jerusalem in Isa. 1:9-10; 3:9; Jer. 23:14; Ezek. 16:44-58; as paradigm for destruction either actual or anticipated in Amos 4:11; Zeph. 2:9; Isa. 13:19; Jer. 49:18.

formula), once in Ezekiel (33:24), and once in Micah (7:20). Isaiah 29:22 introduces a saying addressed to the "house of Jacob" by Yahweh, "who redeemed Abraham." This redemption of Abraham may refer to one or another episode in the Abraham cycle, but it could also testify to an earlier date than suspected for the legend of Abraham's redemption from death at the hands of idolaters in Ur of the Chaldeans (Ur Kasdim), a theme known from the midrash and the *Apocalypse of Abraham,* the latter composed probably in the first century of the common era. But since, in any case, Isa. 29:22 is an appendix to Isa. 29:17-21 immediately preceding, which expresses the eschatological hope of the restoration of the created order, it is certainly late, perhaps as late as the Hellenistic period.[7] The finale of the book of Micah (7:18-20) consoles its readers by reminding them of their God's faithfulness shown to Jacob and his steadfast love manifested to Abraham. The combination of these qualities (Hebrew: *emet* and *ḥesed*) as an abiding characteristic of Israel's God is of frequent incidence in Psalms, the "Hymns Ancient and Modern" of the Second Temple,[8] and is presented as an ethical ideal, an *imitatio dei,* in Proverbs.[9] In the Sinai theophany Yahweh attributes to himself the same characteristics, adding that he is slow to anger and forgiving of iniquity and transgression (Exod. 34:6-7), qualities also presented in the Micah text. This verbal parallelism therefore favors a date in the postexilic period, and the same conclusion is suggested by the liturgical lament in the last chapter of the book.[10] Like Deutero-Isaiah, Micah also consistently refers to contemporary Judeans as Jacob, or the house of Jacob, and to Yahweh as "the God of Jacob" (4:2).

In the book of Amos, the only antecedent of Jacob as ancestor is Isaac, whose name serves as an alternative designation for the prophet's contemporaries in the kingdom of Samaria (7:9, 16). Since all the prophetic books were eventually edited and provided with titles in Jerusalem,

---

7. See Otto Kaiser, *Isaiah 13–39: A Commentary,* OTL (Philadelphia: Westminster, 1974 [1973]), 278; Hans Wildberger, *Jesaja 3. Teilband Jesaja 28-39,* BKAT (Neukirchen-Vluyn: Neukirchener Verlag, 1982), 1127, 1134; Joseph Blenkinsopp, *Isaiah 1–39: A New Translation with Introduction and Commentary,* AB 19 (New York: Doubleday, 2000), 408-10.

8. Pss. 25:10; 40:11; 57:3; 61:7; 85:11; 86:15; 89:14; 115:1; 138:2.

9. Prov. 3:3; 14:22; 16:6; 20:28.

10. Still important is Hermann Gunkel, "Der Micha-Schluss," *Zeitschrift für Semitistik* 2 (1924): 145-78; Eng. "The Close of Micah — a Prophetic Liturgy," in *What Remains of the Old Testament* (London and New York: Griffin, 1928), 115-49. See also Delbert R. Hillers, *Micah: A Commentary on the Book of the Prophet Micah,* Hermeneia (Philadelphia: Fortress, 1984), 83-91.

it remains to be seen from the context whether "Jacob" stands for both kingdoms or, after the Assyrian conquest of Samaria in 722 B.C., for Judah alone. The Judah oracle at the beginning of the book, of Deuteronomistic inspiration (2:4-5), refers to the cult of false gods by Israel's ancestors, an accusation that would match denunciations of the exodus generation rather than Abraham, Isaac, and Jacob, and is found elsewhere with reference to the "out of Egypt" generation, as we shall see. But in any case, Abraham is nowhere referred to in the book.

For Hosea, who may not have survived the siege and capture of Samaria, Israelite origins go back to the exodus and wilderness experience. Yahweh calls his son out of Egypt (11:1-2) and declares himself to be "your God from the land of Egypt" (13:4). Inevitably, given this perspective on the past, Jacob could not fail to be the dominant figure, and, in fact, the book contains a sample of narrative traditions about him (12:2-6, 12). The list begins with the birth of the twins Jacob and Esau, a birth unique in the history of obstetrics if not of legend (cf. Gen. 25:22-26), passing to the struggle with a supernatural being at the Jabbok ford (Gen. 32:22-32), the mysterious encounter at Bethel (Gen. 28:10-22; 33:9-15), and then backtracking to Jacob's forced exile in Aram and his service as a shepherd for a wife — for two wives, as it turned out (Hos. 12:12; cf. Gen. 28:5; 29:15-30). Doubts about the Hosean authenticity of these scraps of tradition have been raised on account of the opening announcement of an indictment on Judah (Hos. 12:2a). It is not to our purpose to decide this question, but even if the hand of a Judean editor is in evidence here, as it is elsewhere in the book, it need not imply more than the reapplication of an older tradition to Judah, referred to as Jacob in Deutero-Isaiah and other postdisaster texts. If, therefore, this retrospective on Jacob is indeed from Hosea, it would constitute a valuable piece of evidence for the antiquity of narrative tradition about Jacob, though not fully identical in every respect with the developed narrative form of the Jacob tradition in Genesis, which (for example) has nothing to say about Jacob weeping.[11]

In the book of Jeremiah Abraham is named only once, in the common triadic formula "Abraham, Isaac, and Jacob," at the conclusion of an oracular statement about the dynastic promise (Jer. 33:14-26). This passage, a

---

11. In addition to the commentaries, see Aage Bentzen, "The Weeping of Jacob," *VT* 1 (1951): 58-59; Peter R. Ackroyd, "Hosea and Jacob," *VT* 13 (1963): 245-53; E. M. Good, "Hosea and the Jacob Tradition," *VT* 16 (1966): 137-45; S. L. McKenzie, "The Jacob Tradition in Hosea xii 4-5," *VT* 36 (1986): 311-22.

variant of Jer. 23:5-6, is absent from the LXX version of the book, which is about one-eighth shorter than the Masoretic Text (MT). Jeremiah 33:14-26 is therefore presumed to belong to a more expansive and later version of the book that can hardly be dated earlier than the mid-to-late Persian period (mid-fifth to late fourth century B.C.), by which time the triadic formula would have been thoroughly familiar. Throughout the book, Judah and its inhabitants are addressed by Jeremiah as "Jacob" (10:25; 30:5-7, 18; 31:7-14), "my servant Jacob" (30:10-11; 46:27-28), and "the house of Jacob" (2:4; 5:20), and their God is "the God of Jacob" (10:16; 51:19). In some of these texts, especially in the section known to commentators as "the Book of Consolation" (chaps. 30–31), which cannot be attributed to the prophet, the language is strongly reminiscent of Deutero-Isaiah where Jacob, "servant of Yahweh" (Isa. 41:8-9; 44:1-2, 21; 45:9), is the most common way of referring to the prophet's Judean contemporaries. Other Deutero-Isaian features that appear in these two chapters of Jeremiah include the call not to be afraid, the call to rejoice and be glad, and the assurance that "I am with you."[12] In sum: neither in the original words of the prophet, to the extent that they can be identified, nor in the extensive additional material in the book, is Abraham identified as a distinct ancestral figure and progenitor of those to whom the sayings are addressed.

I conclude that while the triadic formula was in use from the time of the kingdoms, and therefore Abraham was known to be prior genealogically to Jacob, no narrative traditions about him have survived in written form from that time, and perhaps none were in circulation.

The One and the Many

Abraham begins to emerge from the shadows during the traumatic period that began with the first conquest of Jerusalem by the Babylonians and ended with the conquest of Babylon by the Persians (597-539 B.C.). Our information derives from the prophets Ezekiel and Deutero-Isaiah. Ezekiel records an argument for exclusive possession of the land vacated by those deported to Babylon, including Ezekiel himself, an argument advanced by those left in Jerusalem five or six years after the first deportation, there-

---

12. The call not to fear addressed to Jacob is found in Jer. 30:10; 46:27-28; Isa. 41:10, 13-14; 43:5; 44:2; "I am with you" in Jer. 30:11; Isa. 41:10; 43:5; the call to rejoice in Jer. 31:7, 12; Isa. 54:1.

fore about 592/591 (Ezek. 11:14-21). A similar argument for rights to the land from the survivors of the second deportation, this time supported by a "scriptural" proof from Abraham, is recorded in Ezek. 33:23-29. A few decades later Deutero-Isaiah addressed his hearers as descendants of Abraham, friend of God (Isa. 41:8), urging them to find inspiration in the example of Abraham and Sarah, their progenitors (51:1-2). Since there is general agreement that Deutero-Isaiah was active in the middle years of the sixth century, perhaps a decade or so before the fall of Babylon to the Persian Cyrus II in 539, it was during this half-century, and in response to the extraordinary stress of circumstances at that time, that Abraham first achieved prominence as a distinctive ancestral figure.

In the later of the two Ezekiel texts referred to above, we hear that those who had remained in Judah were appealing to a tradition about Abraham as a way of legitimating their possession of the land, including the estates vacated involuntarily by the deportees. The fact that most of those deported belonged to the professional and aristocratic ranks, and therefore probably left behind large holdings, while most of those not deported belonged to the peasant class, makes the situation look like an incident in class warfare. The text reads as follows (Ezek. 33:24): "The inhabitants of those ruins in the land of Israel are saying, 'When Abraham took possession of the land he was but one; there are lots of us, so the land has been handed over to us as a possession.'" The argument was not simply that if one man could do it, *a fortiori* they could. It was rather that, being no doubt familiar with the "great nation" theme first enunciated in Gen. 12:1-3, those who had escaped deportation were arguing that they, the offspring of Abraham actually resident in the land, the ones in possession, were the only legitimate candidates to inherit the Abrahamic promise. We will probably agree that this "scriptural" argument is not particularly persuasive, and would certainly not have persuaded those forcibly deprived of their land holdings.

The same conclusion is reached and articulated in a more specific way in the earlier of the two reports following on the first deportation (Ezek. 11:14-15): "Your kinsmen and fellow exiles, the whole household of Israel, all of them, are the ones about whom the inhabitants of Jerusalem are saying, 'They have gone far from Yahweh; the land has been made over to us as a possession.'" The argument here is more specific. The command to Abraham to journey to the land of Canaan (Gen. 12:1) implied the obligation to remain in the land unless obliged by necessity to leave it temporarily, for example, during a time of famine. Lot chose to live outside of the Promised Land, and thereby forfeited the opportunity to be Abraham's heir. There was also the older belief that to leave one's own land was to be no longer under the jurisdiction of one's own territorial deity and to come under the jurisdiction of the deity whose writ ran in the land of destination. So, for example, when David was obliged to seek refuge with the Philistines, he cursed those who had driven him out "to serve other gods" (1 Sam. 26:19). It is therefore not surprising to hear the deportees in Babylonia asking, "How can we sing the hymns of Yahweh on foreign soil?" (Ps. 137:4). In Babylonia, jurisdiction was wielded by the imperial deity Marduk, resident in the great Esagila sanctuary in Babylon. The point of the argument of those left behind was therefore that, for reasons unstated, the deportees had been expelled from the Jerusalem cult community, and that the expulsion entailed loss of civil status and forfeiture of property rights. A parallel example would be the situation of those who failed to attend the assembly convoked during Ezra's mission to resolve the intermarriage issue: they were threatened with forfeiture of immovable property, presumably including real estate, and expulsion from "the congregation of the exiles" (Ezra 10:8). This interpretation is confirmed by the rebuttal, placed in the mouths of Ezekiel's fellow deportees, that Yahweh would himself be the sanctuary for them for the short time they were destined to remain in exile (Ezek. 11:16). So they were not expelled from the cult community of Yahweh after all.[13]

We come now to Deutero-Isaiah, the inelegant title modern scholarship has given to the great prophet of the age of disaster and exile: toward the beginning of this section of the book (chaps. 40–55), the survivors of the disaster are addressed as "Israel my servant, Jacob whom I have chosen, the offspring (*zera,* literally 'seed') of Abraham my friend" (Isa. 41:8). Here, finally, Abraham is something more than a name. His intimate relationship with God is expressed by the epithet "friend," and he will continue to be regarded as such in Jewish (e.g., 2 Chr. 20:7; Neh. 9:7), Christian (e.g., Jas. 2:23), and Islamic tradition (*al halil, halil ullahi,* Qur'an 4:124). Use of such titles as "friend" and "servant" suggests that Abraham was a familiar figure by that time, and the same impression is conveyed in the reference to the redemption of Abraham in Isa. 29:22-24, another postdisaster text, as we have seen. Of particular interest is

---

13. On the meaning of *miqdāš mē'at,* see Walther Eichrodt, *Ezekiel: A Commentary* (Philadelphia: Westminster, 1970), 145. The Targum paraphrases: "Therefore I have given them synagogues second only to my holy temple, because they are few in number."

the exhortation the seer addresses to his hearers at a later point in the Deutero-Isaian collection:

> Look to the rock from which you were hewn,
> the quarry from which you were cut;
> look to Abraham your father,
> and to Sarah who gave you birth.
> When I called him he was but one,
> but I blessed him and made him many. (Isa. 51:1-2)[14]

Those addressed are devout people — they pursue what is right and wish to remain faithful to their God (v. 1) — but they are discouraged, as well they might be in the devastating aftermath of the Babylonian punitive campaign. We encounter a similar loss of purpose and sense of identity in the lament in Isa. 63:7–64:12, in which the question is raised whether those lamenting are still known and acknowledged by the ancestors Abraham and Jacob (63:15-16):

> Look down from heaven and see,
> from your holy, glorious, and exalted dwelling!
> Where is your zeal, your power,
> your abundant tender compassion?
> Do not stand aloof, for you are our Father!
> Were Abraham not to know us,
> Israel not to acknowledge us,
> yet you, Yahweh, are our father,
> our redeemer from of old is your name.

Here is expressed a sad sense of disorientation and disconnect from the religious and ethnic traditions essential for preserving a sense of identity and purpose. Jerusalem and the other major cities of Judah were in ruins, the temple gutted, the entire apparatus of state within which Judeans had lived for centuries had been dismantled, and their numbers were drastically reduced. In this situation they were urged, in Isa. 51:1-2, to look to the rock from which they were hewn and the quarry from which they were cut. Without the mention of Abraham and Sarah, we would more natu-

---

14. For "made him many," 1QIsaᵃ, one of the Isaiah fragments, has "made him fruitful" (*w'prhw*). LXX adds "and I loved him" (*kai ēgapēsa auton*).

rally think of the rock and the quarry as metaphors for the God of Israel, as in "the Rock that bore you" in the Song of Moses (Deut. 32:18) and, of course, that great old hymn "Rock of Ages Cleft for Me." But the choice of the rare word translated "quarry" *(maqqevet; hapax legomenon),* from the same verbal stem as *neqevah,* "female," emphasizes the place of Sarah and strengthens the appeal to genealogical origins. This, incidentally, is the only occasion in the Hebrew Bible outside of Genesis where Sarah is named.

The blessing that was to lead to the creation of a people, the "great nation" theme enunciated in Gen. 12:1-3 and elsewhere in the ancestral narratives (e.g., Gen. 18:18), is in the background of the demographic issue expressed or hinted at in symbolic and poetic language throughout the later sections of the book of Isaiah (54:1):

> Sing out, you barren woman, who has borne no child,
> break out in shouts of joy, you who have never been in labor;
> for the children of the wife who was abandoned
> will outnumber those of the wife with a husband.
>
> Your people righteous, one and all,
> will possess the land forever. . . .
> The least will become a thousand,
> the smallest a mighty nation. (60:21-22)

Though Abraham is not named here, we catch the echo of the twofold Abrahamic blessing, demographic and territorial, people and land, in response to the deportations and the fear and anxiety about the possibility of national and ethnic extinction.

Jacob, Foundational Ancestor

One conclusion that can be drawn from our rapid survey of the historical and prophetic writings is that Jacob was from the beginning the primary ancestor. At the most obvious level, Jacob is *the* ethnic and tribal eponym by virtue of his change of name, recorded twice. The first occasion is at Peniel east of the Jordan after his wrestling match with the angel or deity at the Jabbok ford (Gen. 32:28). The second, of Priestly origin, is located at Bethel where Jacob-Israel is blessed by God Almighty (El Shaddai) and receives further assurance that the land will be handed over to him and his descendants (35:9-15). Both versions occur on Jacob's return from a twenty-year exile in Mesopotamia, where a new people, represented by the birth of all of Jacob's sons with the exception of Benjamin, came into existence (29:31–30:24).[15]

Jacob's centrality in the collective memory of origins is confirmed by examples of historical reminiscence encountered, *en passant,* at several points outside of the mainline narrative in Genesis. In asking the king of Edom for right of passage through his territory, Moses gives him an account of Israelite history up to that time, a history that begins with their ancestors, Jacob and his sons, "going down" to Egypt, followed by the oppression, the prayer for help, the rescue by divine act from under the Egyptian yoke, and the wandering in the wilderness (Num. 20:14-16). A similar view of origins is implied in Samuel's valedictory to the people petitioning for the appointment of a king. He reminds them about the beginnings of their history with the appointment of Moses and Aaron and the "bringing up" of their ancestors from Egypt (1 Sam. 12:6-15). An admonition to the Jewish diaspora in Lev. 26:40-45, from the so-called Holiness Code, assures those addressed that, subject to their religious fidelity, God will remember his covenant with their forefathers, the "first ones," the pioneers *(rishonim),* those who were led out from the land of Egypt (v. 45).

The primacy of Jacob is also reflected in the more direct and expressive form of liturgical prayer. Abraham is named in only 2 of the 150 psalms (47:9; 105:6, 9, 42). On one occasion in the psalm collection God addressed is "the God of Abraham" (47:9), but the title "God of Jacob" is much more in evidence. The ancestors are those who came out of Egypt and trekked across the wilderness under the guidance of Moses and Aaron. Psalm 78, which in its final form appears to be anti-Samaritan (vv. 9-11, 67-69), begins its historical survey with the miracles of the exodus and ends with the rejection of Ephraim, the divine choice of Jerusalem, and the election of David. What is sometimes overlooked is that a remarkable number of psalms that contain historical reminiscence of Israel's origins emphasize the sins of the "out of Egypt" generation, which led to its exclusion from the territorial blessing, the possession of the land of promise.[16] Abraham is never named in connection with these tainted origins, and he

---

15. Ephraim and Manasseh, sons of Joseph born to him in Egypt (Gen. 46:27), represent a later and secondary development in the twelve-tribal structure.

16. Pss. 78:56-64; 79:8-10; 95:8-11; 106:6-33.

is also absent from Ezekiel's recital of Israel's past as a history of repeated religious infidelity, a catalogue of "the abominations of their ancestors" (Ezek. 20:4-38). This survey begins with the election of Israel and the self-revelation of Yahweh to Jacob and his sons in Egypt (cf. Exod. 6:2-4). It is unique in tracing Israel's history of infidelity to its origins in idolatrous practices during the sojourn in Egypt, then continuing in the wilderness and after entry into the land, and so down to the present. It ends with the threat that "as I entered into judgment with your ancestors, so I will enter into judgment with you" (Ezek. 20:36). Jacob is, however, named as the preeminent ancestor in a later and more reassuring discourse of the same prophet, according to which "they (a future generation of Israelites) will live in the land that I gave to my servant Jacob, the land in which your ancestors lived" (37:25).

A particularly interesting illustration of Jacob as the ancestor par excellence can be found in the liturgical prayer to be recited at the offering of the firstfruits according to Deut. 26:5-10. It presents something like a canonical form of the religious history of Israel beginning with Jacob:

> My forefather was an Aramean ready to perish[17] who went down to Egypt and lived there as an alien. Though few in number, his family grew into a great, powerful, and numerous nation. When the Egyptians began to treat us harshly and humiliate us by imposing hard labor on us, we cried to Yahweh, God of our forefathers. When he saw our affliction, hardship, and oppression he listened to us and brought us out of Egypt with a strong hand and outstretched arm, with a terrifying display of power, and with signs and portents. He brought us to this place and gave us this land, a land flowing with milk and honey. Now I bring here the firstfruits of the earth which you, Yahweh, have given me.

This "little credo," so named by Gerhard von Rad, is the most formally liturgical of these summaries of salvation history. While the terminology is unmistakably Deuteronomic (or Deuteronomistic), its rhythmic quality — better appreciated if the Hebrew is read aloud — justifies von Rad's suspicion that it reproduces, or is based on, older liturgical usage.[18] The

---

17. The meaning "perish" for the verbal stem *'bd* is well attested in the Hebrew Bible, e.g., Deut. 4:26; 8:19-20; 28:20, 22.

18. Von Rad dealt with this passage in several publications: *Gesammelte Studien zum Alten Testament* (Munich: Kaiser, 1961), 11-16 (first published 1938); Eng. *The Problem of the Hexateuch and Other Essays* (Edinburgh and London: Oliver and Boyd, 1966), 3-8; *Old*

Aramean ready to perish during a time of famine is certainly Jacob. His mother Rebekah, daughter of Bethuel and granddaughter of Nahor the Aramean, lived in Aram-naharaim ("Aram of the Two Rivers," Gen. 24:10, 24), and he himself lived there for twenty years (Gen. 29–31), working for his uncle, Laban the Aramean (Gen. 25:20; 28:5).

There is no mention of Abraham in this recall of origins, but if this quasi-canonical historical summary is compared with the historical prologue to Joshua's covenant discussed earlier, in which the first ancestors are Terah, Abraham, and Nahor (Josh. 24:2), the idea of a development over the course of time by tracing the genealogical line backward from Jacob to Abraham and then linking with Terah, last representative of the old postdiluvial world, will be confirmed. To accept this explanation does not, however, imply that, in the matter of ethnic origins, Jacob and Abraham represent mutually exclusive and competing versions.[19] In the "little credo" itself, the Israelites in Egypt pray to the God of *their* ancestors (Deut. 26:7), and after the offering of the firstfruits there is a further prayer for blessing in accordance with the oath sworn to the ancestors, language evocative of Abraham rather than Jacob (24:15). We return again to a point made earlier, that the earliest narrative traditions about Abraham circulated in response to the disastrous situation leading up to and subsequent to the

---

Testament Theology, vol. 1 (New York: Harper and Row, 1962 [1957]), 121-28; *Genesis: A Commentary* (London: SCM, 1961 [1956]), 156-59. See, apropos of "the little credo," M. A. Beek, "Das Problem des aramäischen Stammvaters (Deut XXVI 5)," *OTS* 8 (1950): 193-212; Leonard Rost, "Das kleine geschichtliche Credo," in *Das kleine Credo und andere Studien zum Alten Testament* (Heidelberg, 1965), 11-25; C. M. Carmichael, "A New View of the Origin of the Deuteronomic Credo," *VT* 19 (1969): 273-89; Andrew D. H. Mayes, *Deuteronomy*, NCB (London: Oliphants, 1979), 332-35.

19. The hypothesis of a combination of two distinct accounts of origins, Moses and exodus on the one hand, Abraham on the other, is defended by Thomas C. Römer in "Les histoires des Patriarches et la légende de Moïse: une double origine?" in *Comment la Bible saisit-elle l'histoire?* ed. D. Doré (Paris: Cerf, 2007), 155-96. Critical comments in Hans-Christoph Schmitt, "Erzvätergeschichte und Exodusgeschichte als konkurrierende Ursprungslegenden Israels — ein Irrweg der Pentateuchforschung?" in *Die Erzväter in der biblischen Tradition. Festschrift für Matthias Köckert,* ed. Anselm C. Hagedorn and Henrik Pfeiffer, BZAW 400 (Berlin: De Gruyter, 2009), 241-66, where he argues that the ancestor and exodus traditions were united as early as Hosea, a view no less contestable. Konrad Schmid, *Genesis and the Moses Story: Dual Origins in the Hebrew Bible* (Winona Lake, Ind.: Eisenbrauns, 2010), 254-59 (Eng. trans. of *Erzväter und Exodus: Untersuchungen zur doppelten Ursprünge Israels innerhalb der Geschichtsbücher des Alten Testaments,* WMANT 81 [Neukirchen-Vluyn: Neukirchener Verlag, 1999]), maintains that these traditions were conflated no earlier than the Persian period, which seems closer to the real state of affairs.

liquidation of the Judean state. They are therefore subsequent to, and in some respects modeled on, the traditions about Jacob. In working through the Abraham story, we shall come across many parallels, some of them verbatim, with incidents in the Jacob cycle consistent with the chronological priority of these Jacob traditions.

The Abraham Story as Part of Genesis

The same fivefold division adopted for the Pentateuch, the book of Psalms, and, somewhat later, the Five Scrolls, or *megillot* (Canticles, Ruth, Lamentations, Qoheleth, and Esther), was taken up as a major structuring device in Genesis and in no other book. Genesis is essentially a history: it has events, characters, and chronology, but the chronology is in the configuration of genealogy, an unbroken genealogical chain from the creation of the world (2:4a) and Adam (5:1) at the beginning to the seventy sons of Jacob who went down to Egypt at the end (46:8-27). This genealogical continuum is arranged in two series each with five units: the first covers the archaic world described in the idiom of myth, with ten generations before and ten after the great deluge; the second chronicles the descendants of Terah and his three sons through four generations, which is to say, Abraham's family. These units are presented under the title "these are the generations . . ." (Hebrew: *elleh toledot . . .*). This word *toledot,* always in the plural, can be translated "generations," "genealogy," or "descendants," while in modern Hebrew it means "history," understandably since history is intimately associated with genealogy.

This introductory *toledot* formula occurs thirteen times in the Hebrew Bible, of which three instances are outside Genesis (Num. 3:1; Ruth 4:18; 1 Chr. 1:29). Of the remaining ten in Genesis, Gen. 36:9 repeats the heading of the Esau unit in Gen. 36:1 and is therefore structurally redundant, but the full complement is restored when we come to the title of the first in the human chain, "this is the book of the *toledot* of Adam" (5:1).

The first fivefold series (pentad), therefore, reads as follows:

2:4a Heaven and earth
5:1 Adam
6:9 Noah
10:1 Noah's three sons
11:10 Shem, Noah's first son

The first is exceptional since it refers both backward and forward: backward to Gen. 1:1–2:3, thus covering the seven-day creation account while leaving the majestic exordium in place (1:1); forward to cover 2:4b–4:26, the vicissitudes of the first human family. One further observation: the third and central panel of the series, the great catastrophe of the deluge, is the most important, serving as the fulcrum on which the structure rests, the watershed — literally — between the old world and the new dispensation in which blessing and a covenant are bestowed on the survivors, an anticipation of the blessing and covenant extended to Abraham and his line. We shall see that the central unit of the ancestral *toledot* plays a similar role.[20]

The ancestral series, the one that is our present concern, reads as follows:

1. 11:27–25:11 Terah (Abraham)
2. 25:12-18 Ishmael
3. 25:19–35:29 Isaac (Jacob)
4. 36:1–37:1 Esau/Edom
5. 37:2–50:26 Jacob (Joseph and his brothers)

A peculiar feature of this pentad is that in 1, 2, and 3 the units deal with the descendants of the eponyms rather than the eponyms for whom the units are named. This peculiarity probably came about because the distribution of genealogical and narrative material available did not necessarily match the relative significance of the ancestors in question. Isaac, in particular, serves more as a genealogical link between Abraham and Jacob than as a subject of biographical interest. The *toledot* of Ishmael and Esau consist exclusively of genealogical lists, but their relationship to Abraham, Isaac, and Jacob is no less significant for that, and their presence in the schema is an important indication of the broader range of the extended family originating with Terah, on which more will be said. The central events of the Jacob story are narrated in the unit named for Isaac in the third and central place, and the stylistically quite different story of Joseph and his brothers is in the unit named for Jacob in the fifth place. The promi-

---

20. On the *toledot* structure, I am drawing on my *The Pentateuch: An Introduction to the First Five Books of the Bible* (New York: Doubleday, 1992), 42-47, 58-93, and *Creation, Un-Creation, Re-Creation: A Discursive Commentary on Genesis 1–11* (London: T. & T. Clark/ Bloomsbury/Continuum, 2011), 4-5.

nence of Jacob, the ancestor of Israel par excellence, in the central panel is self-explanatory, and within the Jacob story his exile in Mesopotamia and return after twenty years is the central event, the fulcrum on which this central panel in the pentad rests. Its relevance for the deportations following on the fall of Jerusalem need hardly be emphasized, but nevertheless will be at the appropriate point of the commentary. Jacob's role in the fifth and last panel was required to link the Abraham story with the next phase consisting of the descent of Jacob and sons into Egypt, the oppression, and subsequent liberation. The relation between these two phases — Abraham, Isaac, and Jacob on the one hand, the generation of the exodus and wilderness on the other — has given rise to important debating points in the current discussion of Israelite origins.

Since we are proceeding on the assumption that the structure of a record like the Abraham story and its place in the larger literary context are essential aspects of its total meaning, we should now at least summarize the relation of the Abraham cycle (Gen. 11:27–25:11) to the mythic history of the archaic world that precedes it, of which Terah may be considered the last representative.

The story of Abraham belongs to the first of the five ancestral *toledot,* the one named for Terah. This should be emphasized, in the first place since Terah and all three of his sons are part of the story. Terah is therefore the primordial ancestor; Nahor, the second son, with his wife Milcah, is the ancestor of twelve ethnic groups (Gen. 22:20-24), the same in number as the twelve-tribal Israelites, the Ishmaelite tribal federation (25:12-15), and perhaps also, originally, the descendants of Abraham and Keturah, another Arabian lineage (25:1-4). Terah and Nahor are also ancestors of the Arameans, counting among their descendants not only Aram (22:21) but also Rebekah, daughter of Bethuel and wife of Isaac (24:15, 24, 47). Laban her brother, with whom Jacob after much trickery and dissimulation on both sides was eventually reconciled (31:43-55), also belongs to the extended Terahite lineage. In his final discourse, Joshua, in fact, numbers both Terah and Nahor among Israel's ancestors (Josh. 24:2). The tradition disposes of Haran, the third son, at an early stage (Gen. 11:28). He dies, but not before fathering Lot, thereby qualifying as ancestor of Moabites and Ammonites. His daughter Milcah is the wife of Nahor, and following Josephus (*Ant.* 1.151) and rabbinic tradition, the other daughter, Iscah, is another name for Sarah, wife of Abraham, an identification to be adopted and defended in the first chapter of the commentary. Abraham himself is the ancestor of both Arabs and Israelites, the former with Hagar and

Keturah (Gen. 25:1-6, 12-18), the latter with Sarah. This at once gives the mission of Abraham a much broader, more inclusive, and irenical character and scope, balancing the more exclusivist and xenophobic elements in other accounts of Israel's origins.

A second consideration starts out from the position of Terah as ninth, and Abraham as tenth, in line from Noah. This links both with the deluge, the near extinction of all life on earth, a mythic image of the fifth and last extinction at the end of the Cretaceous period 65 million years ago. More immediately, it links with the damaged but still intact world that survived it. The link is established genealogically, by way of ten antediluvian and ten postdiluvian generations, the former from Adam to Noah, the latter from Shem, Noah's son, to Abraham. These links of this genealogical chain are strengthened by a chronological scheme that extends into the ancestral history, the sojourn in Egypt, the exodus, and beyond.[21] This linkage broadens the perspective even further, placing Abraham on a vast stage and permitting the conclusion that the mission confided to him is in response to the needs not just of one ethnic group but of the world that survived the great disaster, the postdisaster world we still inhabit. The antediluvian list ends with the three sons of Noah who survived the deluge (5:32), and the postdiluvian list ends with the three sons of Terah, the first of whom is Abraham (11:26). To the blessing pronounced over eight persons — Noah, his wife, his three sons, and his daughters-in-law (9:1) — corresponds the blessing on Abraham, which also extends to the family of which he was a member, also eight in number — Terah, Abraham, Sarah, Nahor, Haran, Lot, Milcah, Iscah (12:2-3). To the covenant God made with the survivors of the deluge, human and nonhuman, there corresponds the covenant with Abraham, both covenants authenticated and represented by a sign (9:8-17; 17:1-14, both from the Priestly writer).

Abraham's place in the greater scheme of things also comes into view when juxtaposed with the dispersion of the descendants of Shem, Ham, and Japheth. The families of the earth that will in some way receive blessing through Abraham (12:3) are the descendants of the three sons of Noah listed in the so-called Table of Nations by their families, that is, their extended kinship groups (10:5, 20, 31, 32). The great name promised to Abraham (12:2) is the antithesis of the name that the builders of the city with its temple-tower in the land of Shinar proposed to make for themselves (11:4).

---

21. On this chronological schema, see, in addition to my *The Pentateuch*, 47-50, the careful and detailed account in Jeremy Hughes, *Secrets of the Times: Myth and History in Biblical Chronology*, JSOTSup 66 (Sheffield: Sheffield Academic Press, 1990).

Shinar is Babylon, where Judean deportees were settled after the Babylonian conquest of Judah in the sixth century B.C.; it is listed explicitly as such in Isa. 11:11. The project of the city and temple builders is represented as an act of hubris, carried out free of constraint from considerations of the common good and the will and purposes of God. The builders talk to each other, God soliloquizes, but there is no communication. The biblical text hints at a connection between this project and the empire-building activities of Nimrod, according to which Babel and the land of Shinar represent the first stage in this imperial expansion (Gen. 10:8-12), and this connection is commonplace in the midrash. In the context of the political life of nations, therefore, Abraham serves as the antithesis to Nimrod, exponent of power politics, embodiment of imperial control, and anticipation of the Babylonian Empire (Babel) that brought the kingdom of Judah to an end.

From Genesis to Exodus, from Abraham to Moses

Though Genesis is both structurally and thematically the most distinctive of the five books of the Pentateuch, beginning as it does with the zero point of the creation of the world and humanity, its conclusion is not nearly so clear and definitive. It could have ended, and perhaps at some point in its formation did end, with the list of Jacob's seventy descendants crossing into Egypt (46:5-27), which is then recapitulated at the beginning of Exodus (1:1-5). The incidents that follow this list — the encounters between Jacob and Joseph and between Jacob and the pharaoh, Joseph's economic policy during a time of famine, the blessings of Jacob on his children and final dispositions leading to his death — are mostly a matter of tying up loose ends. The death of Joseph (Gen. 50:24-26), with which Genesis does end, is also alluded to at the beginning of Exodus (1:6). But since Genesis and Exodus consist of a history of early humanity followed by a prehistory of Israel, the real break between epochs and generations comes toward the beginning of Exodus, in a summary, in one verse, of almost 430 years (Exod. 12:40), or 400 years (Gen. 15:13), or maybe four generations (Gen. 15:16) of life in Egypt (Exod. 1:6-7): "Then Joseph and all his brothers, and all that generation, died. The Israelites were prolific; their numbers increased greatly, and they became so exceedingly powerful that the land was full of them." This is the gap that separates the history of the early ancestors (Abraham, Isaac, Jacob) from the origins tradition featuring Egyptian oppression, rescue under the leadership of Moses and Aaron, the exodus, the journey through the wilderness, and entry into the land. We have seen that this story of oppression and liberation, beginning with the descent into Egypt of "the Aramean ready to perish" (Deut. 26:5), is the primary and canonical myth of origins, that the narrative traditions about Abraham are a later extension backward of the origins story, and that this development is not attested before the disaster of the fall of Jerusalem and collapse of the Judean state. The question now arises: What was behind this extension of the tradition of origins backward, and what does it tell us about the purpose and character of the Abraham traditions?

One approach to an answer might start from the moral judgment passed on the generation of the exodus and wilderness. A liturgical composer of hymns attached to the Second Temple, no doubt a Levite, condemns the ancestors as a stubborn and rebellious generation, and it is apparent that he is referring to the generation miraculously liberated from Egypt and guided by God through the wilderness (Ps. 78:8, 12-55). The same negative assessment is expressed more comprehensively in Ps. 106, which traces a long history of religious infidelity from the ancestors in Egypt to the Babylonian exile. In a sermon addressed to a gathering of Jewish elders in the Babylonian diaspora, dated to 591 B.C., just five years before the fall of Jerusalem, the prophet Ezekiel even denounces "the abominations of the ancestors," with reference to their adoption of local cults during the years spent in Egypt (Ezek. 20:4). There follows a survey of the history from that time to the settlement in the land as a history of religious and moral infidelity (20:5-31). According to a variant of this assessment, the iniquities of the exodus and wilderness generation led to their complete elimination from the scene and exclusion from the ultimate goal, the Promised Land. Psalm 95 ends on a low note:

> For forty years I abhorred that generation,
> I said, "They are a people whose hearts go astray,
> who do not discern my ways."
> I swore an oath in my anger
> that they should not enter my place of rest.[22]

The fulfillment of this oath is marked in the narrative of origins by the episode at Baal-peor recorded in Num. 25:1-18, a key point in the temporal

---

22. For *měnûhâ* ("rest," Ps. 95:11) as a term referring to the Promised Land, see Num. 10:33; Deut. 12:9; 1 Kgs. 8:56.

and spatial coordinates of Israelite origins.[23] It took place in the plains of Moab, which were the last stop before the crossing of the Jordan and entry into Canaan (33:49). In its present form the incident is the last of several purges consequent on religious infidelity recorded in the books of Exodus and Numbers and alluded to in Deuteronomy. The final disappearance of the first generation out of Egypt is made unmistakably clear by the census taken after the Baal-peor incident, on the eve of entry into Canaan (Num. 26). With the exception of Joshua and Caleb, passionate devotees of Yahweh, none of the Israelites listed in the census taken at Sinai (1:1-54) will feature in this second census (26:64-65). This is therefore the second point of transition following on Exod. 1:6-7; these two points divide the story of origins into three phases: the primordial ancestors Terah, Abraham, Isaac, Jacob; the generation of Egypt, exodus, and wilderness; the generation that entered the land.

Reading the Abraham Story in a Collapsed Society

The loss of life, destruction of property, and elimination of the institutions that make social life possible would have left the survivors of the Babylonian conquest in 586 B.C. in a numb and disoriented state. In such a situation, often repeated throughout history, the tendency is to fall back on whatever resources may still be available in the local kinship and family network. With the destruction of the principal political and religious centers and especially the extinction of the Davidic dynasty, we would also anticipate a revival of traditional tribal structures and loyalties, a tendency to which the contentious relations between Judeans and Benjaminites both before and after the disaster provide an important clue.[24] This tendency would bring with it either alienation from the shared past or an urge to establish or re-create genealogical links with the past and to revive the shared myths and traditions of origins.

In many respects, the Abraham story reads like an attempt to respond to this situation. The journey of the Terahite family group from Ur

23. For more on this crucial episode, see my "The Baal Peor Episode Revisited (Num xxv. 1-18)," *Bib.* 93, no. 1 (2012): 86-97.

24. Joseph Blenkinsopp, "Benjamin Traditions Read in the Early Achaemenid Period," in *Judah and the Judeans in the Persian Period,* ed. Oded Lipschits and Manfred Oeming (Winona Lake, Ind.: Eisenbrauns, 2006), 629-45.

to Harran[25] correlates with the sites of the Judean (southern) and Samarian (northern) diasporas respectively. The further stage of the journey undertaken by Abraham with Sarah and Lot from Harran to the land of Canaan matches the return from exile in Babylon either in aspiration or in actuality. The places first visited by Abraham after arrival in Canaan, Shechem and Bethel, played a significant role in the religious and political affairs of Judeans for decades after the disaster. The Abraham narrative also gives its own version of the origins of neighboring peoples who played an important role in Judean affairs under neo-Babylonian and Achaemenid rule: Edomites and Arabs in the first place, but also Moabites, Ammonites, and Arameans, all of whom belonged, together with Abraham, to the many-branched Terahite family. Abraham's relations with these neighboring peoples, and especially with the indigenous populations of Canaan among whom he lived as a resident alien, are respectful and friendly. He offers first choice of grazing land to Lot, ancestor of Moabites and Ammonites; negotiates with Abimelech, later identified as a Philistine ruler (Gen. 21:22-34; 26:1), and therefore a traditional enemy; and insists on following local legal procedures in purchasing a plot of land as a burial site after Sarah's death (23:1-20).[26]

The promise of land, often repeated throughout the history of the ancestors, provided to some in the postdisaster period a charter of land rights, as we have seen, and to others a mandate to return to the land traversed by Abraham and settle there. Closely related to the territorial pledge, and no less relevant to the postdisaster situation, is the demographic promise. It is practically impossible to obtain reliable figures on the population of Judah in this postdisaster period (archaeologically, the transitional period at the end of the Iron Age), and the biblical sources do not agree on the numbers deported by the Babylonians. Results vary, sometimes wildly, but a recent investigation, which may be accepted provisionally and with caution, gives an estimate of 110,000 for the Judean kingdom under the late monarchy, 40,000 for Judah during the remainder of Babylonian rule, and 30,000 for the — much reduced in size — province of Yehud (*yehud medinta*, Ezra 5:8) after the Persian conquest.[27] This loss of population, which must have in-

25. From this point on, to avoid confusion, "Haran" will be the personal name and "Harran" the toponym.

26. Discussed in chapter 10 below and in my "Abraham as Paradigm in the Priestly History in Genesis," *JBL* 128 (2009): 225-41.

27. Oded Lipschits, *The Fall and Rise of Jerusalem* (Winona Lake, Ind.: Eisenbrauns, 2005), 258-71.

duced anxiety about the possibility of ethnic extinction, would have added meaning to the promise of descendants as numerous as the grains of sand or the stars in the sky and the "great nation" theme prominent throughout the story of the first ancestors beginning with Abraham.

The struggle for survival was paramount during that critical period, but sooner or later questions were sure to arise as to why the catastrophe happened, and sooner or later such questioning would be directed at the ancestral deity who had pledged to appoint a place for his people where they might live undisturbed, and for the line of David a throne established forever (2 Sam. 7:8-17). Many simply rejected the "Yahweh alone" option of the religious reformers of Josiah's reign a few decades earlier in favor of the "old religion" of the gods of the earth and underworld and the Queen of Heaven and her court. This was the answer of those Judeans who, following the assassination of Gedaliah, the Babylonian-appointed ruler of the province, fled to Egypt, taking Jeremiah with them (Jer. 44:15-19). Rejecting Jeremiah's preaching of the same message after as before the catastrophe, they placed the blame for the terrible events of the quarter-century since Josiah's death (609-586 B.C.) on the iconoclastic religious reforms and purges carried out during his reign, in effect offering an alternative explanation for the disaster. Note that the women were prominent among the protesters (Jer. 44:16-18):

> "We are not going to listen to you. We will do everything that we have vowed, make offerings to the Queen of Heaven and pour out libations to her, just as we and our forefathers, our kings and officials used to do in the cities of Judah and the streets of Jerusalem. We had plenty of food, lived well, and did not encounter misfortune. But from the time we stopped making offerings to the Queen of Heaven and pouring out libations to her, we have lacked everything and have perished by the sword and famine."

This was one option, but for those who chose to remain faithful to the ancestral traditions and the national deity there remained the task of justifying their choice, to themselves in the first place, but also to those in and outside of their own community who were asking, "Where now is your God?" (Pss. 42:3; 115).

Here, too, the Abraham traditions would have proved relevant. The note of blessing struck right at the beginning of the story reversed the situation in the postdeluge world, the world of Nimrod and Babel (Babylon), mythic counterpart to the postdisaster world in Judah under the imperial rule of Babylon. Abraham, in the tenth generation after the deluge, is God's agent in this reversal; God appeared to him in a far country, and then guided him at each critical point of his life. Abraham and his descendants will be blessed, and the blessing will be shared with "all the families of the earth" (Gen. 12:3).

In effect, this turning point constituted a new dispensation or covenant between God and the remnant of Israel and, by implication, all humanity, parallel to the covenant addressed to Noah and his family ten generations earlier. In neither case is it a covenant containing legally binding obligations that are incumbent on the human partner, on the observance of which God would perform certain benevolent actions. It is rather the expression of the absolutely free and benevolent will of God that not only takes account of the situation the human partner faces but also acknowledges the limitations of the human moral capacity as demonstrated most clearly in the wake of catastrophe. Abraham was called to act as messenger and agent of this new dispensation.

The story of Abraham, composed and in circulation at that time of crisis and uncertainty, aimed to demonstrate that God is not only just but also benevolent, that God is faithful to those who attach themselves to him, and that what God brought about through Abraham, his servant and friend, he could bring about again. The course of history can be reversed; a future can open up even though, like the future foretold to Abraham and Sarah, it may seem to lie beyond human possibilities and calculations.

Beyond the Bible: A Word on "Filling In the Gaps"

We know about Abraham only from the Hebrew Bible since no other independent source of information is currently available, about Abraham either as a literary invention or as a creation of collective memory the origins of which are now irrecoverable.[28] Everything else written about him

---

28. This possibility should not be discounted. Studies in collective memory have demonstrated the remarkable persistence of memories of iconic figures and events, however enhanced or distorted with the passage of time. See Maurice Halbwachs, *La mémoire collective* (Paris: Presses universitaires de France, 1968); Eng. *The Collective Memory* (New York: Harper and Row, 1980); Paul Connerton, *How Societies Remember* (Cambridge: Cambridge University Press, 1989); Jan Assmann, *Religion and Cultural Memory* (Stanford: Stanford University Press, 2006).

is generated in one way or another by interrogating the biblical narrative, probing between its many fissures and fractures, its apparent non sequiturs and aporias, and supplying content for its often glaring omissions. The result is an immense amount of glossing and commentary of varying degrees of plausibility. Not all of this was the production of Jewish scribes, and not all of it was of explicitly religious character. Toward the beginning of this process in the Hellenistic period we note how Abraham was celebrated as a culture hero, having introduced the study of astronomy and mathematics into Egypt, that land of learned sages, scholars, and priests. He was, after all, of Chaldean origin, and the term "Chaldean" was practically synonymous with "astrologer." He was also a descendant of Shem, great mystagogue and expert in astrology. It was known from the sacred writings of the Jews that Abraham had spent some time in Egypt with his wife, so the assumption was that he was there lecturing on astronomy and holding learned seminars with the priests, famed for their erudition. This Egyptian phase must have lasted longer than implied by the episode recorded in those writings (Gen. 12:10-20): five years at least for the author of the Qumran *Genesis Apocryphon* (1QapGen 19:23) and *Jubilees* (12:60; 13:11), twenty according to the historian Artapanus, writing somewhat earlier.[29] Abraham also had the distinction of introducing or reviving the study of the Hebrew language, the language spoken by God, the man, the woman, the snake, and presumably the other animals in Eden. According to the author of *Jubilees* (12:25-27), he studied and copied books written in Hebrew belonging to Terah, his father, no doubt passed down from the learned and pious Shem. From that time he began to speak Hebrew when addressed by God.

For these and other writers who have come down to us from the Hellenistic period and late antiquity, including Berossus and Hecataeus, known to Josephus, Abraham was regarded as one of the great originators and founders of the sciences. Philo, without a doubt the leading commentator on Abraham in antiquity, was part of that world of study and learned inquiry but went beyond it. He held that Abraham, being a Chaldean, believed that the study of the heavenly bodies was the key to a religion in which nature was God, a belief he accepted until he began to discern the truth about God, "the pure beam of light in place of deep darkness."[30] If he is viewed in this way, his true descendants could not be limited to any

---

29. In a fragment preserved by Eusebius, *Praep. ev.* 9.18.
30. *On Abraham* 69-71, 77.

one ethnic category but must include all those who spend their lives in the pursuit of wisdom and the knowledge of God.

In writing the commentary, it seemed better to me to concentrate on the structure, shape, and inner coherence of the life story, without directly referring to the vast amount of commentary from the time of the Hellenistic literati and the rabbis, the medieval schoolmen, and the *illuminati*, down to the present. Since, however, it cannot be ignored, I have provided samples in the last section of each chapter under the rubric "Filling In the Gaps" that could provide a basis for further reading and study.

The Journey

Abraham's Family

The story begins under the heading "These are the descendants of Terah," the first of the five units that provide the skeletal framework for the history of the ancestors. Terah, ninth in descent from Noah, is the most primordial of Israel's ancestors, and is reckoned as such by Joshua at the beginning of his valedictory address to his followers (Josh. 24:2). Before proceeding to the journey, we should take a close look at the members of his family. They are linked to the ancient world, with Terah as ninth and Abraham as tenth in line from Noah and the great deluge, the catastrophe that brought the old world to an end. Like the survivors of that annihilating event — Noah, his wife, his three sons and their wives — they number eight. The world in which they are to act out their lives is a postcatastrophe world, the damaged world we still inhabit. Both Noahites and Terahites are launched into that world with a blessing (Gen. 9:1; 12:2) and a covenantal agreement, a kind of peace treaty between God and humanity that is made with both (9:8-17; 17:1-8). The genealogy from Shem, first of Noah's three sons, to Terah, father of Abraham, is the bridge over which we pass from the world of myth to the world of history, though not history as we understand it today. Terah marks the transition from that archaic world to the damaged but intact world in which we still live, a position signaled by his extraordinary longevity. He died at the age of 205, which no one after him would match, not even Isaac at 180 (35:28), or Abraham at 175 (25:7), much less Moses, who attained only 120 years, dying with "his sight undimmed, his vigor undiminished" (Deut. 34:7).[1]

1. John A. Emerton, "When Did Terah Die (Genesis 11:32)?" in *Language, Theology,*

In keeping with a common feature of this type of familial and ethnic narrative, Terah is assigned three sons — Abraham, Nahor, and Haran, comparable to the three sons of the first parents, Cain, Abel, and Seth; the three sons of Noah, Shem, Ham, and Japheth; and the three progenitors of the Greek peoples, Dorians, Ionians, Aeolians, offspring of Deucalion, the Greek Noah. Three of these names are toponyms, names of settlements known from Assyrian inscriptions in the region of Harran in northern Mesopotamia, Aramean territory. Terah corresponds to *Turāhi,* a place on the Balikh River near Harran; Nahor is identical with *Nahur* in the same region; and Haran, the name of the third son, probably derives from Harran (*harrānu,* Akkadian for "highway"), an important caravan stopover between the Upper Euphrates and the Tigris, on the main north-south, east-west intersection. This is important since it fixes the original homeland of the family, and therefore of Abraham. Lot's name is of unknown derivation, and Abraham is the exception but, like the similar Abiram ("exalted with respect to ancestors"), is certainly Aramean.[2]

Haran conforms to the same basic pattern of three children, in this instance one son, Lot, and two daughters, Milcah and Iscah. Lot is to become, inadvertently, the ancestor of Moabites and Ammonites (Gen. 19:30-38). Milcah becomes the wife of her uncle Nahor. We hear no more about Iscah, but we might take note of the Jewish midrashic tradition, in *Gen. Rab.* 38:14 and other ancient Jewish commentators and adopted by Josephus (*Ant.* 1.151), that Iscah is another name for Sarah. It seems to me that this view is correct and should be adopted. In the first place, the structuring, symmetrical patterning, and functionality common to this type of narrative do not allow for unnecessary characters, that is, characters who have no functional value.[3] The identification also restores symmetry to this compact genealogical table: Haran's daughters provide wives for both

---

and the Bible: Essays in Honour of James Barr, ed. S. E. Balentine and J. Barton (Oxford: Clarendon, 1994), 170-81, raised the issue of the alternative age of 145 for Terah in the Samaritan Pentateuch, the Targum, Philo (*On the Migration of Abraham* 177), and Stephen the Deacon's discourse in Acts 7:4. He reached no definite conclusion, but was inclined to favor MT, supported by LXX, Vulgate, and the Syriac version. This seems to me to be correct, since the alternative age for Terah results from the combination of his age at the birth of Abraham, that is, 70 (Gen. 11:26), with Abraham's age on leaving Harran, 75 (12:4). This conclusion avoided the embarrassment of Abraham leaving his aging father behind in Harran.

2. On the name see Alan R. Millard, "Abraham/Abram," in *ABD* 1:39.

3. The importance of the function of characters in traditional narrative is emphasized in the work of the Russian formalist Vladimir Propp, *Morphology of the Folktale,* 2nd. ed. (Austin: University of Texas Press, 1968). A brief account of the theory and its applicability

of their uncles, thus keeping the marriages within the Terahite kinship group. Finally, the identification is compatible with the names Sarah and Milcah, which are titles used as personal names meaning, respectively, "princess" and "queen." In view of the other neo-Babylonian associations of the Abraham story, to be noted in due course, we might add that *Šarrātu* (princess), cognate with Sarah, is the name of the consort of the moon deity Sin worshiped at Harran under Nabonidus, the last Babylonian ruler, who was replaced by the Persian Cyrus II after the fall of Babylon in 539 B.C. In like manner, *Malkâtu* (queen), cognate with Milkah, is the title of the goddess Ishtar, daughter of the same deity. This would be consistent with the statement in Josh. 24:2, that in times of old the family of Terah lived beyond the Euphrates and worshiped other gods, among whom first in importance was the god Sin worshiped in the Harran region. Iscah *(yiskah),* of unknown etymology and meaning, could therefore have been originally Sarah's personal name.[4]

This type of cross-cousin, uncle-niece marriage, practiced by Isaac and Jacob as well as Abraham (Gen. 24:24; 29:12), was later forbidden in the Levitical laws (Lev. 18:12-14) but was not uncommon in societies based on patrilineal descent. The reason is apparent. In the kind of society that operated on the father-son axis, the household had to import a woman from outside to continue the line. It was therefore important for the oldest son, the future head of the household, to marry a woman close enough to be familiar with the ethos of the household but not so close as to render the marriage incestuous. As the text stands, however, eight individuals are listed at this beginning of this new phase, the same number as those who survived the deluge to face the challenges of a depopulated world.

The passage immediately following the heading "These are the descendants (literally 'generations') of Terah" (Gen. 11:27) is not a straightforward genealogy, which the title may have led us to expect. Its purpose is rather to provide us, the readers, with information essential for understanding the further unfolding of the narrative plot. In the first place: Haran, father of Lot and two daughters, predeceased his father in Ur of the

---

to biblical narrative can be found in my *Treasures Old and New: Essays in the Theology of the Pentateuch* (Grand Rapids: Eerdmans, 2004), 142-44.

4. On this name see Richard S. Hess, "Iscah (Person)," in *ABD* 3:509. That this identification implied that Lot, in addition to being Abraham's nephew, was also his brother-in-law, would not have appeared as problematic. Abraham's claim that Sarah was his father's daughter (Gen. 20:12) could pass for the truth only if "father" is taken to mean "grandfather." She was certainly not the daughter of his, Abraham's, father.

Chaldees (Babylonians). After fathering Lot — who will have a morally ambiguous role to play later in the story — providing his two brothers with wives, and fathering the immediate ancestors of Ammonites and Moabites, he has made his contribution and can be removed from the narrative. Meanwhile his wife, like Lot's wife and daughters, remains nameless. Sarah and Milcah (on the hypothesis proposed above) become wives of the two surviving sons, Abraham and Nahor, respectively. Finally, and most importantly, Sarah is infertile; therefore Abraham has no son. In a narrative that leaves so much unsaid, the implications of this first succinct statement will unfold as the story progresses.

The First Stage of the Journey

At this point, while Terah is still the principal actor, there occurs the journey from Ur of the Chaldees (now Tell al-Muqayyar, about ten miles from Nasiriyah in southern Iraq) to Harran in the extreme north, now in southeast Turkey (Gen. 11:31-32). This journey is to be undertaken only by Terah and the three principals: Abraham, Sarah, and Lot. At this point the careful reader encounters problems. From the outset, the destination was the land of Canaan ("They set out from Ur of the Chaldees to go to the land of Canaan," 11:31). To reach it from Ur, they would first have followed the course of the Euphrates northward, *but not as far north as Harran,* before turning west into Syria in the direction of Damascus and then south into Palestine, following either the Mediterranean coastal highway, the so-called Via Maris route to Egypt, or the central ridge, passing through Shechem and Bethel, the route actually taken by Abraham. Harran, their destination, must therefore have been the result of a deliberate choice to *settle* there rather than make a stopover en route to Canaan (11:31). The party comprised Terah, Abraham, his wife Sarah, and his nephew Lot. Haran died back in Ur. Nahor, in due course to be revealed as ancestor of the Arameans and, specifically, of the wives of both Isaac and Jacob, is left behind.[5]

But there arises another problem of a topographical nature to disambiguate. It has to do with Ur of the Chaldees, a Sumerian city that was ancient at the time in which the Abraham story is set.[6] Haran predeceased

---

5. Later (Gen. 29:5) Laban is said to be the son of Nahor, but "son" must mean "grandson" since elsewhere it is clear that he is the son of Bethuel son of Nahor (28:5).

6. On its rediscovery and the suppositions based on the archaeological data, much

Terah his father in the land of his kin, in Ur (11:28), but his name cannot be dissociated from the place Harran *(harrānu)* in Upper Mesopotamia, between the Euphrates and Tigris, no more than the person Terah can be dissociated from the place *turāhi* on the Balik River near Harran, or the person Nahor — who did not make the northbound journey — from the place Nahur in the same region. Harran is also Abraham's country, where his kin had settled, as he pointed out explicitly in sending his majordomo there to find a wife for his son (Gen. 24:4, 7). This faithful servant then set off for Aram-naharaim ("Aram of the Two Rivers") and Nahor's city (24:10). In the following generation Jacob will be told by his mother Rachel to go to the same region (27:43). This suggests that the phrases "in Ur of the Chaldees" (11:28) and "from Ur of the Chaldees" (11:31) were subsequently added in apposition to "the land of his kin." The motive for the addition may have been to connect with the settlement of the Judean deportees by the Babylonians during and after the conquest of the Judean state (597-586 B.C.) and to link the Abraham traditions with Judean diaspora communities settled in southern Mesopotamia. Apart from these two appositional phrases, Ur is named only in Gen. 15:7 and Neh. 9:7, in both of which the LXX has "the land of the Chaldees" rather than "Ur of the Chaldees."

The connection with the Jewish diaspora finds support in the fact that the first stage of the journey not only starts out from a location associated with the Judean diaspora but also ends in the region in northern Mesopotamia in which Israelites who survived the destruction of the kingdom of Samaria had been settled by the Assyrians 136 years before Judah's deportation.[7] This may be taken to indicate that, at this stage of editorial activity, the hope of the reunion of north and south, the ten dispersed tribes with Judah inclusive of Benjamin, was still alive.

This much-compressed *mise en scène* says no more than is necessary. The number of those who accompanied Terah to Harran, the city in the

---

publicized by Sir Leonard Woolley, including his claim to have found evidence of the great deluge, see Susan Pollock, "Ur," in *The Oxford Encyclopedia of Archaeology in the Near East,* ed. Eric Meyers, vol. 5 (New York: Oxford University Press, 1997), 288-89.

7. Harran was near Gozan (Guzāna, Tell Halāf) on the river Khabûr where Samarian deportees were settled by the Assyrians (2 Kgs. 17:6; 18:11; 1 Chr. 5:26), and where Israelite names have come to light in excavations on the site; on which see Mordechai Cogan and Hayim Tadmor, *II Kings: A New Translation with Introduction and Commentary,* AB 11 (New York: Doubleday, 1988), 197; Lawson Younger Jr., "The Deportations of the Israelites," *JBL* 117 (1998): 201-27.

north, is reduced to the essential three *dramatis personae:* Abraham, Sarah, and Lot. We are told that Sarah was infertile, a condition that will initially afflict all three foremothers (Gen. 11:30; 25:21; 30:1-2), thus demonstrating the life-giving power of the God of Abraham, "who gives life to the dead and calls into existence things that do not exist" (Rom. 4:17). But since Abraham, unlike the reader, did not know what the future held, he would have seen the infertility of Sarah as a mortal threat to the possibility of issue. How grievous this will be, and what consequences it will entail, we will soon be told. It therefore seems likely — and the supposition will be confirmed after the arrival in Canaan — that Lot, Abraham's nephew and also, on the hypothesis about Iscah's other name, his brother-in-law, accompanied Abraham as his heir presumptive. Meanwhile, after a journey of more than 400 miles, they arrived in Harran. How long they settled there we are not told, but long enough for Abraham to accumulate considerable wealth in the form of herds and slaves (Gen. 12:5); this is the first of several indications that the ancestors knew how to prosper living in foreign lands, an example in this respect for their expatriate descendants. Of this aptitude Abraham will provide further demonstrations during his stay in Egypt and on his subsequent return to Canaan (12:16; 13:2). We are told, finally, that Terah died in Harran at the age of 205. Since Terah was 70 years old at the birth of Abraham (11:26), and Abraham was 75 on arrival in Canaan (12:4), Terah lived on for 60 years in Harran separated from his oldest son, predeceasing Abraham by 40 years (25:7) and Sarah by 2 years (23:1).

Abraham Hears the Voice for the First Time

The first of many communications between God and Abraham comes as if out of a void, after a long silence. After the near-death experience of humanity in the deluge, God spoke to Noah, giving him a command and a covenant of promise while bestowing a blessing (Gen. 9:1-17), an earlier parallel to Abraham's experience. But in the course of the ten generations that followed, nothing seemed to go right, and God was silent. The builders of the tower and city of Babel (11:1-9) confer among themselves and the deity deliberates with himself, but they do not interact; there is no communication. The revelation to Abraham comes, then, as a sudden, unanticipated, and profoundly transformative irruption into the course of events. Nothing we have been told about Abraham has prepared us for it, or provided any explanation why it happened to him, or why it happened at that time or in that place. Nor are we told whether the communication came to him in a vision, a dream, an inner voice, or by some other means. It must have had a self-authenticating character for Abraham to obey the voice without demur, pull up roots, and undertake a long journey to an as-yet-unknown destination. In retrospect, it can be seen as the beginning of a long history of frequent interaction either by speech alone, or speech accompanied by a visionary experience, or in the course of an act of worship at a shrine, or in a state of transformed consciousness.

This first revelation to Abraham (12:1-3), the subject of a vast amount of commentary both ancient and modern, consists in a command and an abundance of blessing — the word "bless" or "blessing" occurs five times in this short passage. It is implied that the fulfillment of the blessing is contingent in the first place on obedience to the command: "Leave your country, your kin, and your father's house and go to the land that I will show you. I shall make of you a great nation. I shall bless you and make your name so great that it will serve as a blessing. I shall bless those who bless you, and those who curse you I shall curse. Through you all the families of the earth will receive blessing." This first of many encounters of Abraham with his God, placed here at the beginning, provides the keynote to the story as a whole. It appears that this message and Abraham's prompt response — "so Abram went as Yahweh had bidden him" (12:4a) — have been added to the account of the first leg of the journey (11:31-32), which resumes after the addition with the note of Abraham's age next to that of his father. Abraham is told to go to a land that he will be shown, and therefore a land unknown to him, but we have already learned that from the outset the destination was Canaan (11:31). In keeping with a common literary procedure (a resumptive verse, *Wiederaufnahme*), this information is repeated verbatim when the account of the journey resumes (12:5). At this point we encounter once again the problematic place of Ur of the Chaldees in the story. The voice he hears tells him to leave behind his country, kin, and father's house, but he is in Harran when the message comes to him (11:31). As later events, including the quest for a bride for Isaac, will show, Harran, otherwise referred to as Aram-naharaim ("Aram of the Two Rivers"), is indeed Abraham's homeland, but since the journey originated in Ur, it would be natural to assume that that is where his country was and where his kin resided. Readers of the New Testament will recall that the deacon Stephen, in his defense before the Sanhedrin, saw the problem and resolved it by the simple expedient of locating the revelation in Ur: "The God of glory appeared to Abraham our father in Mesopotamia before he settled in Harran" (Acts 7:2). It is at least clear that this insertion into the journey narrative was intended to provide an explanation in explicitly religious terms for the second stage of the journey.

The voice heard by Abraham provides the first intimation of the far-reaching consequences of this moment of revelation. The God who commands and promises is the God of an Israel that did not exist at that time. The narrator knew that, we the readers know it, but Abraham could not have known it. A revelation to Moses when in Egypt will explicitly deny that the deity revealed himself to the ancestors under the name Yahweh (Exod. 6:2-3). We are therefore to understand the use of the name Yahweh in the Abraham story as reflecting the religious conviction of the narrator and his assumed readers rather than Abraham's own grasp of the situation. We may in any case conclude that there was something self-authenticating for Abraham about the words spoken at that moment in time and at that point in his own life, whatever his past experience may have been.

Abraham, then, is given a command and a promise. He is to abandon his familiar surroundings and leave for a land to which the voice will direct him. The instructions are not given there and then, but in any case Abraham's destination remains the same as the original goal of the journey, namely, the land of Canaan. The promises, which are programmatic for the future and will often be repeated, are that Abraham will be the ancestor of a great nation; that he will be blessed; that his name will serve as a blessing and be the source of blessing; and that this blessing will be for all the families of the earth. After everything that had gone wrong in the damaged world since the great extinction of the deluge, culminating in the abortive attempt to build a city and a temple-tower called Babel, this is good news indeed, like a return to the first creation.

The general sense of the promise is apparent: blessing signifies fullness of life and joy. There is, however, a long-standing debate among biblical scholars, on which we do not need to adjudicate, as to how to parse these promises addressed to Abraham. Among the questions being asked are the following: Which of the promised blessings are original and which secondary? What is the connection between descendants and land? How would the blessings have been understood by the first hearers in light of the exigencies and stresses of their own time, which most critical scholars believe to be shortly after the near extinction of defeat and exile at the hands of the Babylonians? The first of the blessings, the prospect of a great nation that will acknowledge Abraham as founder and forefather, is repeated at a later point in the story (Gen. 18:18), and will begin to be realized in Egypt

(Gen. 46:3; Deut. 26:5; Exod. 1:9). In the course of time, however, it comes about that only after the wilderness generation has passed from the scene will the promise be realized (Exod. 32:10; Num. 14:12). Moreover, the same promise is made of the descendants of Ishmael, Abraham's other beloved son (Gen. 17:20; 21:18). Blessing, a concept much subject to devaluation, is a way of bestowing happiness and well-being. The third promise, that Abraham's name will be great and will be used in pronouncing blessings, is perhaps in deliberate contrast to the builders of the city and tower of Babel who proposed to make a name for themselves in their own way, on their own terms, and by their own efforts (11:1-9). Curses on those who curse and blessings on those who bless serve as a way of assuring good relations and warding off malign influences in advance, as we see from Isaac blessing Jacob (27:29) and Balaam blessing Israel (Num. 24:9). Names can serve as curses as well as blessings. According to Jeremiah, for example, the names of those Judean expatriates tortured and executed (martyred?) by the king of Babylon served that purpose ("May Yahweh make you like Zedekiah and Ahab, whom the king of Babylon roasted in the fire," Jer. 29:22).

The precise meaning of the last and most comprehensive blessing, often repeated, is disputed. One interpretation of the Hebrew verbal theme *(nivreku)* reads it as the passive voice, with the meaning that all the families of the earth will receive blessing in some way because of Abraham; Abraham will be a source of blessing for all peoples (Gen. 12:1-3). This is the meaning according to the LXX, the Vulgate, the Targum tradition, the New Testament (Gal. 3:8), and a good number of modern exegetes. The alternative is to read the verb as reflexive and reciprocal, as if to say, "May you receive blessing in the same measure as Abraham." In other words, Abraham is to be a byword for rather than a source of blessing, though it is not clear why a person cannot be both.[8] On the other hand, the somewhat unusual way of referring to the recipients of blessing as "all the families of the soil" recalls the curse on the soil after the first fratricide (Gen. 4:11-12) and the misplaced ambitions of the "families" of the world in the so-called Table of Nations (10:1-32). Their pretensions culminated in the abortive

8. On Abraham as a byword for blessing, see Erhard Blum, *Die Komposition der Väter-geschichte,* WMANT 57 (Neukirchen-Vluyn: Neukirchener Verlag, 1984), 349-59. Blum cites Ps. 72:17, "Then all will pray to be blessed as he (the king) was," though in this case the verbal theme, Hithpa'el, is different. The issue is discussed in Claus Westermann, *Genesis 12–36* (Minneapolis: Augsburg, 1985), 151-52, and by Jon Levenson in his recent publication *Inheriting Abraham: The Legacy of the Patriarch in Judaism, Christianity, and Islam* (Princeton and Oxford: Princeton University Press, 2012), 24-26.

attempt to build a city and a temple-tower, but since this is Babylon, let us say an empire and a residence for the imperial deity (11:1-9). This is the situation the new initiative of God aims to reverse, bringing blessing to "all the families of the earth." The context of the Abraham story therefore makes it redundantly clear that Abraham is God's agent for a new initiative on behalf not just of one ethnic group but of all humanity. And he is to be not just the standard for what blessing means but the means for the bestowal of blessing.

Like all texts, this one is subject to misunderstanding. One interpretation, ascribed to a certain Rabbi Eleazar, poses the question: "What is the meaning of 'All the families of the earth shall be blessed through you'? The Holy One, blessed be He, said to Abraham, 'I have two good shoots to graft on to you, Ruth of Moab and Naamah of Ammon'" (*b. Yeb.* 63a). Ruth is well known, Naamah was the Ammonite mother of King Rehoboam (1 Kgs. 14:21), and according to Deuteronomic law, Moabites and Ammonites were excluded from Israel in perpetuity (Deut. 23:3). Eleazar, therefore, appears to be promoting a positive attitude to proselytes, not excluding proselytes of Moabite or Ammonite origin, a proposal that is no doubt laudable, but not as an interpretation of the Abrahamic blessing on "all the families of the earth." Blessing on "all the families of the earth" cannot be limited either to proselytes or to diaspora Jewish communities scattered throughout the Near East and the Mediterranean at the time the Abraham story was put together. What is implied in this programmatic statement (Gen. 12:1-4a), following the list of Noah's descendants and the debacle in Babel, is that the blessing of Abraham marks a new beginning for the humanity inhabiting the drastically reduced postdiluvial world. The career of Abraham is to open up a new initiative among the families of the world listed in the Table of Nations in Gen. 10. Jews, Christians, and Muslims will inherit this view of Abraham as "father of all believers" (Rom. 4:11), but the universal implications of the blessing were discerned already in the prophetic writings. Many examples could be cited, but one of the most powerful statements even includes within the blessing the names of two of the most oppressive imperial powers of antiquity with which ancient Israel was intimately acquainted (Isa. 19:24-25): "When that day comes Israel will rank as a third with Egypt and Assyria and be a blessing to the world. This is the blessing the Lord of Hosts will give: 'Blessed be Egypt my people, Assyria my handiwork, and Israel my possession.'"

The Second Stage of the Journey: En Route to Canaan

The narrative of the journey, now under divine mandate, takes up again with the resumptive phrase "they set out to go to the land of Canaan" (Gen. 12:5; cf. 11:31), prefaced by the first of several references to Abraham's age (12:4b-5; cf. 11:31). Recording the passage of time is an especially significant element in any narrative with strong biographical content. In the ancestral cycles, where the temporal aspect calls for close cooperation with the reader, it is done primarily by noting the age of one or another of the principals at important junctures of the plot. Abraham undertakes the journey at age 75 and dies at age 175, giving him exactly a century in Canaan (25:7-8). The intermediate notations of age have several long gaps between them: eleven years to the birth of Ishmael, his first son (16:16); fourteen more to the birth of Isaac (21:5); thirty-seven years to the death of Sarah (23:1-2); and a long stretch of thirty-eight years during which, following the order of events in the cycle, Abraham married Keturah, another Arabian woman, and sired six more sons. (We shall see, however, that according to a traditional reading, Keturah was another name for Hagar, whom Abraham married, or remarried, after Sarah's death.) These are, of course, impossibly high figures. At the time in which the story is set, average life expectancy would have been less than, not more than, it is today. These are schematic ages, and the schema according to which they are calculated is dictated by a view of history as a downward spiral from the greater energy and wisdom available in the dawn of humanity. Apart from that, they function only to manifest relations between individuals and the passing of time between significant events.

In common with biblical narrative generally, nothing is said about the journey itself until the travelers arrive in Canaan. Shechem (Tell Balata, near Nablus in the West Bank) and Bethel (Beitin, about twelve miles north of Jerusalem) lie on one of the two principal north-south routes in Palestine. There is the King's Highway (Num. 20:17), from Upper Mesopotamia to North Arabia and Egypt, vital for the spice trade; the Via Maris, mentioned earlier; and, in between, the central route to Egypt via Shechem, Bethel, and Beersheba. Jacob will follow the same route as Abraham on his return from exile in Mesopotamia, staying long enough in Shechem to purchase a plot of land (Gen. 33:18-34:31), then visiting the Bethel sanctuary on his way to Beersheba and, eventually, reaching Egypt.

"The place Shechem" (12:6)[9] was destined to play an important role in Israelite history. The route taken by Abraham passed through the valley in which Shechem lay, situated between the mountains of Ebal and Gerizim. In the conquest narrative, the first religious act of the Israelites after entering the Promised Land was to build an altar of unworked stone on Mount Ebal, sacrifice on it, and set up on the mountain plastered stones on which laws had been inscribed (Josh. 8:30-35, in obedience to Deut. 11:29-32). According to one reconstruction of this defining moment, a covenant ceremony took place on the site involving representatives of the twelve tribes and featuring solemn curses on violations of the twelve laws promulgated (Deut. 27:1-26). Another version of the Shechem covenant concludes Joshua's activities and the book named for him (Josh. 24:1-28). Increasing alienation between Jerusalem and Samaria, in evidence during the governorship of Nehemiah (Neh. 13:28), led to open hostility toward the temple at Gerizim built, according to Josephus, shortly after the Macedonian conquest (*Ant.* 13.256), leading eventually to its destruction by John Hyrcanus in 129 B.C. (13.255-256). It is therefore no surprise to come across examples of anti-Shechemite, and therefore anti-Samaritan, bias in biblical texts, including the brief and disastrous rule of Abimelech as king of Shechem in Judg. 9 and the rape of Dinah by the city ruler and the subsequent plundering of the city and slaughter of its inhabitants in Gen. 34.[10]

The sacred tree associated with the sanctuary in the account of Abraham's itinerary (Gen. 12:6) is also mentioned without comment in Deut. 11:30. It was either a terebinth or an oak, and the name could suggest a con-

---

9. For *māqôm*, "place," as a designation for a sanctuary, see, e.g., Deut. 12:5, 11, 21, with reference to Jerusalem; Ezra 8:17; 9:8 with reference to Casiphia in southern Mesopotamia.

10. Among obscure and debatable allusions to Shechem some scholars count the reference to "Melchizedek king of Salem" (*melek šālēm,* Gen. 14:18). While the reference in the mind of the writer was certainly to Jerusalem, there existed an alternative tradition of uncertain age and origin about a place called Salem in the vicinity of Shechem. In Gen. 33:18 we read that "Jacob came to Salem, a city of Shechem," a reading supported by the LXX. No other reading seems likely, least of all with the adverbial sense of "peacefully." There is also the tradition, if that is what it is, passed on by Pseudo-Eupolemus (fragment 1:56) from Eusebius (*Praep. ev.* 9.17.6), that "Abraham was treated as a guest by the city in the temple Argarizin which means 'Mount of the Most High.'" On the excavations at Mount Gerizim from 1979 to the present and the dedicatory inscription from the fourth and third centuries B.C., see Yitzaq Magen, "Mount Gerizim — a Temple City: Summary of Eighteen Years of Excavations," *Qadmoniot* 33 (2000): 74-118, and Jan Dušek, *Aramaic and Hebrew Inscriptions from Mt. Gerizim and Samaria between Antiochus III and Antiochus IV Epiphanes,* Culture and History of the Ancient Near East, vol. 54 (Leiden: Brill, 2012).

nection with oracles; it is perhaps identical with the "oak of the diviners" during the disastrous reign of Abimelech at Shechem (Judg. 9:37). Since the veneration of trees associated with different *numina* was practiced in Canaan, it was probably Abraham's oak or terebinth that inspired the explanatory and exculpatory comment that "at that time the Canaanites were in the land" (Gen. 12:6). This, by the way, was one of the texts that persuaded Abraham ibn Ezra in the twelfth century that, contrary to orthodox opinion at that time and for long afterward, Moses could not have written the entire Pentateuch.

At Shechem, the first stopping place in Canaan, Abraham heard the same voice he heard in Harran, this time accompanied by a vision. Since he had now obeyed the command to go on the journey, there is added the promise of a place to live, if not for himself, then for his descendants. This promise will recur as a leitmotif throughout the history of the ancestors. In recognition of this further sign of benevolence, Abraham built an altar to the deity whose voice he had heard and obeyed. There is a hint here of the practice of setting up an altar in newly occupied territory, a way of staking a claim. Saul, for example, set up his first altar after defeating the Philistines in their own territory, which he would then take over (1 Sam. 14:35). But there was something more momentous at issue with Abraham's altar-building activity. It signified the introduction of the worship of the one, true God into a pagan world of which the Canaanite inhabitants of the land were a part. The parallel in Islamic lore would be the command to Ibrahim and his son Isma'il to set up the Kaaba, the house of prayer, in Mecca (Qur'an 2:127).

Abraham's next stop was at Bethel. This holy place, principal sanctuary of the kingdom of Samaria after its secession from Solomon's united monarchy, associated closely with the Jacob traditions, survived both the Assyrian conquest (2 Kgs. 17:24-28) and the reforming zeal of Josiah (23:15-20) to serve an important role in the postdisaster period as a major sanctuary and substitute for the Jerusalem temple then lying in ruins.[11] At Bethel, site of an ancient Canaanite sanctuary, Abraham invoked the name of Yahweh, an expression that implies an act of worship but not necessarily sacrifice.

---

11. This chapter in the history of Bethel is discussed in my "Bethel in the Neo-Babylonian Period," in *Judah and the Judeans in the Neo-Babylonian Period,* ed. Oded Lipschits and Joseph Blenkinsopp (Winona Lake, Ind.: Eisenbrauns, 2003), 93-107.

Filling In the Gaps

A narrative that is so compressed and leaves so much unsaid will inevitably provoke all sorts of questions. Why did Terah, patriarch of the family, decide to undertake such a long journey from Ur to the land of Canaan, and then settle at the halfway mark in Harran where, it seems, he spent the rest of his life? Why did the revelation happen to Abraham, about whose antecedents we are told nothing, and why did it happen in Harran rather than in Ur where he is said to have lived long enough for his brother Haran to have three grown children before dying in that city? Did something happen in Ur of the Chaldees or in Harran that might explain his role in the biblical story of the ancestors? Contemporary readers are, on the whole, content to take the story as it is without being unduly concerned about such questions. In the world of Jewish midrashists, however, such probing was essential to getting at the inner meaning. Their inclination was rather to follow the principle of interpretation current in the school of Hillel: "Turn it, and turn it again, for everything is in it" (*m. Avot* 5:22). This final section of the chapter, and that of the chapters that follow, presents only a small selection of such "turnings" from the midrash and other ancient sources.

Starting with the Hebrew Bible itself, attentive readers of the Abraham story would have found of interest the opening statement of Joshua's valedictory address mentioned earlier. It begins with Terah and his sons Abraham and Nahor living beyond the Euphrates and worshiping other gods; hence these three, rather than Abraham, Isaac, and Jacob, are the primal ancestors — a point to be kept in mind. From this situation Abraham was rescued, taken from beyond the River, and led by divine guidance into the land of Canaan (Josh. 24:1-3). A prayer, attributed in the Septuagint to Ezra, praises God for bringing Abraham out from Ur of the Chaldees, and does so in language calculated to bring to mind the exodus from Egypt, in some texts described as deliverance from an iron furnace (Neh. 9:7; cf. Deut. 4:20). The tradition is reproduced in Pseudo-Philo (*Liber antiquitatum biblicarum* 6), in terms reminiscent of the Maccabee martyrs (2 Macc. 6:18-31; 7:1-42) and of some later Christian martyrologies.

Some ancient commentators on Gen. 11:31–12:3 were anxious to correct the impression given in the Joshua text that, as a member of Terah's family, Abraham also "served other gods." This required setting him apart from his idolatrous father and the rest of his kin. *Jubilees* (11:4-17) has him, aged fourteen, trying to talk his father out of the worship of idols and, on failing to do so, getting his attention by burning down the house in which the idols were worshiped. A similar tradition is taken up in Islam, recording Ibrahim's unsuccessful attempt to win over his father Azar from paganism (Qur'an 19:42-47). The young Abraham's recourse to arson could also account for the absence of Haran after the departure from Ur since, according to one tradition, Haran died in the fire trying to save the idols. Other commentators present Abraham as a youth propagating the worship of the one true God, activity that led to his being cast into a fiery furnace by Nimrod, who then ruled the land, thus sharing the fate of the three youths in Dan. 3.[12] Josephus tells us that after miraculously surviving this trial, he was expelled from Chaldea (*Ant.* 1.155-157).

In the first section of the *Apocalypse of Abraham* (1-8), a work that has survived only in Palaeoslavonic but is thought to have been composed in Hebrew in the first or second century of the common era, these various themes are combined into a kind of novelistic *Bildungsroman* in which the young Abraham's vicissitudes and adventures in the service of mono-theistic faith are recorded in a fast-moving narrative. It all ends with his last-minute rescue, by divine intervention, as Terah's house with everyone and everything in it goes up in flames. Terah's addiction to idolatry and his work as a professional idol maker also absolved Abraham from the charge of parental neglect in abandoning his father, then 145 years old, when Abraham left for the land of Canaan (*Gen. Rab.* 39:7).

We find a different line of interpretation in Philo and early Christian writers. For the latter, what called for comment above all was Abraham's immediate and unconditional obedience to the summons from God, mak-ing him a model for those answering the call to Christian discipleship.[13] In his treatise *On the Migration of Abraham,* Philo read Abraham's journey as symbolic of the quest for enlightenment and true wisdom in the spirit of Plato's allegory of the cave in the *Republic* (514a-520a). It involves progress from imprisonment in the world of sense impressions to self-knowledge, and from self-knowledge to knowledge of God, "the mind of the universe" (§§ 1-4). You cannot find enlightenment by staying where you are. Like Abraham, you must be a Hebrew in the etymological sense of one who "crosses over," one who moves on; in other words, a *peratēs* ("migrant,"

12. *Gen. Rab.* 38:13; *Tg. Neof.* on Gen. 11:31; more in Louis Ginzberg, *The Legends of the Jews*, vol. 1 (Philadelphia: Jewish Publication Society of America, 1961), 198-203.

13. Matt. 16:24; 19:27; Mark 10:28; Luke 14:26. For samples of early Christian com-mentary on Gen 11:27–12:9, see Mark Sheridan, *Ancient Christian Commentary on Scripture: Old Testament II; Genesis 12–50* (Downers Grove, Ill.: InterVarsity, 2002), 1-6.

§20). So Abraham journeyed from Chaldea, a country famous for astrological knowledge attained by physical observation, to Harran, the stage of self-knowledge, and finally to the Promised Land of the knowledge of the one true God (§§ 189-197).

· 2 ·

Sarah and Lot, Wife and Nephew

Sarah Preserved, Lot Eliminated

The focus now moves to the roles assigned to Sarah and Lot, both so far silent actors in the drama set in motion by the words spoken to Abraham and the journey to Canaan. Of the original eight characters, Haran is dead, Terah has been left behind in Harran, Nahor and Milcah will reappear later after Isaac meets Laban and Rebekah in Aram-naharaim (i.e., Harran), and Iscah is another name for Sarah. We left Abraham at Bethel setting up an altar and invoking the name of the deity whose voice he had heard before leaving his own country (Gen. 12:8). How soon after this he set out on another journey, this time to the Negev, the desolate region to the south of Canaan (*negev* means "south"), we are not told. Here and throughout the history of the ancestors the time element must be supplied by the reader. The Negev was not outside the boundaries of the land that was Abraham's destination. It was included in the census that got David into trouble (2 Sam. 24:7), and settlements in the Negev are listed as part of the tribal territory of Judah and Simeon, incorporated into Judah (Josh. 15:20-32; 19:1-9). After the extinction of the Judean state toward the end of the sixth century B.C., however, it was occupied by Edomite and, eventually, Idumean and Qedarite Arabs, on which more later. At this point, the narrator needed to place Abraham in the Negev in close proximity to Egypt where famine would provide him with justification for a temporary absence from the land. Egypt served as the traditional refuge during severe droughts and famines that have been the lot of Palestine, on average once every seven years, some lasting seven years, since time immemorial.[1]

---

1. Gen. 26:1; 41–43; 45:6, 11; 2 Kgs. 8:1.

The famine is the cue for two early complications of the plot, the first involving Sarah, the second Lot. The first narrates how Abraham endangered the life and honor of his wife Sarah when in Egypt on account of the famine and, by doing so, placed in jeopardy the future fulfillment of the promises (Gen. 12:10-20). The second presents Lot as voluntarily taking himself out of contention as the heir presumptive of Abraham by choosing to live not only outside the land of promise but also among people of bad repute (13:1-18). The consequence of this self-interested choice was that he ended up as collateral damage in the War of the Nine Kings, one of the most curious narratives in Genesis, which called for his rescue by Abraham and his allies (14:11-16). His elimination from a central role in the future anticipated in the promises is marked by a more comprehensive repetition of the territorial promise made at Shechem, to be inherited by Abraham's as-yet-nonexistent descendants (13:14-18).

We delay to a later point in our survey consideration of the misadventures of Lot after settling in his new habitat (19:1-38). In connection with the endangering of Sarah in Egypt (12:10-20), it will also be convenient to take account of a similar episode in Philistine territory involving Abraham, Sarah, and a foreign ruler (20:1-18), one certainly modeled on the Egyptian version, as we shall see.

Trouble in Egypt

The Egyptian episode (12:10-20) provides an illustration of the way the story of the ancestors was put together by several hands over a considerable period of time. Abraham's progress from Bethel to the Negev and thence to Egypt (12:8-9) is repeated in reverse order immediately after his return from Egypt (13:1-4), putting him back at Bethel. This bracketing technique is an example of the way individual type-scenes have been slotted into the genealogical framework of the history. The brief Bethel phase of the Abraham cycle will come to an end after Sarah emerges unscathed from Egypt and Lot disqualifies himself as Abraham's heir by choosing to live in Sodom, therefore outside of Canaan. At this point, after an especially emphatic repetition of the promise of land (13:14-17), Abraham moves farther south to another religious sanctuary, Mamre, with its sacred trees, near Hebron in the southern highlands, where he will remain for much of his remaining time (13:18).

Bethel, a few miles north of Jerusalem, is the principal center for Jacob, Abraham's grandson, but Mamre is destined to be the burial plot for all the ancestors beginning with Sarah and Abraham. Bethel is primarily associated with Jacob, and the Jacob story is the original nucleus around which the other characters and their stories have been arranged, Abraham and Isaac preceding it, the sons of Jacob-Israel, eponym of the twelve tribes, following it. Abraham's move from Bethel to Mamre can be seen as one aspect of the process by which the traditions about Abraham, author of blessing for all the families of the earth, were combined with the traditions about Jacob-Israel by genealogical extension backward. Abraham's purchase of the burial plot at Mamre, after lengthy negotiations (23:1-20), also serves to illustrate the importance of the link between the living and dead members of the kinship group. It explains the attachment of later generations to the ancestors who, though long dead, continue to shape the identity of their descendants and live on in their memory.[2] Mamre, near Hebron, like other burial sites, may also have been one of the principal loci for the preservation of the rich fund of traditions about Abraham that have survived.

Only Abraham and Sarah are named as seeking survival in Egypt, but the caravan would have included retainers, other dependents, and the slaves mentioned earlier. It would have been inconceivable, not to say suicidal, for two people, a man and his wife, to travel alone through the vast Sinai Peninsula, especially in a time of drought. The narrator is silent about Lot, no doubt to avoid distraction from the one theme with its focus on Sarah, a theme that will be stated with the greatest economy of words and characters.[3] The attentive reader will however note that Abraham arrived in Egypt as a resident alien (Hebrew *ger*) rather than as a settler, whereas we are informed that Lot *settled* among the Cities of the Plain, and specifically in Sodom (13:2; 14:12; 19:29). "Now there was a famine in the land. So Abram went down to Egypt to reside there as an alien, for the famine was severe in the land" (12:10). It is thereby emphasized that Abraham's stay in Egypt was unavoidable and temporary, and that therefore, unlike Lot, he had not voided the promises by moving outside of the land of Canaan.

2. On the importance for the extended kinship group of burial on patrimonial domain, see Herbert Brichto, "Kin, Cult, Land and Afterlife — a Biblical Complex," *HUCA* 44 (1973): 1-54; Francesca Stavrakopoulou, *Land of Our Fathers: The Roles of Ancestor Veneration in Biblical Land Claims* (London and New York: T. & T. Clark, 2011).

3. In keeping with a characteristic of popular traditional narrative that concentrates on one principal character at a time and avoids complicated scenarios; see the classical treatment of Axel Olrik, "Epische Gesetze der Volksdichtung," *Zeitschrift für deutsches Altertum* 51 (1909): 1-12.

The brief record of trouble in Egypt begins with Abraham's instructions to Sarah before departure: "When he was about to enter Egypt, he said to his wife Sarai, 'I know that you are a woman beautiful in appearance; and when the Egyptians see you they will say, "This is his wife"; then they will kill me, but they will let you live. Say you are my sister, so that it may go well with me because of you, and that my life may be spared on your account'" (12:11-13). It goes on to relate how it turned out as Abraham had feared, with Sarah in Pharaoh's harem (vv. 14-16). It ends with the discovery of the deceit and the ignominious dismissal of Abraham by the pharaoh — "Here's your wife; take her and go" (vv. 17-20). There is nothing uplifting in this terse account, and there is no dialogue. Sarah, in particular, is silent throughout.

Abraham begins his briefing of Sarah by acknowledging that she is a beautiful woman, which involves ignoring her "schematic age," according to which she was then in her late sixties (12:4b; 17:17; not that a woman in her late sixties cannot be beautiful). He is afraid that when they see her with him they will assume she is his wife and will kill him in order to possess her. The solution: tell them that you are my sister, so that all may go well with me and my life may be spared on your account. At one time, some commentators believed they had found a key to this wife-sister issue in a curious marriage custom among the Hurrian population of Nuzi, situated in what is now the Kurdish region of northern Iraq. The date would be the second half of the second millennium B.C. (1500-1200 B.C.), archaeologically the Late Bronze Age, which seemed to fit very well with what was, at one time, the preferred date for the biblical narratives about the ancestors. Briefly: according to this custom the wife was adopted by the husband as his sister, a legal fiction that gave her higher status and better protection. This seemed at first to fit the situation in Egypt quite well, but such an early dating of the Genesis episode has been abandoned by the great majority of scholars, and in any case the bearing of the practice on the biblical texts has never been convincingly demonstrated. This explanation is therefore no longer heard.[4]

An even less plausible explanation is by appeal to the practice, famil-

---

4. On this Nuzi custom see Ephraim A. Speiser, "The Wife-Sister Motif in the Patriarchal Narratives," in *Biblical and Other Studies,* ed. A. Altmann (Cambridge: Harvard University Press, 1963), 15-28; Ephraim A. Speiser, *Genesis: Introduction, Translation, and Notes,* AB 1 (Garden City, N.Y.: Doubleday, 1964), 91-93. The relevance of this material to the "endangering of the ancestress" passages has often been criticized, most comprehensively by Thomas L. Thompson, *The Historicity of the Patriarchal Narratives,* BZAW 133 (Berlin:

iar from the Song of Songs, of referring to the wife or betrothed as sister ("My sister, my bride!" [Song 4:9, 10]), especially since it seemed to enable him to avoid lying while giving the impression that his claim is to be taken in the literal, biological sense. But apart from the distinct possibility that the Egyptians, to whom this usage was well known, would easily have seen through the deceit, there is no evidence that the practice was familiar in Abraham's own environment.

There are questions arising from these instructions that the reader might wish to raise, among them the following: Why was Abraham so sure that the Egyptians would act in this way? Even if they believed his story, how would this discourage an Egyptian attracted by Sarah's great beauty from killing the brother escorting her in order to possess her? How could an Asiatic, one of many such foreigners notoriously unwelcome in Egypt, as is apparent from the inscriptions (see also Gen. 43:32), come so readily to the attention of the pharaoh and his officials? How, to state the main point, could the Abraham we are beginning to get to know be so incredibly callous?

From the brief account of what actually happened (vv. 14-16), it seems that trouble arose only with the appearance on the scene of the powerful of the land, when Sarah came to the attention of Pharaoh's attendants, leading to her induction into the royal seraglio. Perhaps mindful of David's seduction of Bathsheba and murder of her foreign husband (2 Sam. 11–12), the author notes that, rather than simply ordering Abraham's death, the standard solution to the problem, the pharaoh compensated him for the loss of his "sister" in the usual currency: sheep, oxen, donkeys, camels, and male and female slaves. Silver and gold, mentioned somewhat later (13:2), were probably also taken from Egypt, in one aspect anticipating the "plundering of the Egyptians" during the exodus (Exod. 12:35). Precious bullion also features in the later version involving Abraham and the king of Gerar (Gen. 20:16), and is mentioned in the imaginative retelling known as the Qumran *Genesis Apocryphon* (1QapGen 20:31). What is especially striking here, in contrast to the David-Bathsheba episode, where we are told that "the thing that David had done displeased Yahweh" (2 Sam. 11:27), is the lack of authorial comment. The events are allowed to speak for themselves.

The resolution of the problem left Sarah free from her Egyptian bondage, thus keeping the promised future open at the cost of Abraham's

---

De Gruyter, 1974), 234-47; John Van Seters, *Abraham in History and Tradition* (New Haven: Yale University Press, 1975), 68-85.

public shaming (Gen. 12:17–13:1). Yahweh inflicted "great plagues" on Pharaoh, probably a disfiguring skin disease of a serious nature (cf. Lev. 13:1-59), which he, or his court diagnosticians, at once identified as the consequence of his accepting a married woman as one of his wives, albeit unknowingly.[5] How this connection was established we do not know, but we assume that Pharaoh's positive reaction had the desired result of a cure. Abraham was summoned, and had to listen in silence to Pharaoh's reproaches and contemptuous dismissal. Abraham, morally compromised and punished, moved on to deal with a dispute between his herdsmen and those of Lot. It seems very likely that Pharaoh had sexual relations with Sarah; this is implied in his reproach that, in consequence of Abraham's deceit, he took her for his wife. But since Yahweh had not yet opened her womb, there was no issue, and so the future still lay open.

Several interpreters have noticed that Abraham in Egypt serves as a kind of preview of Jacob and his sons going to Egypt during a famine in Palestine (Gen. 42:1-2; 46:5-7). Like Abraham, they suffered deprivation there (Exod. 1:8-22), for which Pharaoh and his people were afflicted with plagues (Exod. 5–11). In due course they left loaded down with silver, gold, and other goods from Egypt (12:35-36), as did Abraham before them. Since this can hardly be coincidental, it will serve as another indication of the primacy of the Jacob traditions as ethnogenesis to which the Abraham story came to serve as a prelude.

Trouble in Philistine Country

Critically considered, this second of three incidents in which an ancestress is the object of unwelcome attention from a ruler in a foreign land (Gen. 20:1-18) would be considered a synoptic narrative variant of the other two (12:10-20; 26:1-11). At the purely literary level this is so, but read in the narrative context as a whole, it is a distinct incident, a repetition of the experience in Egypt anticipated by Abraham before setting out from Harran. This, at any rate, is the way Abraham explained to Abimelech,

---

5. From its position in the sentence, most commentators conclude that *wĕ'et-bêtô* ("and his household") is an insertion, perhaps suggested by the parallel Gerar version in 20:17. According to the Qumran *Genesis Apocryphon* (20:16-17), Pharaoh and all his household were affected, resulting in general impotence among the male palace personnel. Hence Pharaoh's inability to have sexual relations with Sarah even though she remained with him for two years.

ruler of Gerar, how this could have happened again after the humiliating conclusion to the episode in Egypt: "When God set me wandering from my father's house, I said to her (Sarah), 'There is a duty towards me which you must loyally fulfill: wherever we go, you must say that I am your brother'" (20:13). Both this second occasion and the third, involving Isaac and Rebekah, took place in Gerar, which was ruled by the Philistine Abimelech. So now Abraham and Sarah are, for reasons unstated, in Gerar, a settlement situated on the southern boundary of Canaan (10:19), perhaps on the site of Tell Haror, about twenty kilometers west of Beersheba, between Beersheba and Gaza.[6]

The isolation of this incident in its narrative context is apparent from the opening sentence, which says Abraham journeyed *from there* to the Negev but does not indicate his point of departure. The last location named is Mamre/Hebron (18:1, 33), and on this occasion no reason is given for leaving Canaan. Since, however, the episode in Gerar represents another trial survived and another problem overcome, it has been strategically placed after the final exclusion of Lot, now identified as ancestor of Moabites and Ammonites, Israel's neighbors, which is to say, enemies (19:37), and before the birth of a son to Sarah in her old age (21:1-3). It is also situated between the announcement of the birth of this son (18:10) and the actual miraculous event when Sarah was ninety years old (21:5-7; cf. 17:17). In noting these structural arrangements and interconnections, we see how these stories were put together as a work of bricolage, an assemblage of different incidents and type-scenes strung together to make a more or less coherent story.

One solution to the many questions to which the "endangering of the ancestress" theme gives rise is to read this second instance as a purely scribal creation, gridded on to the Egyptian episode on the one hand and the similar story involving Isaac, Rebekah, and the same ruler on the other (26:1-11). All three are clearly instantiations of the same type-scene exploiting elements of customary law concerning marriage, adultery, consanguinity, affinity, and brother-sister relations in particular. All three exhibit

---

6. Eliezer D. Oren, "Gerar (Place)," in *ABD* 2:989-91. It is not clear why Abraham is said to have first settled between Kadesh and Shur (Gen. 20:1). The famous oasis of Kadesh in the Sinai is located on the southern boundary of Judah, but at what period of Judah's history is uncertain (Josh. 15:1-3). Shur was an Ishmaelite settlement in the northern Sinai (Gen. 25:18; 1 Sam. 15:7), situated a good distance from Gerar (Tell Haror). We shall see that it may not be coincidence that Hagar's destination after her expulsion was also at an oasis between Kadesh and Shur (Gen. 16:7).

motifs and procedures found in oral folktales, but none of the three is a written-up folktale. That 20:1-18 betrays familiarity with 12:10-20, and that its author is aware of the moral ambiguities of Abraham's situation as described there, is beyond reasonable doubt. In the present episode Abraham explains to Abimelech that Sarah really is his sister, daughter of his father but with a different mother (20:12), thus removing or at least mitigating the lie in the Egyptian episode, though perhaps at the cost of telling another lie. The author of the Gerar episode also abbreviates Abraham's self-serving admonitions to Sarah, predates them to the Harran period, and even has Abraham hinting that the deity was really responsible since it was the deity who caused him to wander from his native home (20:13). The stratagem is also justified on the grounds that the local Philistine population was not religiously minded (i.e., God-fearing) rather than by appealing to the irresistible charms of his wife. The attempt to give the Gerar episode a higher moral tone than the Egyptian parallel is also apparent in the relations between Abraham and the local ruler. Abimelech brought Sarah into his palace but, in contrast to the Egyptian ruler, did not have intimate relations with her and, in the course of an encounter with a deity in a threatening and premonitory dream (vv. 3-7), defended himself by pointing out that both Abraham and Sarah misled him, vigorously protesting his innocence, and asking rhetorically, "Lord, will you destroy an innocent people?" (v. 4), a rhetorical question that anticipates Abraham's own plea to God preparing to destroy Sodom: "Will you sweep away the innocent together with the wicked?" (18:23). Abimelech's confrontation with Abraham after the discovery of the ruse, his reaction to Abraham's self-justification, and the very generous terms on which the matter was settled are also in notable contrast to the curt dismissal of Abraham by the pharaoh.

According to the documentary hypothesis in its original formulation, the Abraham in Gerar episode is assigned to the Elohist source (E), while 12:10-20 and 26:6-11 (Isaac and Rebekah in Gerar) belong to the basic Yahwist (J) narrative strand.[7] From the beginning, the principal criterion was the incidence of divine names, and "Elohim" is used throughout 20:1-18, with the exception of the last verse, a superfluous addition to the

---

7. Hermann Gunkel, *Genesis* (Macon, Ga.: Mercer University Press, 1997), 218-25; Martin Noth, *A History of Pentateuchal Traditions* (Englewood Cliffs, N.J.: Prentice-Hall, 1972 [1948]), 38-41, 228-35; Otto Eissfeldt, *The Old Testament: An Introduction* (Oxford: Blackwell, 1956), 200-204.

narrative. Another feature of the Abraham in Gerar narrative deemed to be characteristic of the Elohist writer is its more elevated religious and moral tone compared with the first of the three variants, the Egyptian episode. Also cited is Abraham's concern about the absence of "the fear of God" in Gerar — which, as it turned out, was at least not true of the ruler. Then there are the language of sinning against God or against others (20:6, 9), the dream as a medium of revelation, and the efficacious intercessory prayer of Abraham the prophet, all deemed characteristic of the Elohist narrative strand. As far as 20:1-18 is concerned, much of this can be conceded, but the Elohist has never clearly and convincingly emerged as a coherent source or narrative strand, and the date assigned to it in the early monarchy is no longer in favor, and for good reason. Two examples: the expression "the fear of God" *(yirat elohim),* deemed to be characteristic of the Elohist, occurs on numerous occasions in Proverbs and Job, both late texts, and intercessory prayer occurs with almost equal frequency in the Deuteronomistic History and Jeremiah.

Abraham and Lot Go Their Separate Ways

Lot, *l'homme moyen sensuel,* one of those people destined repeatedly to make bad choices, seems to have been in Egypt after all, unless the phrase "and Lot with him" is a gloss anticipating Gen. 13:5-7. According to the Qumran *Genesis Apocryphon* (1QapGen 20:21-29), he not only accompanied Abraham and Sarah but negotiated with a local official the termination of the pharaoh's affliction and the return of Sarah to Abraham. So the three principals, Abraham, Sarah, and Lot, leave Egypt for the Negev (13:1), and the narrative moves on from the Egyptian episode resulting in the preservation of Sarah to the dispute about *Lebensraum* between uncle and nephew resulting in the elimination of the latter (13:1-13). Allusion to Abraham's wealth after leaving Egypt parallels the exodus of the Israelites from Egypt with great possessions,[8] while preparing for the dispute between these two, both rich in flocks, herds, and tents. As the text stands, the place where Lot looked around and chose the Jordan Valley was Bethel (13:3-4). It may be that the Jordan Valley is visible from Burg Beitin, just outside the village of Beitin (Bethel), an observation made by

---

8. Exod. 3:21-22; 12:33-36. The same theme, expressed in similar language, occurs with reference to the exodus in Gen. 15:14.

George Adam Smith long ago and often repeated in commentaries, but the southern end of the Dead Sea where Lot settled is far more readily visible from a location in the Negev. It seems more likely, therefore, that this further stage of Abraham's wanderings, from the Negev back to Bethel, deliberately relocates this critical event at the most important religious center in Canaan for the ancestors, and for Abraham in particular prior to his move to Mamre/Hebron (13:18).

Disputes about grazing rights, wells, and the watering of animals must have been frequent among pastoralists. The reminder that Canaanites also lived in the land (see also 12:6), now accompanied by Perizzites,[9] no doubt explains further why a dispute about pasture land could have arisen. Judging by the somewhat disjointed way in which it is narrated, the incident seems to be based on, and is practically verbatim with, the account of the separation between the pastoralists Jacob and Esau in Gen. 36:6-8, another example of the linguistic and thematic links between Abraham and Jacob traditions. In the Jacob incident, the land was insufficient to support both families and their abundant livestock, so Esau moved into the hill country of Seir, another name for Edom.[10] As the story unfolds, it becomes apparent that the dispute is a literary stratagem to explain how Lot moved out of the land of Canaan, therefore out of contention as Abraham's heir, into the Rift Valley, more specifically, to Zoar at the southern tip of the Dead Sea where, under unusual circumstances, he became the ancestor of Moabites and Ammonites, Transjordanian neighbors and remote kin of the Israelites. In this respect, the story about Lot serves to display the interest of the ancestral narratives in ethnic origins and Israel's kinship relations with its neighbors. Lot is the ancestor of Moab and Ammon, Nahor and Bethuel of Arameans, and Esau, Jacob's brother, of Edomites. Abraham, with Hagar and Keturah, is the ancestor of different branches of the great Arab people.

9. Perizzites *(pĕrizzî)*, a formation of the same order as Kenizzites, the Hurrian envoy Perizzi, and a ruler of Qatna called Ahizzi mentioned in the Amarna Letters from the late fourteenth century B.C., were a residue of the penetration into Palestine in the second millennium B.C. of the Hurrians, a non-Semitic, non-Indo-European people whose homeland lay in the mid-Asiatic region now inhabited by Kurds. References in my *Gibeon and Israel: The Role of Gibeon and the Gibeonites in the Political and Religious Life of Early Israel* (Cambridge: Cambridge University Press, 1972; digital edition 2009), 129.

10. Note the close parallelism between 12:5, "Abram took Sarai his wife, Lot his nephew, all their possessions *(rĕkûšām)* which they had accumulated *(rākāšû)* and all the persons *(nepeš)* they had acquired in Harran," and 36:6, "Esau took his wives, his sons, his daughters, and all the persons *(napšôt)* of his household, his cattle, livestock, and all the property he had accumulated *(rākaš)* in the land of Canaan."

The next phase in the dispiriting story of Lot is his capture by the four-nation coalition and his rescue by Abraham (14:1-24), to be discussed in the following section of this chapter. Subsequently, we will hear of the unintended consequences of his residence in Sodom: a second rescue, this time from homosexual rape and death by fire and brimstone, and a further relocation, this time to Zoar, thence to a cave where his daughters ply him with drink and have relations with him resulting in the birth of Moab and Ben-ammi (19:1-38). The renewed promise of land, located between phases in the story of Lot (13:14-18), anticipates the richer and more complex account in 15:1-21. The first fully stated promise of land in 13:14-18 has been placed here advisedly since it is only now that Abraham is free of Lot's copresence in the Promised Land.

Abraham, Lot, and the War of the Nine Kings

This strange episode, or assemblage of episodes (14:1-24), is introduced abruptly with no obvious link with the preceding passage. Continuity is established only with the sack of Sodom, Lot's domicile (13:12), leading to his capture and his eventual rescue by Abraham. Lot's hold on the narrative line is, therefore, quite tenuous, and is overshadowed by events that serve, for the one and only time, to place Abraham actively in the context of international affairs.[11]

A close reading reveals breaks in narrative continuity that suggest that this episode is composite. There is, in the first place, a report about a campaign launched by a coalition of four kings, the greatest in the region, against five heads of small settlements in the region of the Dead Sea (14:1-3, 8-11). Into this account has been inserted a report of the suppression by the same coalition of revolt among tribes in the region south of Judah, the Negev and Sinai (vv. 4-7). Continuity between the two segments of the mainline narrative, vv. 1-3 and vv. 8-11, is smooth; when vv. 4-7 are removed, the text does not bleed. There is no account of the actual battle that took place in the Valley of Siddim,[12] in the region around the Dead Sea (vv.

---

11. John A. Emerton, "The Riddle of Genesis XIV," *VT* 21 (1971): 403-39, suggested that Lot had been added to the narrative since he is introduced at a late point (v. 12). But Abraham's pursuit was undertaken with the purpose of rescuing Lot, and the episode is connected with the fate of Sodom, yet another rescue of Lot, and how he became ancestor of Moabites and Ammonites.

12. LXX, Vulgate, and *Vetus Latina* associate this valley with the Salt Sea. The pres-

3, 8), or perhaps — according to the author — on land later covered by the Dead Sea. The first named of the four kings is Amraphel of Shinar (another name for Babylon, v. 1), but the punitive expedition is led by Chedorlaomer of Elam, and is in a quite different location (vv. 5-7). Lot is introduced only after the defeat of the five "kings" (more realistically tribal chieftains) and the sack of Sodom, after which we have a continuous narrative featuring Abraham, Lot, and the king of Sodom that records Abraham's victory over the four kings, the rescue of Lot, and negotiations between Abraham and the king of Sodom (vv. 12-17, 21-24). The appearance of the priest-king Melchizedek (vv. 18-20) interrupts the encounter between Abraham and the king of Sodom since the latter goes to meet Abraham before the insertion but only addresses him after it, and Abraham declines the offer of booty, or goods recovered from the enemy, yet is able to offer Melchizedek "a tenth part of everything."

This "bizarre synthesis of diverse elements"[13] may have been influenced by Assyrian and Babylonian royal inscriptions dealing with military campaigns, as has often been suggested, but the differences — especially the use of third rather than first person — are as much in evidence as the similarities. A closer parallel can be found in the biblical story of David's rise to power. In 1 Sam. 30, Ziklag, one of David's cities, is attacked and sacked, and its people, including David's two wives, are taken captive. David pursues the aggressors with six hundred of his followers; they split into two unequal groups; the people, including his wives, are rescued; much booty is taken; and there is a big issue about the disposal of the spoils of war. No priest intervenes, but in similar situations a proportion of war booty would be assigned to a sanctuary (2 Sam. 8:11-12; 1 Chr. 26:27).

This narrative pattern is not greatly concerned with historical verisimilitude. It strains credulity, in the first place, that Abraham should have 318 retainers,[14] born in his household, who are armed by him and sent into battle, who traverse the entire country as far north as Damascus. With this tiny force, even when divided into two separate contingents, he is able to rout the armies of Babylon, Assyria, Elam, and either the Hittites of Asia

---

ence of the article has also given rise to the emendation of *'ēmek haššēdîm,* "the Valley of the Demons" or "the Valley of Ancestral Spirits."

13. Claus Westermann, *Genesis 12–36* (Minneapolis: Augsburg, 1985), 192.

14. The suspicious nonrounded number has whetted the curiosity of some commentators; it is perhaps a reference to Eliezer of Damascus (15:2), whose name, by gematria, adds up to 318, or perhaps an allusion to some esoteric astrological calculation.

Minor or a Hittite kingdom in Syria,[15] then return loaded with booty. At this point, the king of Sodom, having lost everything after the sack of his city, magnanimously requests only the return of his people taken away by the coalition, no doubt as slaves. Abraham, however, outdoes him by declining to accept the spoils, yet is able — in the insertion — to offer a tithe to Melchizedek from the bounty he had just renounced.

It has been acknowledged from the early days of critical exegesis that this account of military campaigns, defeats, and pursuits is basically historical fiction from the pen or stylus of a scribe with strong antiquarian interests matched with a lively imagination.[16] A postexilic date is, in the first place, apparent in its dependence on Deuteronomy. It lists the five cities and their five kings attacked by four powerful imperial overlords, but it is only in Deuteronomy (29:22) that the distinct variants Sodom and Gomorrah (Gen. 18:20) and Admah and Zeboiim (Hos. 11:8) are combined, and even later that one more was added to make the Cities of the Plain into a pentapolis.[17] Likewise, most of the tribal groups subdued by the fourfold coalition under Chedorlaomer are taken from the antiquarian glosses in the introductory chapters of Deuteronomy.[18] Affinity with late works that purport to be historical is not difficult to detect. Esther is one of several such works that provide a clue to their genre in the opening sentence ("It happened in the days of a certain king or kings"). Judith also begins by introducing a story about a great king ("It was the twelfth year of the reign of Nebuchadnezzar," Jdt. 1:1), and has a narrative sequence remarkably

15. Amraphel, not to be identified with Hammurapi, is of uncertain origin. Shinar is Babylon (cf. Gen. 10:10; 11:2; Isa. 11:11; Zech. 5:11; Dan. 1:2). Ellasar is uncertain, but Arioch occurs as a Babylonian name in Dan. 2:14-15, so perhaps it is Assyria since Babylon is already accounted for. No Chedorlaomer is known to history, but *kudur* corresponds to an Elamite word for "son." Tidal is taken to be a corruption of Tudhaliaš, a name borne by several Hittite kings. The mysterious *gôyîm* (peoples) may refer to the neo-Hittite kingdoms established in north Syria after the collapse of the Hittite empire.

16. Gunkel, *Genesis*, 273-84: from the Persian or Hellenistic period; Noth, *History of Pentateuchal Traditions*, 154: "a late scholarly composition"; M. C. Astour, "Political and Cosmic Symbolism in Genesis 14 and in Its Babylonian Sources," in *Biblical Motifs: Origins and Transformations*, ed. A. Altmann (Cambridge: Harvard University Press, 1966), 65-112; Van Seters, *Abraham in History and Tradition*, 112-20.

17. Wisdom of Solomon 10:6-8 refers to Lot, unnamed but described as a righteous man, escaping the fire that descended on the pentapolis.

18. Rephaim, mythical, quasi-historical in Deut. 2:11, 20; 3:11, 13; Ashteroth-karnaim, Deut. 1:4; Zuzim (= Zamzummim?), Deut. 2:20; Emim, Deut. 2:10-11; Horites, Deut. 2:12, 22; El-paran, Deut. 1:1. Other names not well-known occur only in Gen. 14.

close to Gen. 14 in which the Assyrian army under Holofernes is defeated by a much smaller Israelite force and is pursued beyond Damascus as far as Hobah, the final point of the pursuit in Gen. 14:15 and the only other occurrence of this toponym in the Hebrew Bible. The victors return with a great quantity of booty, and the high priest comes out to witness the scene and pronounce a blessing (Jdt. 15:3-10).

While the War of the Nine Kings serves to carry forward the history of Lot's vicissitudes, it has much more to say about Abraham than about Lot. Its presentation of Abraham as warrior and hero is uniquely distinctive. Only here is he described as a Hebrew (*ivri*, Gen. 14:13), which is significant in that in biblical usage this designation is restricted to situations of contact with Egyptians, Philistines, the sailors on board the ship in which Jonah was attempting to flee from the presence of the Lord (Jonah 1:9), and other foreigners. Only here is Abraham put on the stage of international affairs, as a figure of international significance, rather than serving as ancestor of his people and model for those attempting to establish a new community and identity after the disaster of the fall of Jerusalem.

Melchizedek

It will be apparent from the present section, as in those preceding it, that the story of Abraham reached its final form by a process of incremental expansion and updating covering a significant period of time. In some instances it was a matter of artful arrangement of different narrative themes and pericopes; for example, by locating the War of the Nine Kings, which, with the exception of the brief Melchizedek episode in 14:18-20, is basically secular in character and international in scope, between two theophanies, or two variants of a theophany, giving further assurance about the promise of land and descendants to one ethnic group (13:14-18; 15:1-21). In the present episode a scribe has taken the opportunity of adding another facet to the profile of Abraham by bringing the priest-king Melchizedek into contact with the great ancestor (14:18-20):

> King Melchizedek of Salem brought out bread and wine; he was priest of God Most High. He blessed Abram and said:
>
> > "Blessed be Abram by God Most High,
> > Maker of heaven and earth;

and blessed be God Most High,
who has delivered your enemies into your hand!"

Then Abram gave him a tenth of everything.

The interpolation awkwardly interrupts Abraham's encounter with the king of Sodom in the Valley of Shaveh, or the Valley of the King,[19] but makes sense in the narrative context as a whole. The issue is the disposal of war booty, and it would occur to a pious scribe, especially a temple scribe, that tradition dictated that some part of it should go to the clergy and the temple.

Contrary to what some commentators have argued,[20] this brief appearance of Melchizedek is not the climax and raison d'être of the chapter. The War of the Nine Kings contributes to the Abraham story as an incident in a narrative sequence that connects Lot's departure from the land of Canaan and residence in Sodom with his relocation in Zoar, last of the five cities listed in 14:2, and the incident in the cave that follows. After this point Lot disappears from the history — not a moment too soon, we are tempted to add. The Melchizedek appearance is therefore no more than an appendix to the mainline narrative.

Who, then, is this mysterious priest-king of Salem *(shalem)* — certainly understood by the author to be Jerusalem[21] — who makes such a sudden entrance into the story? The name Melchizedek occurs in the Hebrew Bible only here and in Ps. 110, where the Davidic ruler is addressed as "a priest forever according to the order of Melchizedek" (v. 4). The conquest account in Joshua (10:1-5) lists Adonizedek of Jerusalem among the thirty-one "kings" conquered by Joshua. His name is of the same type as

19. The Valley of the King, also mentioned at 2 Sam. 18:18, is probably the southern end of the Kidron Valley, east of Jerusalem, rather than Beth-hakkerem as in the *Genesis Apocryphon* 22:14. Beth-hakkerem is usually identified with Ramat Rahel, south of Jerusalem, which, as the name suggests, is on high ground.

20. Gerhard von Rad, *Genesis: A Commentary* (London: SCM, 1961 [1956]), 174; Emerton, "Riddle of Genesis XIV," 403-39; Michael C. Astour, "Melchizedek (Person)," in *ABD* 4:684.

21. Identified with Jerusalem in *Genesis Apocryphon* 22:13, *Targum Onkelos,* and Josephus, *Ant.* 1.180, it is in parallelism with Zion in Ps. 76:2. In the Egyptian Execration Texts from the nineteenth century B.C. and the Amarna Letters from the fourteenth century B.C., Jerusalem is *uru-šalim,* bearing the name of the god Šalim, also mentioned in the Ugaritic texts (*KTU* 1:23). This deity is the theophoric element in the names Absalom and Solomon, and in other nonbiblical Semitic names. See Herbert B. Huffmon, "Shalem," in *DDD* 755-57.

Melchizedek, meaning "Zedek is my lord." Both names are theophoric, identifying the bearers as devotees of Zedek, another deity associated with Jerusalem in its pre-Israelite (or pre-Judean) stage.[22] Yet a third deity is El Elyon ("God Most High"), designated as supreme deity by virtue of the attribute of universal creator, whom Melchizedek served in his capacity as king of Jerusalem. In speaking to the king of Sodom, Abraham refers to "Yahweh El Elyon." This has been understood by some scholars as an example of syncretism in keeping with the common process of consolidating the functions and attributes of different deities, either in premonarchic times or in some later period. Such processes are well attested throughout the history of Israel, but the God of Israel is also frequently addressed as "Elyon," or "Yahweh Elyon," or "Elohim/El Elyon," especially in Psalms. This usage suggests that, whatever earlier practice may have been, *'elyôn* ("Highest," "Supreme") was in liturgical use in Israel as an epithet for Yahweh.[23]

Melchizedek therefore comes from Jerusalem to meet Abraham bringing bread and wine. This could hardly have been intended as nourishment for the victorious Abraham and his allies since they had just returned laden with booty. The bread and wine were more probably elements in a ceremonial act connected with or preparatory to the blessing. The blessing itself is clearly liturgical, doxological, and rhythmic in character:

> "Blessed be Abraham by God Most High,
> Creator of heaven and earth.
> Blessed be God Most High,
> who delivered your enemies into your hand!"

In response to the blessing, Abraham gives Melchizedek one-tenth "from everything," presumably from all the booty taken during the blitzkrieg against the four kings. Since *ma'ăśēr* (one-tenth) is also the word for "tithe," this sequel to the priest-king's intervention, which has its parallel in Jacob's promise to give one-tenth of his possessions to the Bethel sanctuary (Gen. 28:22), has often been read as an etiology and legitimation of the

---

22. The obvious affinity of the name with *sedeq, sĕdāqâ,* etc., the language of justice, suggests that this deity may have been worshiped as a hypostasis of the solar deity Shamash, arbiter and guarantor of human justice. See Bernard F. Batto, "Zedek," *DDD* 929-34.

23. *'elyôn,* Deut. 32:8; 2 Sam. 22:14 = Ps. 18:14; Pss. 78:17; 91:9; *YHWH 'elyôn,* Pss. 7:17; 47:2; *'ēl 'elyôn,* Ps. 78:35, 56. The corresponding Greek title *hypsistos* occurs frequently in the New Testament, Apocrypha, and Pseudepigrapha.

practice of tithing by virtue of its great antiquity. Abraham's action would certainly have been understood in this way, even though tithing implies a well-established sanctuary (e.g., Deut. 12:5-7, 11) and a settled agrarian economy, conditions that do not fit the Abraham story. That Abraham offered one-tenth "from everything" could also imply something analogous to but more primitive than the practice of tithing, namely, the offering of part of war booty to a sanctuary and its personnel who do not take part in military action. So, for example, the Chronicler's David and his followers dedicated part of their war booty for the upkeep of the "house of Yahweh" (1 Chr. 26:27), wherever that may have been.

It is no surprise that there is no consensus on the date and purpose of the Melchizedek episode. The proposal that it dates to the very early monarchy, of which there are several variants, suffers fatally from the lack of textual or solid archaeological support.[24] The presence of genuinely ancient names of deities and kings, here and elsewhere, demonstrates only that elements of ancient tradition can survive for centuries in the collective memory, or among the literati, to be taken up and used by writers with an interest in ethnic and national origins. If a postexilic date is accepted for the narrative into which the Melchizedek episode in Gen. 14:18-20 has been inserted, as argued above, then, *a fortiori,* the insertion itself must be of at least equal antiquity. Some commentators have suggested that the incident reflects the period of Hasmonean ascendancy since the Hasmoneans claimed both royal and priestly status. Josephus describes Hyrcanus as "high priest of the Most High God" (*archiereus theou hypsistou, Ant.* 16.163), and this title for the deity, *Hypsistos,* the translation of the Hebrew *elyon* in the Septuagint and elsewhere, was in common use from about that time. The Hasmonean connection cannot be ruled out, but much uncertainty remains.[25] It may be more prudent to propose in general terms that the

24. One of the more interesting arguments for an early date claims that Zadok, David's priest, whose name is etymologically related to Melchizedek, began his career as a Jebusite priest of El Elyon in pre-Israelite Jerusalem. See Harold H. Rowley, "Zadok and Nehushtan," *JBL* 58 (1939): 113-41; Harold H. Rowley, "Melchizedek and Zadok," in *Festschrift Alfred Bertholet* (Tübingen: Mohr, 1950), 461-72; C. Hauer, "Who Was Zadok?" *JBL* 82 (1963): 89-94; see also the critical comments of Saul Olyan, "Zadok's Origins and the Tribal Politics of David," *JBL* 101 (1982): 177-93. Ronald E. Clements, *God and Temple* (Philadelphia: Fortress, 1965), argued that El Elyon was the principal deity of pre-Israelite Jerusalem, identified with Yahweh during the ascendancy of David.

25. The acrostic on the name *šim'ōn,* standing for Simon Maccabee, which Gustav-Wilhelm Bickell in the late nineteenth century claimed to find in Ps. 110:1-4, was rejected by Gunkel, *Genesis,* 280, but revived by Robert H. Pfeiffer, *Introduction to the Old Testament*

figure of Melchizedek, as the one conferring blessing on Abraham, was intended to assert the high status and antiquity of the priesthood of the Second Temple, the office of the high priest in particular, and the priestly control and disposal of the tithe.

Filling In the Gaps

The temporary loss of Sarah in Egypt was the third of the ten trials to which God subjected Abraham, beginning with the command to leave his native land, followed by the famine (Gen. 12:10), and ending, according to variant rabbinic traditions, with either the command to sacrifice Isaac or the death of Sarah.[26] Temporary relocation in Egypt, accompanied by his wife, was occasioned not only by famine, according to Josephus (*Ant.* 1.161), but also by Abraham's desire to engage the Egyptian priests in learned conversation. Abraham was warned in a dream that the Egyptians, notorious for sensuality (already in biblical texts; see Ezek. 16:26; 23:8, 19-20), would want to kill him in order to possess Sarah (*Genesis Apocryphon;* 1QapGen 19). We even have a rather amusing addition to the story in *Gen. Rab.* 40:5, according to which Abraham attempted unsuccessfully to get his wife safely into Egypt by concealing her in his luggage. Whatever her age, Sarah was a stunningly beautiful woman, one of the four most beautiful women in the Bible together with Rahab (Josh. 2:1), Abigail (1 Sam. 25:3), and Esther (Esth. 2:7), more beautiful even than Eve (*Gen. Rab.* 40:5). Her charms, described enthusiastically and in detail to the pharaoh by his officer Hirkanos in *Genesis Apocryphon* (1QapGen 20:1-8), had however been noted by the chaste Abraham only en route, after he saw her reflection in a pool of water (*Tg. Yer.* on Gen. 12:11), which then became the occasion for the brother-sister arrangement. Though Sarah remained with the pharaoh for two years,[27] in answer to her prayer God preserved her from his

---

(London: A. & C. Black, 1952), 630. The hypothesis is highly speculative and, in any case, the relevant letters do not come at the end of consecutive verses. Much the same can be said for Pfeiffer's claim to find an acrostic reading "for Yanni (Alexander Jannaeus) and his wife" in Ps. 2:7. See Pfeiffer, 628.

26. *Pirqe Abot* 5:3; *Pirqe R. El.* 26; *Abot R. Nat.* 34:94-95; cf. *Jub.* 19:8.

27. 1QapGen 20:17-18, preceded by five years with Abraham in Egypt (1QapGen 19:23; *Jub.* 13:11), therefore seven years in all (1QapGen 22:28). The historian Artapanus (fragment 1 preserved in Eusebius, *Praep. ev.* 9.18) gives Sarah a twenty-year stay, probably to allow Abraham more time to teach astronomy to the Egyptians.

attentions by means of a beating administered by an angel (*Gen. Rab.* 41:2) or, according to an alternative account, a disease that rendered him and his attendants impotent. Rabbinic tradition is, in any case, unanimous that Sarah emerged from her ordeal intact (*Gen. Rab.* 41:2; cf. Philo, *On Abraham* 19). After negotiations between Hirkanos and Lot, Abraham healed the pharaoh (1QapGen 20:21-31). As for the pharaoh's returning Sarah to Abraham, the Targum tradition replaces the contemptuous dismissal of the biblical text with the spectacle of a pharaoh practically groveling before Abraham. He explains that, moved by affection rather than lust, he had actually written Sarah a marriage contract deeding the province of Goshen to her together with much gold and silver and, as a bonus, an Egyptian maid whose name was Hagar (*Tg. Ps.-J.* to Gen. 26:1).

In the narrative context, the strife between the herdsmen of Abraham and those of Lot served the purpose of narrowing the options by removing Lot from contention as Abraham's heir, and therefore heir to the promises. The reason given in the text, that the increase in their wealth as pastoralists, in part as a by-product of the Egyptian episode, had created a serious problem of overgrazing, would seem to provide an adequate explanation of the ensuing tension. For some rabbinic commentators, however, the situation called for further probing. According to one view, Lot's herdsmen neglected to muzzle their animals so that they ate more than Abraham's herds. Moreover, Lot had reckoned — mistakenly, as it happened — that Abraham was sterile and that therefore he, Lot, would in due course take over all Abraham's possessions, which gave him a certain right to precedence there and then. His self-serving attitude could also be explained by his previous career as a usurer, a detail on which the biblical text is silent (*Gen. Rab.* 41:5-6). Abraham, by contrast, is presented as a model of consideration and peaceful accommodation.[28] Josephus may be hinting at something similar in Lot's choice of Sodom, since he adds that it was a flourishing city with great wealth before it was laid waste by fire and brimstone (*Ant.* 1.171).

In rabbinic tradition Lot's unsavory reputation continues right to the

---

28. Zohar 1:79a adds another reason: being a prophet, Abraham foresaw that Lot would be the ancestor of Ruth the Moabite, and therefore of David. For other rabbinic opinions on Lot, see Louis Ginzberg, *The Legends of the Jews,* vol. 5 (Philadelphia: Jewish Publication Society of America, 1955), 240 n. 171. For the more moralistic interpretations of early Christian writers — John Chrysostom, Ambrose, Augustine — see Theresia Heither, O.S.B., and Christiana Reemts, O.S.B., *Biblische Gestalten bei den Kirchenvätern, Abraham* (Münster: Aschendorff, 2005), 51-59.

end. *b. Naz.* 23a and *b. Hor.* 10b record a somewhat outré interpretation of the last verse of Hosea — "The Lord's ways are straight; the righteous walk in them but sinners stumble and fall" (Hos. 14:9) — with reference to Lot and his two daughters in the cave at Zoar (Gen. 19:30-38). The righteous are the daughters who, believing they were the only survivors on earth (19:31-32), piously fulfilled the creation commandment to increase and multiply. Though inebriated, Lot on the other hand contemplated a sexual crime.

Since the War of the Nine Kings is already manifestly legendary in character, not much expansive comment seemed to be called for. On the identity of the four kings from the east, the principal addition was to identify Amraphel with Nimrod (*Gen. Rab.* 42:4). According to the haggadah, Nimrod was the leader of the builders of the Tower of Babel, which was undertaken as an act of defiance against God. He was also Abraham's enemy from of old, having thrust him into the fiery furnace while still in Mesopotamia, from which he was miraculously delivered (*Gen. Rab.* 38:13). The attack on the Cities of the Plain, carried out under the leadership of Chedorlaomer, to whom Nimrod was now subordinate, was motivated by the presence of Lot in Sodom, since his capture would be an injury and defeat for Abraham (*Gen. Rab.* 41:7-8). Predictably, the rabbinic commentators and midrashists were intrigued by Abraham's 318 armed followers. According to one narrative embellishment, his attendants were afraid to follow him into battle on account of his admonition that none who had sinned should take part. The only one who qualified was Eliezer of Damascus (Gen. 15:2), who was invested with the strength of 318 men (*b. Ned.* 32a). The more plausible allusion, however, is to the six letters of his name that, by gematria, add up to 318 (*Gen. Rab.* 43:2). A Christian version of the same procedure, first proposed in the *Epistle of Barnabas* (9:8), would discover behind this intriguing number the monogram for Jesus. Working with the Greek script for numerals, Barnabas read the letters of the alphabet corresponding to 10 and 8 as IH, a familiar abbreviation for IHΣΟΥΣ (Jesus), and 300 as T, signifying the cross on which Jesus died.

One obvious problem with this episode is to imagine how Abraham with 318 followers could have defeated the combined forces of four imperial powers. This proved to be no problem for the haggadic commentators. Abraham was assisted by the angel Lailah ("Night"); God repositioned the planet Jupiter to provide light to finish off the enemy; and Abraham himself was transformed into a giant as tall as seventy men set on end.[29] By

---

29. *Gen. Rab.* 42:3; *b. Šabb.* 196b; *b. Sanh.* 96a.

contrast, Josephus presents a fairly sober account of a campaign in which Abraham with his 318 followers and three associates defeated an Assyrian army near Dan in the Golan and pursued them as far as Oba (Hobah, Gen. 14:15) in Syria (*Ant.* 1.176-178).

Commentators have been greatly exercised over the unannounced appearance in the narrative of this mysterious personage Melchizedek. He is a priest but, as the author of the Epistle to the Hebrews puts it (Heb. 7:1-3), he lacks genealogical identity and is therefore an object of wonder and speculation. He is also said to be king of Salem, which is identified with Jerusalem by most commentators, though some, perhaps with Samaritan attachments, have proposed an alternative location near Shechem. The ruler addressed in exalted language in Ps. 110 as a priest forever according to the order of Melchizedek, the only other reference to this person in the Hebrew Bible, does nothing to dispel the mystery. Melchizedek brings bread and wine that, according to the *Genesis Apocryphon* (13:14-17), are intended to nourish Abraham's entire army on its return. Philo (*On Abraham* 235) agrees, stating that it sufficed handsomely for all of them, and Josephus (*Ant.* 1.181) rather incongruously has Melchizedek blessing Abraham in the course of a banquet — more like a toast than a blessing. The combination of the two equally obscure and portentous texts, Gen. 14:18-20 and Ps. 110:4, resulted in making Melchizedek a figure of transcendental status. For some Qumran sectarians he is eschatological judge, vindicator, and savior, and his place is with the divine council.[30] Others identified him with Shem, a great power in heaven, a source of arcane knowledge for gnostic or gnosticizing groups both Jewish and Christian. But when all is said and done, he remains a mystery.[31]

---

30. 11Q13 (11QMelch); 4Q401:11.1-3 (*Songs of the Sabbath Sacrifices*).

31. On the Qumran Melchizedek see Annette Steudel, "Melchizedek," *EDSS* 1:536-37; Paul J. Kobelski, *Melchizedek and Melchireša'*, Catholic Biblical Quarterly Monograph Series 10 (Washington, D.C.: Catholic Biblical Quarterly, 1981). On the Nag Hammadi Melchizedek texts, see James M. Robinson, *The Nag Nammadi Library*, 3rd rev. ed. (San Francisco: Harper and Row, 1988), 438-44. Also recommended is the recent comparative study of the Melchizedek episode by Emmanouela Grypeou and Helen Spurling, *The Book of Genesis in Late Antiquity: Encounters between Jewish and Christian Exegesis* (Leiden and Boston: Brill, 2013), 199-239.

The Promise

Staking a Claim to Land

On the assumption, often argued or simply taken for granted, that Gen. 14, to which we gave the title "The War of the Nine Kings," is among the latest additions to the book of Genesis, we can reconstruct an earlier stage in the formation of the Abraham story with three parallel and consecutive narratives dealing with the theme of promise. The first (13:14-18) states explicitly the promise of land formerly only hinted at or mentioned in passing; the second (15:1-6) deals with the demographic promise, the creation of a people, and therefore in the first place with the possibility of an heir for Abraham; the third and most complex combines both themes (15:7-21). This threefold series makes an important contribution to the theme of the Abraham cycle as a whole, which moves toward its terminus by way of the successive removal of obstacles to the fulfillment of commitments made to Abraham in Harran (12:1-3). Following the preservation of the endangered Sarah and the self-disqualification of Lot as the surrogate heir, the first leaves Abraham unchallenged as heir, if not to the land itself, then to the promise of land for his descendants; the second excludes the choice of another surrogate heir from Abraham's household; and the third reiterates the territorial promise. Beyond this point there will be other complications and crises, including the need to provide a proxy wife for Abraham, the birth of her son Ishmael the Arab, and, finally, the command to sacrifice the heir.

Since the Abraham narrative cycle has been prefaced to the story of Jacob by extending the genealogical chain backward, it is not surprising that this first of our three passages draws on the promise of land made to Jacob (28:10-17) by transposing it into an earlier setting. Compare the parallel versions:

Abraham (13:14-16)	**Jacob** (28:13-15)
Raise your eyes and look around from the place where you are to the north, the south, the east, and the west.	You shall spread abroad to the west, the east, the north, and the south.
All the land you see I give to you and to your descendants forever.	The land on which you lie I give to you and to your descendants.
I shall make your descendants countless like the dust of the earth.	Your descendants shall be countless like the dust of the earth.

The promise addressed to Jacob takes place at Bethel while he is on his way to exile in Mesopotamia, and to Bethel he will return twenty years later, where it will be renewed (35:12). In the Abraham story the scene is transposed to a place unnamed, but the most recent location mentioned is in fact Bethel (13:3-4), from which in due course Abraham would move farther south to Hebron by the sacred oak of Mamre (13:18).

Throughout the ancestral story, Bethel and Hebron/Mamre are the principal topographical centers of the Jacob and Abraham traditions respectively. Following on the promise, Abraham is told to walk the length and breadth of the land (13:17). A clue to understanding the implication of this command can be found in Joshua's allotment of tribal territories after the conquest of Canaan (Josh. 18:1-10). Three men from each of the tribes still without territory were told to "walk about" through the land. This "walkabout" reflects an ancient custom for staking a legal claim to land by walking through its length and breadth or along its boundaries; this practice was known to republican Rome and is somewhat similar to the ancient English custom of "beating the bounds."[1] The allusion in both the Jacob and Abraham passages to the four points of the compass may indicate the same practice with reference to the land as a quadrant, analogous to the symbolic topography of the allotment of land sanctified and fecundated by the temple at its center in the so-called Law of the Temple in Ezek. 40–48.

A date for this first of the three passages (Gen. 13:14-18) later than the

---

1. In both Gen. 13:17 and Josh. 18:4, 8 the same theme of the verb "to walk" (Hithpāʿēl of *hlk*) is used with this technical sense.

formation of the Jacob cycle is also suggested by the language in which the revelation to Abraham is couched. The invitation to take in the four points of the compass in 13:14 and 28:14 is close to, and probably dependent on, Deut. 3:27, where Moses is told to view the land "from the west to the north, the south, and the east." This command, spelled out with topographical precision, came to him on the last day of his life.[2] The hyperbolic language about a future people as numerous as the (specks of) dust of the earth, less evocative than comparison with the stars in the sky, occurs in both the Abraham and the Jacob version. This first definitive promise of land was communicated to Abraham once Lot removed himself from contention as Abraham's heir by moving outside the Promised Land. It concludes with Abraham settling in Hebron (Gen. 13:18): "So Abram moved his tent, and came and settled by the oaks of Mamre, which are at Hebron; and there he built an altar to Yahweh."[3] Abraham had already "walked about" the land, from Shechem to Bethel and from there to the Negev, retracing his steps as far as Bethel after his return from Egypt (12:6-9; 13:1-4). His setting up altars at these ancient pagan cult centers, including now one at Mamre (13:18), reinforces the idea of staking a claim to territory on behalf of his descendants, even though Abraham himself would become the owner of only a field and a cave.

In light of the situation at the time the main lines of the Abraham traditions were set down, during the neo-Babylonian or early Achaemenid (Persian) period, from the mid–sixth century to the mid–fifth century B.C., Abraham's choice of Hebron for a residence immediately after staking a claim to the land is particularly significant. By that time Hebron was probably within the expansive sphere of influence of Arabian tribes, soon to be part of Idumea, and eventually coming under the control of the Qedarite tribal federation that, led by Geshem, would create serious problems for Nehemiah. Hence, Abraham's move south to Hebron, staking a claim to disputed territory, may reflect the loss of this city and the surrounding region during the decline and final extinction of the Judean monarchy.[4]

2. Moses is here being shown the land he was not permitted to enter (Deut. 34:1-4). The arc of vision from Mount Nebo took in Gilead, Dan, Naphtali, Ephraim, and Manasseh to the north, Judah to the west, and the Negev to the south. No part of the land lay to the east.

3. The Masoretic Text has the plural, "oaks of Mamre," signifying a grove, but LXX, Syriac, and Vulgate have the singular. The plural may have been intended to disguise the common practice of venerating sacred trees.

4. We can get an idea of the mixed population of the region between Lachish and Hebron at that time by noting the personal names in Aramaic ostraca said to originate in

Another Surrogate Heir Excluded

This threefold series is not the only instance in which originally parallel traditions are set out sequentially, as distinct episodes. The parade example is, of course, the narrative theme about the endangered ancestress (12:10-20; 20:1-18; 26:6-11). Since Wellhausen, this second of our three passages about promise (15:1-6) is recognized by most scholars as a text originally distinct from the rest of the chapter to which it is attached. Its distinctive character is indicated in the first place by the way it is rounded off as it opens with a reference to the reward for Abraham's obedience to the prompting of his God.[5] The new revelation that follows is, moreover, of a quite different kind, dealing with territory rather than posterity (15:7-21). The first revelation takes place at night (15:5), the second in the evening, at sunset (15:12). The first ends by noting Abraham's faith and trust in the God who had spoken to him (15:6); in the second he is still seeking to be reassured (15:8).

Genesis 15:1-6, the second of the three passages, addresses from a different perspective and with different emphases the theme of the promise. It describes a vision and opens with a phrase familiar from prophetic revelations: "the word of Yahweh came to Abram." It consists in a message of reassurance opening with the traditional exhortation, necessary for one still in a new and unfamiliar environment, to put aside fear. God will be his shield and his very great reward. The metaphor of the shield occurs predominantly in psalms. Throughout Ps. 18, repeated in the David story (2 Sam. 22), the shield is closely associated with salvation, being safe with God, as the outcome of fidelity. When David, in the course of his psalm, re-

---

that southern part of the country, the majority of which are Edomite or Arabian. See André Lemaire, "Nabonidus in Arabia and Judah in the Neo-Babylonian Period," in *Judah and the Judeans in the Neo-Babylonian Period,* ed. Oded Lipschits and Joseph Blenkinsopp (Winona Lake, Ind.: Eisenbrauns, 2003), 290-91.

5. This conclusion is widely accepted. See, *inter alios,* John Skinner, *A Critical and Exegetical Commentary on Genesis,* 2nd ed. (Edinburgh: T. & T. Clark, 1930), 276-77; Otto Kaiser, "Traditionsgeschichtliche Untersuchung von Gen 15," *ZAW* 70 (1958): 107-26; L. A. Snidjers, "Genesis 15: The Covenant with Abraham," *OTS* 12 (1958): 261-79; Gerhard von Rad, *Genesis: A Commentary* (London: SCM, 1961 [1956]), 177-78; Norbert Lohfink, *Die Landverheissung als Eid. Eine Studie zu Gn. 15* (Stuttgart: Katholisches Bibelwerk, 1967); Moshe Anbar, "Genesis 15: A Conflation of Two Deuteronomic Narratives," *JBL* 101 (1982): 39-55; Claus Westermann, *Genesis 12–36* (Minneapolis: Augsburg, 1985), 214-16; Christoph Levin, "Jahve und Abraham in Dialog: Genesis 15," in *Gott und Mensch in Dialog. Festschrift für Otto Kaiser zum 80. Geburtstag,* BZAW 345/1-2 (Berlin: De Gruyter, 2005), 237-57.

joices that Yahweh rewarded him according to his (David's) righteousness (2 Sam. 22:21), we are not far from the reassurance addressed to Abraham at the conclusion of this second text, that "Yahweh reckoned his faith to him as righteousness" (Gen. 15:6). So now, after the exclusion of Lot from consideration as Abraham's heir, Abraham proposes another candidate. The state of the text does not permit us to establish the identity of this person about whom so far we have heard nothing. To make matters worse, a textual problem is at once apparent in the duplication of Abraham's complaint addressed to God in successive verses (15:2 and 15:3). If the latter was intended to clarify the meaning of the former, which is practically unintelligible, we could at least conclude that, in the absence of a son, a member of Abraham's household — not necessarily a slave, as the Vulgate and some modern translations assume — will be his heir and inherit his property. But since Eliezer is the only clearly intelligible word in the second half of the previous verse, this may be the name of the prospective candidate, as the traditional Jewish exegesis assumes, but we cannot be sure. The ancient versions also had trouble with these two verses. According to the LXX, he is "the son of Masek of my household," and the Vulgate identifies him as a *vernaculus,* one born in his household, generally a slave. But apart from the name, we know nothing about this person and are given no clue as to how he became a surrogate heir to the childless Abraham.[6]

This brief encounter between Abraham and his God ends as it begins with a word of commendation: "He believed in God (Yahweh), and God reckoned it to him as righteousness." Believing or not believing in others is normally a question of believing or not believing what they say. Believing is intimately associated with trust. Without independent evidence about what people we do not trust say, we do not believe them. Not surprisingly, then, the Hebrew verb most commonly used for "believing" is found in parallelism with the verb for "trusting."[7] The acknowledgment

---

6. The obscurity surrounding *ben-mešeq* has occasioned many guesses: "servant," C. H. Gordon, "Damascus in Assyrian Sources," *IEJ* 2 (1952): 174-75; "steward," H. L. Ginsberg, "Abram's 'Damascene' Steward," *BASOR* 200 (1970): 31-32; "usurper," Snidjers, "Genesis 15," 261-79; "cup bearer," Henri Cazelles, "Connections et Structure de Gen XV," *RB* 69 (1962): 221-49; other options in Westermann, *Genesis 12–36,* 220. A connection with Damascus mentioned in passing in the "War of the Nine Kings" (14:15), supported by Eliezer's number by gematria, is proposed in *Gen. Rab.* 44:9 and, for different reasons, by Thomas C. Römer, "Genèse 15 et les tensions de la communauté juive postexilique dans le cycle d'Abraham," *Transeu* 7 (1994): 118.

7. See, for example, Mic. 7:5 and Ps. 78:22.

that Abraham's believing in God, that is, in the word spoken to him by God, is reckoned to him as righteousness (or as "a righteous act") is subject to the misinterpretation that it is entered on the plus column of God's ledger of righteous and unrighteous deeds. This misreading of the verse has had, as we know, an unfortunate impact on Christian theology and, indirectly, on commonly held but often unexamined ideas and perceptions about the biblical God. A better reading can be found at the beginning of the long prayer in Neh. 9:6-37, attributed in the LXX to Ezra. The prayer is addressed to the God who chose Abram, brought him out from Ur of the Chaldees, changed his name to Abraham, and found his heart faithful in God's presence. Use of the word "faithful" (or "believing," *ne'eman,* from the same verb, *'mn*) points unmistakably to Gen. 15:6, and occurs in a statement that defines Abraham's attitude not just at this juncture but throughout his life. The same verse has had, as we know, powerful resonance in early Christian writing about our relationship to God.

Let us add that trusting another can be more than just believing what the other says. There are relationships on which much depends, which have a self-authenticating quality and call for commitment, but also involve accepting the risk of being led into an unknown future. This was the situation of Abraham at this point of his life.

The Third Episode: Visionary Experiences

The third episode seems at first reading to be continuous with the second since the dialogue between Abraham and the deity whose voice he hears continues. It is certainly possible to read it that way, but we have just seen reason to believe that 15:7-21 is a distinct episode dealing with a separate, if closely connected, issue, that of territory. Other considerations — inconsistencies and aporias that cannot be ignored — lead to the further conclusion that this third passage has itself received considerable editorial attention. The ceremony involving dismembered animals and the nocturnal trance experience of Abraham that follows are interrupted by a prediction that the fulfillment of the promise will be delayed for 400 years (vv. 13-16). But the problem then arises that the revelation about fulfillment long after Abraham's death does not make a good answer to his question about how he is to know that he will possess the land (15:8).[8] The final paragraph (vv.

8. Thomas C. Römer, "Abraham and 'the Law and the Prophets,'" in *The Reception*

18-21), which describes the ceremony as a covenant, was also probably added, by a Deuteronomistic or post-Deuteronomistic hand, to judge by the language. It was intended to serve as a final clarification of a distinctly arcane episode. It opens with the typically Deuteronomic terminology for "cutting" (i.e., making) a covenant.[9] The boundaries of the Promised Land, from the river of Egypt to the great river, which is the Euphrates (15:18), reproduce the land's ideal boundaries in texts of Deuteronomistic origin or inspiration,[10] and the listing of indigenous peoples is also characteristic of the same source.[11] Perhaps not coincidentally, the boundaries correspond roughly to those of the trans-Euphrates satrapy under Persian rule (sixth to fourth century B.C.). Finally, the statement "To your descendants (literally 'seed') I give this land" has a quasi-juridical, one might say performative, character, as it has in Deuteronomistic texts.

The distinctiveness of 15:7-21 as a whole is further indicated by the solemn exordium: "I am Yahweh who brought you from Ur of the Chaldees to give you this land as a possession" (15:7). This is a declarative statement modeled on the often-repeated self-identification of Yahweh as the God who brought Israel out of Egypt, a designation that also introduces both forms of the Decalogue (Exod. 20:2; Deut. 5:6). A particularly close example occurs in connection with the jubilee and sabbatical laws, closely associated as they are with land ownership: "I am Yahweh your God who brought you from the land of Egypt to give you the land of Canaan and to be your God" (Lev. 25:38). The asseveration can therefore be taken as one more indication that the Abraham story in Genesis is constructed on the foundation of the exodus–wilderness–land occupation account of ethnic and national origins, and that the generation that "went down" to Egypt

---

and Remembrance of Abraham, ed. P. Carstens and N. P. Lemche (Piscataway, N.J.: Gorgias, 2011), 87-101, questions the conclusion that vv. 13-16 are an addition on the grounds that (1) without this passage Abraham's question in v. 8 remains without an answer, and (2) birds of prey portend bad news and, absent vv. 13-16, no bad news follows. In answer to the first objection: the ceremony itself is intended as the response, a not unusual procedure in visions; as for the second objection: birds of prey, attracted by the sight and smell of dead flesh, do not have to portend bad news. Take, for example, the scene of Rizpah protecting the impaled bodies of Saul's sons from birds of prey (2 Sam. 21:10-12). Römer's parallel from *Aeneid* 3.225-230, following von Rad, *Genesis,* 182, has to do not with birds of prey but with the dreaded Harpies, females with wings.

9. Deut. 4:23; 5:2, 3; 7:2; 9:9; 29:13, 25; 31:16.

10. Deut. 1:7; 11:24; Josh. 1:4; 2 Kgs. 24:7.

11. Deut. 7:1; 20:17; Josh. 3:10; probably also Exod. 3:8, 17; 13:5. Variance in number, from seven to ten, is immaterial.

with Jacob and the one that was eventually "brought out" from there were long considered the original ancestors. We see once again how traditions about Abraham represent a genealogical extension backward in time, and emerge at a later date in response to different circumstances. Consider, for example, the historical review offered by the prophet Samuel in which he reminds his people that the story begins with the fathers who went down to Egypt (1 Sam. 12:6-8), or, much later, Ezekiel's review of a history of repeated religious infidelity that begins with the forefathers in Egypt (Ezek. 20:1-44). In neither of these is there any mention of Abraham.

Abraham's anxious expostulation — "How can I know that I will possess it?" — receives a nonverbal response in the ceremony that follows (Gen. 15:9-12 + 17). This strange episode proceeds in three phases. In the first, which takes place during daytime, Abraham is told to make the necessary preparations by assembling a heifer, a she-goat, and a ram, all three years old, together with a turtledove and a pigeon. He is to dismember the land animals but not the birds and dispose the pieces opposite each other. This leaves him with the task of scaring off the birds of prey inevitably attracted by the sight and smell. Abraham's immediate and unquestioned obedience to this extremely odd command anticipates his response to the far more demanding and wrenching command to sacrifice his son (Gen. 22). The second stage takes place at sunset when he enters into a trance state, a state of great and fearful darkness. This state is expressed by the Hebrew term *tardemah,* which describes the state into which the man in the Garden of Eden was cast during the creation of the woman. It connotes no ordinary sleep but a state of transformed consciousness. The third phase takes place in darkness, a darkness lit by a smoking brazier and burning torch passing between the severed limbs of the animals. If the intervening prophecy about the 400-year hiatus is an interpolation, Abraham would also have witnessed the fiery phenomenon in a state of trance.

About the interpretation of this strange ceremony there is no consensus. The only access we have to an actual event is through this text, which has no great concern to be reader-friendly. In the first place, there is the question whether the entire episode, all three "moments," is the record of a visionary experience, or the visionary element is confined to the smoking brazier and flaming torch seen by Abraham. The more immediate question, however, is about the point and purpose of the ceremony. According to the final paragraph (vv. 18-21), it is a covenant ritual by which Yahweh guarantees possession of the land by Abraham's descendants, and so it has been read in midrash and rabbinic commentary. In Gen. 15:17 it is referred to as "the covenant of the pieces" *(berit haggezarim).* It has therefore been the almost universal practice among commentators to pair Gen. 15 with Gen. 17 as contrasting accounts of covenant making, the former J (Yahwistic), or a combination of J and E (Yahwistic-Elohistic), the latter P (Priestly); this practice will not be followed here. Commentators have noted a close connection with the reference in Jer. 34:18-19 to passing between the severed parts of a calf as symbolic of punishment for violation of the terms of a covenant. The analogy does not, however, survive close inspection. If Gen. 15:17 is to be read as the climax of a covenant ritual, both parties to the pact should take part in the symbolic passing through the "pieces." Furthermore, since the smoking brazier and flaming torch of Gen. 15:17 symbolize the presence and activity of a divine being, an anticipation of the numinous, divine presence on Mount Sinai in smoke and fire (Exod. 19:18), it is incongruous to suppose that the deity can take on a commitment under a penalty that can be represented symbolically by the dismemberment and death of animals or, for that matter, can be placed under sanctions of any kind.[12]

An alternative explanation, generally advanced in a much more tentative manner, is to read the ritual as a sacrifice. Sacrifice can certainly accompany treaty making and covenant making, as in the covenant between Jacob and Laban in Gen. 31:43-54. In Gen. 15, however, sacrificial language is absent, there is no altar, no sacrificial meal, and no burning of the victims, an essential element. In addition, the sacrificial hypothesis does not explain the most singular features of the ritual: the cutting in half and disposal of the parts, the brazier and torch, and the passing between the dismembered parts of the animals. The only possible connection with sacrifice would be that the animals and birds are acceptable for sacrifice, but this may simply be a way of making sure that they are ritually clean.[13]

12. Gerhard F. Hasel, "The Meaning of the Animal Rite in Gen 15," *JSOT* 19 (1981): 61-78, pointed out that Jer. 34:18-19 is in any case textually insecure. It agrees with Gen. 15:17 only in one respect, that one person passes through the pieces. In Jer. 34:18-19, however, the inferior party is involved, but in Gen. 15:17 it is the deity who self-evidently cannot be subject to sanctions. See also on this issue D. J. McCarthy, *Treaty and Covenant,* AnBib 21 (Rome: Pontifical Biblical Institute, 1963), 52-54, 93-94; John Van Seters, *Abraham in History and Tradition* (New Haven: Yale University Press, 1975), 100-103, 249-78; Westermann, *Genesis 12–36,* 247-50.

13. Hermann Gunkel, *Genesis* (Macon, Ga.: Mercer University Press, 1997), 176-83, combines the sacrificial element with an acted-out oath and self-imposed curse. J. Henninger, "Was bedeutet die rituelle Teilung eines Tieres in zwei Hälften?" *Bib.* 34 (1953): 344-53, and S. E. Loewenstamm, "Zur Traditionsgeschichte des Bundes zwischen den Stücken," *VT* 18 (1968): 500-506, argued that originally there was only one animal; the addition of

We understand why commentators have focused on the covenantal and sacrificial aspects in the animal rite, but we see that neither interpretation is free of problems. It seems more in keeping with the specific features of the account, and with the Abrahamic narrative as a whole, to read it as an acted-out form of asseveration, an oath confirmed in the strongest possible terms in visual form as it is verbally throughout the history of Israel's origins. It has long been customary to reinforce this interpretation, with different variations and emphases, by adducing rites from the ancient Near East and beyond, in which oaths are sworn as confirmation of a treaty or agreement of some kind and one or several animals are killed, symbolizing unequivocally the punishment awaiting the party found in violation of the stipulations of the agreement. None of these correspond closely with the specific features of the rite in Gen. 15, but they serve to profile a type of ritual act into which the "covenant of the pieces" may be seen to fit.[14]

A different kind of analogy may be proposed, namely, the prophetic sign-act. We encounter cases where, when words no longer suffice, the prophet acts out the message or, in the case of Ezekiel, even has recourse to what we might call street theater; he acted out, in the view of a public unreceptive to verbal threats, the anticipated siege of Jerusalem and the miserable conditions the witnesses could expect as deportees in the near future (Ezek. 4). In something of the same way, the author of Gen. 15:7-12, 17 has found a way, beyond verbalization, of presenting the commitment of the deity and the receptivity and obedience of Abraham.

There remains the prediction, delivered to Abraham after sundown during his catatonic trance, about the delay in the fulfillment of the promise (vv. 13-16):

> "Know this for certain, that your offspring shall be aliens in a land that is not theirs, and shall be slaves there, and they shall be oppressed there

---

others made it into a sacrifice; similarly Westermann, *Genesis 12–36*, 225. Hasel, "Meaning of the Animal Rite," 70, calls the ceremony "a covenant ratification sacrifice."

14. In the example often cited from the Mari correspondence (eighteenth century B.C.), the animals — a donkey, goat, and young dog — are simply killed. In the treaty between Abba-AN and Yarimlim in the following century, the oath is accompanied by slitting the throat of a sheep. In the vassal treaty between Ashurnirari V of Assyria and Mati'ilu of Arpad in north Syria, almost a millennium later, a lamb is decapitated and its shoulder torn off. In none of these often-cited, rather gruesome cases are the animals cut in two, nor is the scene lit up by a smoking firepot and a flaming torch. References for these animal rites in Van Seters, *Abraham in History and Tradition*, 100-103.

for four hundred years; but I will bring judgment on the nation that they serve, and afterwards they shall come out with great possessions. As for yourself, you shall go to your ancestors in peace; you shall be buried at a good old age. And they shall come back here in the fourth generation; for the iniquity of the Amorites is not yet complete."

This statement, which is a later addition, as we have seen, deals with a contradiction in the existing narrative inclusive of the Deuteronomistic conclusion (vv. 18-21). Yahweh solemnly renews the promise of land to Abraham, and in response, Abraham asks for reassurance that he will indeed possess it. But it turns out that his descendants, not Abraham himself, will be the beneficiaries. The author was familiar with the tradition about the settlement of Jacob and his sons in Egypt, the exodus, and occupation of the land, and was therefore aware that Abraham ended his life in possession of no more than a field and a cave. The history is therefore presented in outline as a way of reconciling the initial promise made to Abraham personally with the larger narrative. The prediction also serves to prepare for the animal rite interpreted as guarantee and pledge that this future will come about. The intent of this prediction is therefore clear in spite of some unevenness. There is, first of all, Abraham's death and burial "in peace."[15] More problematically, the return in the fourth generation contradicts the 400 years of servitude in Egypt. In antiquity 30 years is about the maximum for a generation, as we gather, for example, from Egyptian genealogical lists (e.g., in Herodotus 2.142) and other ancient records. We can only conclude that the author is using the term "generation" more loosely for a long period of time, as long as a century. The 400 years also looks like a rounding out of the 430 years for the sojourn in Egypt in Exod. 12:40-41, a text commonly assigned to the Priest-author (P). Needless to say, neither of these estimates is based on historical sources. Both contradict what we are told about the chronology of the life of Moses, during the sojourn in Egypt (Exod. 2:1-2), but not at the beginning since his birth took place after the accession of a new pharaoh (Exod. 1:8). He died at age 120, toward

---

15. To die and be buried "in peace" *(běšālôm)* is to be buried on your own plot, your ancestral domain; hence Abraham's insistence on purchasing the field and cave at Machpelah (Gen. 23). The further implication is that the deceased will be "gathered to his ancestors," which implies aggregation to the totality of the kinship group, including dead and living members. This is what is stated and implied in the account of Abraham's death and burial (25:8), and it can happen even following a violent death or for one "not full of years," as was the case with King Josiah, who also died "in peace" (2 Chr. 34:28).

the end of the trek through the wilderness (Deut. 34:5-7). The 430 years, on the other hand, are calculated to fit the overall chronological schema in the Pentateuch, probably based on a world epoch or "Great Year" of 4,000 years.[16]

Filling In the Gaps

The conclusion to the second of our three passages, "He (Abraham) believed Yahweh, and it was reckoned to him as righteousness" (Gen. 15:6), has served throughout the history of interpretation as a summary of Abraham's attitude to God and of Abraham himself as the model for the believer. For the Christian, it will more often than not be read as interpreted by Paul in Romans and Galatians in connection with Hab. 2:4: "The righteous live by their faith" (NRSV), or "the righteous will live by being faithful" (REB), or "the righteous man is rewarded with life for being faithful" (JPS).[17] But this statement about the relation between faith, righteousness, and reward was noticed much earlier than Paul. According to Ps. 106:31, the intervention of Phinehas at Baal-peor in bringing the plague to an end, though reprehensible and repugnant for the modern reader, "was reckoned to him as righteousness," winning for him the reward of a covenant of perpetual priesthood (Num. 25:10-13). A prayer attributed in Neh. 9:6 LXX to Ezra praises Abraham because of his faithful heart (vv. 7-8), though the sequel appears to suggest that the righteousness was reckoned to the righteous God who fulfills his promises rather than to Abraham. Ben Sira also links Abraham's faithfulness to observance of law and covenant (Sir. 44:19-20).[18] On his deathbed, Mattathias, father of the Maccabee brothers, urges his

16. See my *The Pentateuch: An Introduction to the First Five Books of the Bible* (New York: Doubleday, 1992), 47-50, references on 53 nn. 12-15. The 400 years and the fourth generation exemplify the biblical preference for the number four and its multiples, especially 40 (e.g., Deut. 1:3; Judg. 3:11; 8:28; 13:1; 1 Sam. 4:18; 1 Kgs. 2:11). See the observations of S. Von Kreuzer, "430 Jahre, 400 Jahre, oder 4 Generationen — zu den Zeitangaben über den Ägyptenaufenthalt der 'Israeliten,'" *ZAW* 98 (1986): 199-210.

17. The verse is cited in Rom. 4:3; 9:22; Gal. 3:6; Jas. 2:23. In Rom. 3:21-26, one of the key passages in the letter written with Gen. 15:6 in mind, *dikaiosunē* occurs six times and *pisteuein/pistis* four times. In the Qumran pesher on Habakkuk (1QpHab VII, 17–VIII, 3), the righteous of Hab. 2:4 are those who observe the law according to the interpretation of the Teacher of Righteousness, in striking contrast to Paul's interpretation of the text.

18. On Ben Sira's Abraham, see B. C. Gregory, "Abraham as the Jewish Ideal: Exegetical Traditions in Sirach," *CBQ* 70 (2008): 66-81.

sons to be faithful to the ancestral laws in imitation of Abraham, for "was he not found faithful when tested, and it was reckoned to him as righteousness?" (1 Macc. 2:51-52). The same connection with law observance as the way leading to righteousness, meaning acceptance by God, is behind the allusion to Gen. 15:6 in the Qumran *Halakhic Letter* (4Q398, fragments 14-17, col. II, line 7), where the author assures his readers that if they are faithful to the works of the Torah — as interpreted by the author and his school — it will be reckoned to them as righteousness. This reading of the text is not so different from the Epistle of James, which cites Gen. 15:6 as proof that Abraham won divine approval as a result of doing, not just believing. But if we attend to the narrative context of Gen. 15:6, we will assign priority to Abraham's persistent faith and trust, even in desperate situations, in the truth of the messages he receives from God, and therefore in God. It is this more than anything else that accounts for Abraham's greatness.[19]

The "Covenant of the Pieces" could hardly fail to be a subject of fascination and a source of speculation for early readers, as it still is for readers of Genesis today. The slaughtered animals, all acceptable for sacrifice, the smoke, and the fire led several to interpret the scene as a sacrifice, in spite of features that clearly do not fit this interpretation, as we have seen. The author of *Jubilees* (14:9-19) attempted to solve the problem by locating the episode beside the oak of Mamre where Abraham had built an altar (Gen. 13:18). The blood was therefore poured out and the victims consumed in the fire, together with the appropriate fruit offering and libation. In keeping with the intense interest in calendric matters in this work, the author adds that the sacrifice took place in the middle of the third month. Josephus (*Ant.* 1.183-185) also turns it into a sacrifice *(thusia)* offered on an altar, and does so by the simple expedient of omitting all the details peculiar to the event, including the passing between the pieces.[20] While

19. Other discussions of Gen. 15:6 in Bruce Chilton, "Aramaic and Targumic Antecedents of Pauline Justification," in *The Aramaic Bible: Targums in Their Historical Context,* ed. D. B. G. Beattie and Martin J. McNamara (Sheffield: JSOT, 1994), 379-99; Manfred Oeming, "Der Glaube Abrahams: Zur Rezeptionsgeschichte von Gen 15,6 in der Zeit des zweiten Tempels," *ZAW* 110 (1998): 16-33; Rudolph Mosis, "Gen 15,6 in Qumran und in der Septuaginta," in *Gesammelte Aufsätze zum Alten Testament* (Würzburg: Echter, 1999); James L. Kugel, *Traditions of the Bible: A Guide to the Bible as It Was at the Start of the Common Era* (Cambridge: Harvard University Press, 1997), 308-11.

20. Thomas W. Franxman, *Genesis and the "Jewish Antiquities of Flavius Josephus,"* BibOr 35 (Rome: Biblical Institute Press, 1979); Louis H. Feldman, *Josephus's Interpreta-*

accepting this sacrificial reading, Philo was more concerned to interpret the animals allegorically; for example, the two birds stand for divine and human reason respectively (*Who Is the Heir?* 125-128). According to one rabbinic interpretation that draws on the four kingdoms theme in the book of Daniel, the animals serve as political allegory: the heifer is Babylon, the she-goat Media, the ram Greece, and the "deep and terrifying darkness" of 15:12 is Edom, code name for Rome.[21]

Abraham's vision seen during this deep and terrifying darkness of his ecstatic state[22] provided the occasion to some readers for introducing "out of body" experience and soul travel into the "covenant of the pieces." The Targum (*Tg. Neof.* on Gen. 15:17) and *Liber antiquitatum biblicarum* (23:6-7) interpret the fire passing between the pieces as the fire of Gehenna prepared for the unrighteous. In the course of his night vision, Abraham also saw the temple (*Gen. Rab.* 44:21; *2 Bar.* 4:34) and, beyond that, the final consummation (*4 Ezra* 3:13-15). On this relatively sober foundation the *Apocalypse of Abraham*, composed probably about the same time as *2 Baruch* and *4 Ezra* (late first or early second century A.D.), constructs a phantasmagoric scenario. Overcome by emotion, Abraham collapses but is assisted by an angel who guides him to the chosen place followed by the three animals and the two birds. He is told to slaughter the animals, and is then taken up on the wing of one of the birds, where he is told to count the stars in the sky (cf. Gen. 15:5). He sees the Garden of Eden, the fall of Jerusalem and destruction of the temple, and the chariot throne with the four living creatures, and returns to earth in time to rebuff the demon Azazel, who has appeared in the guise of a bird of prey (*Apoc. Abr.* 15–29). These and similar readings are not much concerned to determine the *intentionality* of the text, to get at what it means in itself, in the context or contexts in which it came into existence. A critical reading of texts should not exclude the possibility that a text can mean a great deal more than it intends to this or that reader, but there is still space for attempting to arrive at what it has to say within its own terms of reference.

---

tion of the Bible (Berkeley and Los Angeles: University of California Press, 1998), 223-89; Louis H. Feldman, *Flavius Josephus: Translation and Commentary,* vol. 3, *Jewish Antiquities 1-4* (Leiden: Brill, 2000).

21. *Gen. Rab.* 44:14-15, 17; *Tg. Neof.* on Gen. 15:12; *Pirqe R. El.* 28.

22. LXX translates *tardēmâ* with *ekstasis;* on which see Philo, *Who Is the Heir?* 258.

• 4 •

Hagar and Ishmael

Another Expedient

The next chapter in the history, narrated in Gen. 16:1-6, describes another expedient for solving the problem of issue for Abraham in decidedly unpromising circumstances: an infertile wife and advanced age, Abraham being seventy-five and Sarah sixty-five on their arrival in Canaan (16:1-6). At the beginning, Abraham's nephew Lot was to be the surrogate heir, but he quickly eliminated himself from contention (13:2-13). Then another candidate, Eliezer of Damascus, one of Abraham's household servants, was proposed but brusquely set aside (15:2). In the meantime, only divine intervention prevented Abraham from losing to a foreign potentate the wife who was to bear his child (12:10-20). After the threefold confirmation of the promise of posterity and territory (13:14-18; 15:1-6; 15:7-21), we are back where it all began with the arrival in Canaan a decade earlier with no solution in sight. The stage is therefore set for another attempt, this time by means of a surrogate wife rather than an adopted heir.

This latest expedient brings on to the stage a new *dramatis persona*, Hagar, an Egyptian slave, but by no means servile, as will become apparent. The terminology used in this episode (16:1-6) defines Hagar's status in relation to Sarah rather than Abraham: Sarah is the mistress *(gevirah)*, and Hagar is a slave, but in a privileged position as her personal assistant in attendance on her, a *shiphah,* like Bilhah with Rachel and Zilpah with Leah (30:1-24). The point about social status may be illustrated by an Isaian text about the end time when all such distinctions will be obliterated, when "it will be as with the slave *(eved)* so with his master *(adon),* as with the maid *(shiphah)* so with her mistress *(gevirah)*" (Isa. 24:2). The same point is made, with some exaggeration, in the proverbial saying that "a *shiphah* who takes over the position of a *gevirah* is one of three things which make the earth tremble" (Prov. 30:23). Hagar, therefore, belongs to Sarah, and is therefore only indirectly answerable to Abraham. The further point, that she is Egyptian, reminds the reader of what is already known, that Abraham left Egypt richer than he was before going there, after receiving gifts from the pharaoh, including female slaves (12:16). The Qumran *Genesis Apocryphon* goes a step further in affirming that Hagar, who will later have an Egyptian daughter-in-law (Gen. 21:21), was given to Sarah by the pharaoh as reparation together with silver, gold, and a fine new wardrobe (1QapGen XX, 31-32). Hagar, however, is an Arabian personal name well attested in Palmyran, Nabatean, and Safaitic inscriptions, and her son Ishmael is certainly an Arab.[1] She was therefore probably a member of a group formerly resident in Egypt, but basically an Egypto-Arab.

The expedient proposed by Sarah was of frequent recourse in the ancient Near East and Levant, and since it was open to serious abuse in practice, it was also the object of legislation. In his commentary on Genesis, Ephraim Speiser cited an adoption and marriage contract from Late Bronze Age Nuzi (Yorgan Tepe in northeastern Iraq) reflecting practice among the local Hurrian population, but probably not confined to them. According to the terms of this contract, if the wife bears children the husband may not take a second wife, but if she fails to do so the wife must procure for the husband a slave woman as her surrogate. If children result from this union, they will legally be the children of the childless wife.[2] Another law frequently cited is from the Code of Hammurapi (§146), which deals with the case of the slave woman who serves as a surrogate wife, bears children, but then aspires to equal status with the childless wife, or — one supposes — is accused of doing so. The ruling is that she is to be branded with the slave mark and reduced to the rank of an ordinary slave but may not be sold. But this stipulation appears to be a special case applying to a category of female temple officiants *(nadītu),* and it is not certain that it

---

1. E. Axel Knauf, *Ismael,* 2nd ed., ADPV (Wiesbaden: Harrassowitz, 1989), 16-35, 49-53, 144-45; E. Axel Knauf, "Hagar (Person)," in *ABD* 3:18-19. A relation between the personal name and the pastoralist tribe of Hagrites in the upper Transjordanian region (1 Chr. 5:10, 19-20; 27:30-31; Ps. 83:6) has been proposed but remains uncertain. See David F. Graf, "Hagrites," in *ABD* 3:24.

2. Ephraim A. Speiser, *Genesis: Introduction, Translation, and Notes,* AB 1 (Garden City, N.Y.: Doubleday, 1964), 119-21. For Speiser's translation of the text, see AASOR 10 (1930), 31-32, which can be compared with that of Theophile J. Meek, *ANET,* 2nd. ed., 220.

was of general application. A third case is from a contract from the Old Assyrian period (nineteenth century B.C.), according to which a wife who is childless after two years of marriage must purchase a slave woman as a surrogate but, contrary to the ruling in the Hammurapi Code, after she bears a child she may be sold.[3] We do not know whether any of these legal stipulations were known to the author of Gen. 16, but they at least give us grounds for concluding that the situation described in Gen. 16 had legal consequences and fitted a familiar pattern of customary law.

Unlike previous expedients, the proposal to make use of a substitute wife comes from Sarah, not Abraham. This is the first time we hear her speak; previously she was addressed but did not answer, or others spoke about her, or made decisions that affected her, including such major decisions as leaving for Egypt. Like Hannah at Shiloh (1 Sam. 1:5-6), she attributes her inability to have children, a huge blow to self-esteem for women of marriageable age in that culture, to Yahweh, who opens wombs but also sometimes closes them, as he closed the wombs of the women in Abimelech's household (Gen. 20:18). Sarah is not sure it will work; maybe she will have children by Hagar, but Abraham accepts, Hagar becomes pregnant, and after ten years of waiting it looks as if Abraham will have an heir at last, at the age of eighty-five.[4]

As on previous occasions, however, at the moment when it seemed about to succeed, the plan was frustrated — in this instance by Hagar's attitude to her mistress. Like Peninnah with the childless Hannah at Shiloh

---

3. For Hammurapi §146, see *ANET,* 2nd ed., 172, and Martha T. Roth, *Law Collections from Mesopotamia and Asia Minor* (Atlanta: Scholars Press, 1995), 109. For the Old Assyrian text see *ANESTP* 543; and for these laws in general, John Van Seters, "The Problem of Childlessness in Near Eastern Law and the Patriarchs of Israel," *JBL* 87 (1968): 401-8; John Van Seters, *Abraham in History and Tradition* (New Haven: Yale University Press, 1975), 68-71. The rabbinic ruling that a husband may give his wife a bill of divorce if she remains childless after ten years is based on the ten years Abraham spent in Canaan before Sarah offered him Hagar as a surrogate wife (*Gen. Rab.* 45; *b. Yeb.* 64a).

4. The time element in the Abraham cycle is indicated primarily by his age, as follows (age is in the third column):

12:4	From Harran to Canaan	75
16:3	Conception of Ishmael	85
16:16	Birth of Ishmael	86
17:1	Covenant of circumcision	99
17:24	Abraham circumcised	99
21:5	Birth of Isaac	100
23:1	Death of Sarah aged 127	137
25:7	Death of Abraham	175

(1 Sam. 1:6-7), she looked down on Sarah (verbal stem *qll;* literally, "she made light of her"). The relevant stipulation of the Code of Hammurapi shows that this conduct could have serious judicial consequences for one who, though privileged, was still a slave; that Sarah was aware of this can be deduced from her reaction. In the first place, she addresses not Hagar but Abraham in his capacity as head of the household, a position that entailed considerable discretionary powers and judicial reach. She says three things: first, "It is your responsibility to right the wrong done to me";[5] then the complaint: "I have lost status in her eyes" (literally, "I have been insignificant in her eyes"); then, finally, the appeal: "May Yahweh adjudicate between you and me," a formula used only in extreme situations. Referral to the ultimate court of appeal is made only when one is certain about the justice of one's cause. Abraham accepts responsibility, gives Sarah leave to deal with Hagar as she sees fit, Sarah ill-treats her, and Hagar runs away — another act that, for a slave, could have grave consequences.

Hagar in the Wilderness; the Birth of Ishmael

Unlike the situation in the later, very similar incident of expulsion into the wilderness (Gen. 21:1-21), nothing is said on this occasion (16:7-16) about provisions for the journey, or even about the journey itself up to the point of the encounter on the way to Shur, one of the two north-south routes to Egypt together with the Via Maris along the Mediterranean coast. We do not know what destination Hagar had in mind. Wandering about in the Sinai wilderness is not an option, least of all for a pregnant woman. Egypt as Hagar's destination comes to mind, but the wilderness, and more specifically the wilderness between Havilah and Shur, was probably Ishmael's birthplace, and in any case will in due course be Ishmaelite territory (21:20; 25:18). The choice of geographical location for the encounter may therefore have been dictated by these considerations.[6]

In biblical and other ancient narrative, significant characters not

---

5. The substantive *ḥāmās,* usually translated "violence," can also refer to such unjust acts as spreading a false or malicious report about another, an act subject to judicial penalty (Exod. 23:1; Deut. 19:16).

6. According to Exod. 15:22, the Israelites passed through the wilderness of Shur on their way from Egypt to the Promised Land and, like Hagar, had trouble finding water. By the time of the composition of the basic narrative in Gen. 16, the Qedarite Arabs had

infrequently encounter messengers, supernatural visitants from another world. The function of such encounters will frequently be to reveal what is to be the destiny of the one encountered, for example, in the appointment of Gideon as leader in the fight against the Midianites (Judg. 6:12-24), or to prevent some harmful action, for example, by barring the way to Balaam and his donkey (Num. 22:22-35). In the present episode, the angel-messenger could have been taken for a passing fellow traveler who asks Hagar a guileless question, "Hagar, slave-girl of Sarai, where are you coming from, and where are you going?" though Hagar must have wondered how he could have known her name and that of her mistress. After this first exchange, the threefold repetition in rapid succession of the introductory "the messenger from Yahweh said to her" (vv. 9, 10, 11) persuaded some rabbinic readers that Hagar encountered three or more angel-messengers (*Gen. Rab.* 45:7). Contemporary exegesis would more probably assume that the text is overloaded as a result of incorporating three different responses: first, she is to return, resume her previous status, and wait for the birth of her child (v. 9); second, she is motivated to do this by the prediction that from her son will proceed a nation too numerous to be counted (v. 10); and, finally, the occasion calls for a portentous birth oracle (vv. 11-12):

> "Now that you have conceived, you shall bear a son,
> you shall call him Ishmael,
> for Yahweh has heeded your affliction.
> He will be like the wild ass,
> his hand will be against everyone,
> and everyone's hand against him.
> He will live at odds with all his kin."

The birth oracle is a well-attested genre consisting in a portentous announcement; the name of the child to be born; the significance of the name, often with an etymological wordplay; and a prediction of the child's destiny. How persistent this ancient practice is may be seen in the announcement of the angel to Mary mother of Jesus, which reproduces the same pattern (Luke 1:26-38). Examples from the Hebrew Bible, often cited, are the announcements of the birth of Samson in Judg. 13:2-7 and of the

---

succeeded the Ishmaelites in control of that region. On the history of the Ishmaelites, see E. Axel Knauf, "Ishmaelites," in *ABD* 3:513-20.

child to be named Immanuel in Isa. 7:14-16, though the former lacks the name[7] and in the latter the one announcing is a prophet rather than a messenger from God, and the announcement is to the house of David, not to the mother. The reference in the oracle to the wild ass (Gen. 16:12) is not derogatory, as it is in much rabbinic comment. The wild ass (onager) is an animal that is at home in the wilderness and in desolate, uninhabited places (Isa. 32:14; Jer. 2:24; Hos. 8:9), wants nothing more than to be free, and is practically untamable (Job 39:5-8). The oracle, therefore, celebrates in advance the freedom-loving Bedouin lifestyle of Ishmael and his tribe and their often contentious relations with the settled population in their vicinity.

The sequel to the oracle presents serious problems on account of textual corruption and a history of alterations and additions. A preliminary translation might read as follows (Gen. 16:13-14):

> Hagar named the Lord who had spoken to her: "You are El Ro'i, the God who sees me,"
> [for she said, "Have I indeed seen God and am still alive after seeing him?]
> Therefore the well is called Bĕ'ēr Lahai Ro'i, "The Well of the Living One who sees me";
> it lies between Kadesh and Bered.

This sequel to the birth oracle consists of three brief statements. First, Hagar gives a name to the numen[8] who had appeared to her in keeping with her understanding of what had happened; second, a later reader attempted to give an interpretation of Hagar's statement (in brackets); third, another scribe has used the statement to identify a particular well in the Sinai and provide it with an etiology. It may not be so important that the incident happened in the proximity of a spring rather than a well, since springs and wells are often found together. A well is the site of Hagar's encounter with the angel-messenger in the parallel expulsion account in 21:1-21 (21:19), and both springs and wells are frequently associated with religious shrines and their traditions. Hagar's naming of the

---

7. The name Samson *(šimšôn)* is omitted on account of its association with the sun *(šemeš),* hence with a solar deity.

8. "YHWH," translated here as "the Lord," cannot be the original reading since the Hagar of the narrative could not have know the name of the God of Israel that, we will learn later, was not revealed to the first ancestors (Exod. 6:3).

well is her way of responding appropriately to the reassuring oracle. In keeping with the practice of attaching a specific attribute to El, the basic denominator of deity by appending an epithet — Olam, Elyon, Shaddai, etc. — Hagar refers to this local numen as El Ro'i. The explanation that follows takes the epithet in the primary and literal sense of "seeing," and since it is accepted that no one can survive seeing or being seen by God, it was natural for Hagar to express astonishment that she was still alive. In the context, however, it is more natural to assume, rather than simple visual contact, the sense of careful and loving solicitude, a meaning well attested for the common verb "to see" *(ra'ah, lir'ot)*.[9] Finally, there is the etiology of the well named *Bĕ'ēr Lahai Ro'î*. Whatever the original meaning of the name, it serves in this context to express Hagar's positive response to the birth oracle. It is now, in effect, "the Well of the Living One who provides for me."

If this is so, the explanation of the deity's name, according to which Hagar sees God and survives, breaks the connection between the name of the deity and the name of the well. It has therefore almost certainly been inserted by a scribe who shared the common belief that no one could see God and survive, as in Moses' reaction to the theophany in the burning thornbush (Exod. 3:6) or at Sinai (Exod. 33:20, 23). The scribe therefore felt obliged to interpret the obscure name of the well accordingly.

The conclusion to this incident in the wilderness that, as occurs often in stories about ancestors, deals with conception, continuity, and defiance of death, records the birth of Hagar's son and his naming by Abraham, then aged eighty-six. It contradicts the oracle that stipulated that Hagar should name her son, and thus shifts the focus from Hagar to Abraham, and from the wilderness to Abraham's settlement at Hebron/Mamre. We note in passing that mention of Abraham's age at the birth of his firstborn son in Gen. 16:16 (i.e., eighty-six) is consonant with the chronological data in the following chapter where Abraham is ninety-nine years old and Ishmael thirteen when both are circumcised (17:1, 24-25), but it creates a problem when applied to the story of Hagar's second expulsion in 21:1-21. Ishmael was born fourteen years before Isaac (16:16; 21:5), to which we should add three or four years for Isaac to be weaned (21:8) since, in Israel as in many ancient and traditional societies, infants were breast-fed for three years or

---

9. For example: when God saw Leah's affliction and she gave birth to a son (Gen. 29:32), or when God saw the misery of his people in Egypt and delivered them (Exod. 3:7, 9). Other examples: 1 Sam. 1:11; 2 Sam. 16:12; 2 Kgs. 20:5; Pss. 10:14; 25:18-19.

longer.[10] At the time of the second expulsion, therefore, Ishmael would be sixteen or seventeen years old — too big to be carried on Hagar's shoulder (21:14), or put under a bush (21:15), or even to be crying loud enough to be heard in heaven (21:17).

The Birth of Isaac

In view of the distance between the account of the flight of Hagar (16:1-16) and her expulsion (21:8-21), and the close parallels between these two episodes, the first task will be to fit the events recorded in this chapter within the narrative logic of the Abraham story as a whole. With the birth of Ishmael (16:15-16), the expedient proposed by Sarah and accepted by Abraham seems to have worked after all. For the next thirteen years, from Abraham's eighty-sixth to his ninety-ninth year (16:16; 17:1), and from the birth of Ishmael to the birth of Isaac (16:15-16; 21:1-3), Ishmael's status as heir presumptive is never challenged. He was regarded as, biologically and legally, Abraham's heir and therefore heir to the promises, and there is no hint that it was taken to be a temporary expedient. Toward the end of this thirteen-year period the situation changed radically with the promise that Sarah would herself bear a child for Abraham after all (17:15-22; 18:1-19), and the child to be born would, in keeping with customary law, have legal precedence over a child born to the surrogate wife. The second endangering of Sarah recorded in the chapter immediately preceding (20:1-18) would therefore have taken place under circumstances significantly different from the first, and at a more advanced stage in the dramatic development of the story. The vicissitudes of Abraham and Sarah in Gerar in 20:1-18 are nevertheless dependent on and in some respects parallel with the earlier troubles in Egypt in 12:10-20, just as the expulsion of Hagar in 21:1-21 is dependent on and in some respects parallel with her flight into the wilderness in 16:1-16. Accepting this as a literary datum does not, however, absolve us of the task of determining the place of each of these episodes within the context of the Abraham story and the broader context of the ancestral history as a whole.

Another strand in the Abraham story comes into view with the observation that the record of Hagar's expulsion and her encounter with the

---

10. Mayer I. Gruber, "Breast-Feeding Practices in Biblical Israel and in Old Babylonian Mesopotamia," *JANESCU* 19 (1989): 61-83.

messenger of God in the wilderness is spliced into a rather lengthy account of Abraham's uneasy relations with Abimelech while residing as an alien in the Negev (20:1-18 + 21:22-34). The first part of this story (20:1-18) concerns the rescue of Sarah, now pregnant, from the attentions of Abimelech, thereby preparing for the announcement of the birth of Isaac immediately following (21:1-7). At this point, finally, Sarah comes alive, starts talking, and begins to assert herself. The Abraham-Abimelech strand then takes up again with a nonaggression pact between Abimelech the ruler and Abraham, a resident alien in territory controlled by Abimelech (21:22-24). This arrangement is followed by the settlement of a dispute about wells that provides the occasion for bringing one more holy place within Abraham's orbit. The agreement involves the gift of seven ewe lambs to Abimelech, and is accompanied by the swearing of oaths in confirmation of Abraham's ownership of a well. Since "seven" and the verb "to swear" share the same stem in Hebrew, the swearing and the seven lambs provide alternative etiologies of the name of the ancient sanctuary of Beersheba ("The Well of the Seven" or "The Well of the Oath"). This account, too, has its parallel in the Isaac cycle, in a dispute about wells involving Isaac, the Philistines, and their ruler Abimelech with his army commander Phicol, an incident in which Isaac's wife Rebekah is endangered, and which ends with yet another etiology of Beersheba (26:1-33).

Abraham stayed a considerable amount of time in the Negev, more specifically in Beersheba, where he planted a tamarisk tree and offered cult to the local numen under the title El Olam (God Everlasting, 21:33-34). To Beersheba he then returned after the near sacrifice of Isaac in "the land of Moriah" (22:19). Abraham's association with this holy place completes the chain of sanctuaries from north to south — Shechem, Bethel, Mamre, Beersheba — now dedicated to the worship of Abraham's God and serving as a pledge and surety for the fulfillment of the promises.

We return to 21:1-7. The birth of a son to Sarah is announced in advance in parallel passages, the first in the account of the covenant of circumcision (17:15-22), the second in the lead-up to the destruction of Sodom, and the final phase in the history of Lot (18:1-15). These pronouncements are parallel in theme and often in language: a child is promised to Sarah, formerly Sarai (17:16; 18:10, 14); in both pronouncements laughter anticipates the birth of Isaac (17:17, 19; 18:12-15); the advanced age of the mother is noted in both (17:17; 18:11-12); as also is the appointed time for the birth (17:21; 18:10). The account of the birth in 21:1-7 refers back unmistakably to these predictions. Yahweh dealt with Sarah as he had foretold; she gave birth to her child at the time appointed; the child was given a name by Abraham, as he had also named Ishmael; he circumcised the child on the eighth day as prescribed (17:12); and now Sarah can laugh with joy and others can laugh with her.[11] All this laughter is, of course, a play on the name of the child. The name Isaac *(yiṣḥaq)* is an abbreviated form of *yiṣḥaq-'el* ("May God smile on this child"), a common northwest Semitic formulation.

This momentous event is dated to Abraham's 100th year, the year following the announcement of Sarah's pregnancy (17:1), corresponding in the overall chronological schema of the Pentateuch to the year 2046 *anno mundi*.[12] With the immemorial theme of the birth of the child, Gen. 21:1-7 therefore brings to a point of definition and finality a history filled with tension and ambiguity. Its recapitulatory character leads to the conclusion that it comes from a very late stage in the development of the Abraham tradition. It is not surprising, therefore, that exegetes who adhere to the classical but now rather outdated source criticism have found evidence in this brief passage of all three Genesis sources, J, E, and P.[13]

The Second Expulsion of Hagar with Her Son

This episode (21:8-21) runs parallel in structure and theme with Hagar's flight and her encounter with Yahweh's angel-messenger near a spring in the wil-

---

11. The wording of 21:6 is ambiguous. The only other occurrence of *sĕḥōq*, "laughter," Ezek. 23:32, in which Oholibamah/Jerusalem is an object of derision, is certainly derogatory, and the verb followed by the preposition *lamed (yiṣḥaq-lî)* suggests "laughing at" rather than "laughing with"; see Gunkel's comment: "The old woman is ashamed to have become a mother at her age" (*Genesis* [Macon, Ga.: Mercer University Press, 1997], 225). But derisive laughter usually takes a different verbal theme (Piel rather than Qal) and, more importantly, the immediate context, especially Sarah's exclamation in the following verse, suggests joyful laughter.

12. See the time chart in Blenkinsopp, *The Pentateuch: An Introduction to the First Five Books of the Bible* (New York: Doubleday, 1992), 48.

13. John Skinner, *A Critical and Exegetical Commentary on Genesis,* 2nd ed. (Edinburgh: T. & T. Clark, 1930), 320-21; Gunkel, *Genesis,* 225, 267; Gerhard von Rad, *Genesis: A Commentary* (London: SCM, 1961 [1956]), 226-27; Otto Eissfeldt, *The Old Testament: An Introduction* (Oxford: Blackwell, 1956), 188, 199-200; Claus Westermann, *Genesis 12–36* (Minneapolis: Augsburg, 1985), 331. There are of course variations in detail, but general agreement that 2b-5 is P, most or all of the rest J, not much if anything for E. As Skinner, *Genesis,* 321, remarked: "There remains for E the solitary half-verse 6a."

derness (16:1-16). In the narrative context of the Abraham cycle, however, it is a distinct episode that took place some time later but has been written up with the flight narrative in mind. The passage of fourteen years between the two events, calculated according to the chronological schema of the Pentateuch, predictably created problems, in the first place with respect to the relative ages of Ishmael, now a sturdy teenager, and the infant Isaac. We can make sense of the activity of the characters at this juncture only by ignoring Ishmael's "schematic" age and thinking of him as a young child.

The description of Isaac's infancy is traditional and unexceptional; compare, for example, the birth and infancy of Samuel (1 Sam. 1–2) or of Samson (Judg. 13:24), both children of initially infertile mothers. The child would have been weaned no earlier than the third year. This was common practice, no doubt in view of high mortality rates during the first few years, and perhaps also as a way of spacing successive pregnancies. With the infant Samuel, the time of weaning is indicated by the offering of a three-year-old bull (1 Sam. 1:24), and the mother of the Maccabee martyrs reminds the last of her seven sons that she weaned him when he was three years old (2 Macc. 7:27). Weaning was also an event to celebrate, as Elkanah and Hannah celebrated at Shiloh (1 Sam. 1:24-28), and now Abraham with his "great feast" for Isaac. It marked in the first place the child's survival of the first few dangerous years of life during which, at that time, and for centuries later, survival could by no means be taken for granted. It was also a kind of rite of passage, the end of infancy and the beginning of childhood.

We are probably meant to understand that it was in the course of this day of celebration that trouble once again raised its ugly head. By chance Sarah observed the son of Hagar the Egyptian whom she had borne to Abraham, here unnamed, playing with the newly weaned Isaac.[14] "Playing" (verb *tsahaq*) creates another play on the name Isaac, but this hardly explains Sarah's violent reaction to what she saw. Rabbinic interpreters propose a wide range of reprehensible ways of playing attributable to Ishmael, and some of the moderns have proposed a less innocent form that the semantic range of the Hebrew verb in question certainly permits, namely, sexual abuse of a minor.[15] The context, and especially Sarah's peremptory

---

14. Adding "with her son Isaac" with the LXX *(meta Isaak tou huiou autēs)* and some manuscripts of the Vulgate *(cum Isaac filio suo)* to the MT where it is lacking.

15. There is a sexual connotation attached to the verb ṣḥq in Gen. 26:8; 39:14, 17; Exod. 32:6; and perhaps Judg. 16:25.

and angry appeal to Abraham, suggests rather an issue of status. Sarah's concern that Ishmael, in making himself at home in the Abraham household, could supplant Isaac as heir, explains the contemptuous tone of her address to Abraham: "Cast out this slave woman and her son, for the son of this slave woman must not inherit with my son Isaac" (Gen. 21:10). Hagar is no longer the personal attendant *(shivḥah)* of Sarah, as in the incident leading to Hagar's flight into the wilderness. She has been "reduced to the ranks," in this case the rank of a slave woman, an ordinary female slave *('amah),* like so many others. While Abraham, desolate at the prospect of losing his son by Hagar, was casting about for an answer to Sarah, he received yet another message. He is told to do what Sarah says since it will be through Isaac that the name of Abraham will be perpetuated. This was to be expected, but he is also told not to grieve over Ishmael. This was really too much to ask, even though God will make a great nation of the slave woman's son since he is also Abraham's son, and the elder son, though now deprived of the legal privileges of that position.

It may seem strange that Abraham, attached to Ishmael as he clearly was, should have surrendered so meekly to Sarah's demand to expel both him and his mother. It is true that with respect to matters of inheritance in the situation obtaining, that is, in the situation in which the wife gives birth to a son after procuring a proxy for her husband, legal custom favored Sarah. Yet it still required a supernatural intervention for Abraham to comply with his wife's demand. And so, no doubt with a heavy heart, he gave Hagar provisions for the journey and sent her and her son on their way. Hagar's destination was the wilderness of Beersheba, a Negev settlement dedicated to the cult of a local El deity no doubt accompanied by a female consort.[16]

If we take in the ancestral history of Beersheba as a whole, we see

16. Beersheba, one of the cult centers condemned in Amos 5:5; 8:14, was the residence of a deity in whose name oaths were taken and who is referred to enigmatically as "the Way of Beer-sheba" (*derek bĕ'ēr-šeba'* [Amos 8:14]). Some have taken this to refer to the anthropomorphized or theomorphized pilgrimage route, the *via sacra* of Beersheba (e.g., REB, "the sacred way to Beersheva"), but a female fertility deity is much more probable, perhaps Ashima, named in the same Amos text. The word *derek* has a secondary meaning with reference to sexual potency or sexual activity in general, as in Prov. 31:3 ("Do not give to women your vigor / your 'ways' [*dĕrākêkâ*] to women who destroy kings") and Jer. 3:13 ("You [Judah] have scattered your favors [*dĕrākayik*] among strangers under every green tree"). A connection with the goddess Darketu worshiped in Ashkelon in the Hellenistic period has also been suggested. See Saul M. Olyan, "The Oaths of Amos 8:14," in *Priesthood and Cult in Ancient Israel,* ed. Gary A. Anderson and Saul M. Olyan, JSOTSup 125 (Sheffield:

that this city is associated primarily with Isaac, as Hebron/Mamre was with Abraham and Bethel with Jacob. On his way to Egypt, Jacob offered sacrifice to the god of his father Isaac at Beersheba, and, in response, this local deity revealed himself as the god of Jacob's father (46:1-4). Isaac offers his own etiology of Beersheba following on disputes and settlements about wells with the local Philistines and their ruler Abimelech, as at the time of Abraham (26:12-33).[17] The account of Hagar and Ishmael in the wilderness interrupts a record of Abraham's sometimes contentious dealings with Abimelech, a Philistine ruler (20:1-18; 21:22-32), and this concludes with Abraham planting a tamarisk tree and setting up cult to Yahweh El Olam (Yahweh Everlasting God) at Beersheba. It was at Beersheba, then under Philistine control,[18] that he continued to reside as an alien, and it was there that he returned and continued to live after the near sacrifice of Isaac (22:19).

Since we are given no explanation for Abraham's relocation from Hebron/Mamre to Beersheba, it would not be out of place to connect this move with the destination of Hagar and her son in the same region, the wilderness of Beersheba (21:14). The sequence of events is by no means clear, but convergence at the same destination could be seen as one more indication of the close attachment of Abraham to his other beloved son, his firstborn, who came close to death in the wilderness. The juxtaposition of the near-death experience of Ishmael in the wilderness with that of Isaac in the land of Moriah immediately following (22:1-19), both of which were Abraham's doing, followed by Abraham's return to Beersheba after the sacrifice of the ram in the land of Moriah, provokes further reflection and will call for comment in a later section.

What happened in the wilderness is described with great pathos and

---

JSOT, 1991), 121-49; Shalom M. Paul, *A Commentary on the Book of Amos,* Hermeneia (Minneapolis: Fortress, 1991), 271-72; Hans M. Barstad, "Way, דרך," in *DDD* 895-97.

17. "He called it Shivah, therefore the name of the city is Beer-sheva to this day" (Gen. 26:33). Similarity with the verbal stem *šbʿ*, "swear an oath," would suggest a connection with the negotiations of Isaac with Abimelech (26:26-31), but a link with the discovery of water immediately preceding would be contextually more likely. Vulgate translates *abundantia,* but unfortunately the appropriate verbal form does not occur in classical Hebrew.

18. Philistine hostility to Abraham seems to have been the cause of his problem with Abimelech (26:12-16), which concluded with a negotiated settlement, after which Abimelech returned to the land of the Philistines (21:32). Philistine ware was recovered from Beersheba, specifically from Early Iron Age stratum IX of Bir es-Sebaʿ, site of the ancient settlement. On the archaeology of the site, see Zeʾev Herzog, "Tell Beersheba," in *NEAEHL* 1:167-73; Dale W. Manor, "Beer-Sheba," in *ABD* 1:641-45.

admirable brevity. Her water flask empty and no help in sight, Hagar places her son tenderly under a bush to protect him from the sun and, unable to watch him die, sits down opposite him but some distance away and weeps. The rescue by supernatural intervention appears to be told in alternative versions. According to the main narrative line, God (Elohim) heard the child crying, and intervened by showing Hagar a well full of water, so she went, filled her flask, and gave the child a drink (vv. 17a + 19). The interpolated version (vv. 17b-18) conforms to the same pattern as in the flight narrative: a simple question addressed to Hagar, a command, and an assurance of ultimate success (16:7-12). In this version the intervention comes from the angel-messenger of God. Hagar is told not to be afraid since God has heard the sound of the child crying. She is not offered assistance, but told to take the child in her arms in the assurance that all will be well. God will make of Ishmael a great nation.

The episode concludes with a statement of approval of Ishmael: God was with him, as he was with the young Samuel (1 Sam. 3:19); he grew up and lived and moved around in the wilderness of Paran in the eastern Sinai,[19] a skilled hunter with the bow, the prototype of the Bedouin no doubt well familiar to the narrator. It is hardly surprising that his mother procured an Egyptian wife for him since she is routinely referred to as "Hagar the Egyptian" (Gen. 16:1, 3; 21:9; 25:12), and the wilderness of Paran is contiguous with Egyptian territory. What is said here of Ishmael is of course said of him as the model or paradigm of the people who bore his name, members of the Ishmaelite confederacy consisting of the twelve Arab tribes listed in the second of the five ancestral *toledot* (25:12-18).[20] Of these twelve, the most numerous and powerful were the descendants of Qedar (Qedarites, Gen. 25:13; 1 Chr. 1:29), who succeeded the Ishmaelites. By the Persian period, when Gen. 21:1-21 probably attained its final form, they controlled a vast area in the Sinai, the Negev, and the Transjordanian region. From scattered allusions to Ishmaelites elsewhere in the Hebrew Bible, we learn that they were camel nomads (Gen. 37:25; 1 Chr. 27:30); traders in gum, balm, and resin (Gen. 37:25), as well as slaves (Gen. 37:27-

19. Ishmaelites were to be found "from Havilah to Shur, opposite Egypt, on the way to Asshur" (Gen. 25:18), in the same region as Amalekites (1 Sam. 15:7). Before moving to Gerar, Abraham settled for a while "between Kadesh and Shur" (Gen. 20:1), while Hagar fled to a place near Kadesh, on the way to Shur (16:7, 14). The identification of Havilah, Shur, and Asshur is uncertain, but we assume that these locations correspond to what was known or surmised about tribes in the Negev and Sinai at the time of writing.

20. On the names in the list see E. Axel Knauf, "Ishmael," in *ABD* 3:513-20.

28; 39:1); and recognizable by their gold earrings (Judg. 8:24). They also intermarried with Edomites (Gen. 28:9; 36:3), Simeonites (1 Chr. 4:25), and no doubt other southern tribes related to Judah.

A concluding note. One of the most impressive features of the Abraham story is the close bond between the patriarch and his firstborn son Ishmael. Even after hearing that he will have issue from Sarah, he pleads that Ishmael may be the chosen one (Gen. 17:18). He is grievously distressed at having to lose him after Sarah's demand that the "slave woman" and her son be expelled from the household (21:11). And, finally, it is a curious coincidence that on both occasions when Hagar has to leave to avoid the hostility of Sarah, Abraham is described as relocating in the same region. On the first occasion, Hagar ended her journey on the way to Shur near Kadesh (16:7, 14) and Abraham settled between Kadesh and Shur (20:1). After the expulsion of Hagar and her son, her journey ended in the wilderness of Beersheba (21:14), and it was at Beersheba, apparently about the same time, that Abraham set up a cult site (21:33), settled there (21:34), and returned after the near sacrifice of his other beloved son, Isaac (22:19). The relation between Abraham and Ishmael will call for further comment in chapter 8 below.

Filling In the Gaps

Since Hagar is described as an Egyptian in the Abraham story (Gen. 16:1, 3; 21:9; 25:12), the author of the *Genesis Apocryphon* concluded that she must have been given to Sarah by the pharaoh while still in Egypt (1QapGen XX, 32). Either inadvertently or deliberately, the author ignored the fact that female slaves were among the compensatory goods given to Abraham, not Sarah (12:16). Jewish tradition of a later date goes further in identifying Hagar as Pharaoh's daughter who is handed over to Sarah as a slave as part of the marriage agreement (*ketuvah, Gen. Rab.* 45:1; *Pirqe R. El.* 26; *Tg. Ps.-J.* on Gen. 16:1). There existed, however, a tradition that Sarah must have made Hagar a free woman before offering her as surrogate wife to Abraham, since it would be unseemly for Abraham to have intimate relations with a slave.[21] Hagar takes the initiative in this expedient, and makes it clear that she wants children for herself, not just for Abraham, whose plight was extreme since, according to another rabbinic maxim,

---

21. *Gen. Rab.* 45:6; *Tg. Yer.* on Gen. 16:3.

"whoever does not have a child is like one who is dead and destroyed" (*Gen. Rab.* 45:2). Rabbinic commentators are divided on Hagar's character, with some maintaining that she was initially righteous like her mistress, but that after she bore a child she began to spread false rumors about her. She spread the word that Sarah looks pious but cannot be, for "if she were a righteous woman she would have got pregnant by now, while I got pregnant in a single night" (*Gen. Rab.* 45:4). There is, however, something close to a consensus on Abraham's attachment to her. According to one well-attested opinion, Abraham not only remarried Hagar after the death of Sarah, but he fathered six more sons with her, a remarkable feat since his "schematic" age at that time would have been 137 (23:1), with another 38 years to go (25:7). This exegetical tour de force was made possible by the simple expedient of identifying Hagar with Keturah, the other Arab woman who bore him six children.[22] These Arabian eponyms, including Midian, could therefore claim Abrahamic descent, but according to one tradition, reported in *Gen. Rab.* 61:5, the marriage did not work out well since they turned out to be idol worshipers.

That the union between Abraham and Hagar took place after Abraham had lived in Canaan for ten years (Gen. 16:3) is contemporized and explained by R. Ammi in the name of R. Shim'on ben Laqish with reference to the rabbinic precept that if one has married a woman and lived with her for 10 years without issue, he must divorce her and marry another.[23] At that time Abraham was, schematically, 85 years old, and 15 more years would pass before the birth of Isaac (21:5). The biblical text tells us only that Isaac's birth occurred in Abraham's 100th year, but this was not enough for some early readers. According to the *Book of Jubilees* (16:13), this defining moment coincided with the Feast of Weeks (Shavuoth) in the third month (Sivan), but later opinion preferred Passover in the first month (Nisan), and, more precisely, at noon of the first day of the festival (*Gen. Rab.* 43:6). A tradition represented by *Pirqe R. El.* (21:4) maintains that Abraham's great feast was to celebrate not the weaning of Isaac but his circumcision on the eighth day, contrary to the explicit statement of the biblical text (Gen. 21:8). This view seems to have been shared by Josephus, who adds that Abraham's feast marks the origin of the practice of circumcising on the eighth day (*Ant.* 1.214). It was, in any case, quite a party. Guests came from far and wide, including Abimelech and his army commander Phicol,

---

22. *Gen. Rab.* 61:4; *Pirqe R. El.* 30; *Tg. Yer.* on Gen. 25:1.
23. *Gen. Rab.* 45:3, with reference to *b. Yeb.* 64a.

thirty-one other kings, among them Og, king of Bashan, he of the famous bed. Even Terah and Nahor checked in from far-distant Harran.

It seems that trouble leading to the expulsion of Hagar and her son began during the festivities. One explanation maintained that Sarah was afraid Ishmael would harm Isaac (Josephus, *Ant.* 1.215). Elaborating on this fear, some rabbis held that Ishmael, an expert bowman, was in the habit of playfully shooting arrows at the infant (*Gen. Rab.* 53:11; *t. Sotah* 6:6). Not impossibly, traditions of this kind may be behind Paul's statement that "the natural-born son persecutes the spiritual son" (Gal. 4:29). Another surmise, based on Gen. 21:9, has Ishmael playing and dancing during the festivities, thereby charming Abraham but infuriating Sarah (*Jub.* 17:4). Jealous of the attention Abraham paid to Hagar's son, Sarah put the evil eye on Ishmael with the result that he fell into a fever, had to be carried, and drank all the water from Hagar's flask (*Gen. Rab.* 53; *Tg. Yer.* on Gen. 21:16).

Descriptions of Ishmael in Jewish tradition reflect something of the fear and contempt of those living in a more settled urban situation than that of the desert Arabs. Ishmael embodies this profile in traditional Jewish commentary as a wild man, "his fist against everyone and everyone's fist against him" (Gen. 16:12). The polemical note intensified after the rise of Islam,[24] and has continued residually down to the present. Early Christian reflection on Hagar and Sarah, their contentious relationship, and the birth of Ishmael and Isaac is for the most part either allegorical — as in Paul's allegory of the two women in his epistle to the Galatians — or moralistic. Typical of the latter type is the concern to explain how Abraham could have contracted a second marriage or even engaged in extramarital relations. In his treatise on Abraham (1.4.23), Ambrose of Milan excused him on the grounds that the law forbidding adultery had not yet been enacted and, in any case, Abraham was motivated not by sensuality but by the desire to have a son in keeping with the divine plan.[25]

---

24. C. T. R. Hayward, "Targum Pseudo-Jonathan and Anti-Islamic Polemic," *JSS* 34 (1989): 77-93; D. J. Zucher, "Conflicting Conclusions: The Hatred of Isaac and Ishmael," *Judaism* 39, no. 1 (1990): 37-46; C. Bakhos, *Ishmael on the Border: Rabbinic Portrayals of the First Arab* (Albany: State University of New York Press, 2006); Emmanouela Grypeou and Helen Spurling, *The Book of Genesis in Late Antiquity: Encounters between Jewish and Christian Exegesis* (Leiden and Boston: Brill, 2013), 239-59.

25. Citations from early Christian commentary in Mark Sheridan, *Ancient Christian Commentary on Scripture: Old Testament II; Genesis 12–50* (Downers Grove, Ill.: InterVarsity, 2002), 41-50, 89-99; Theresia Heither, O.S.B., and Christiana Reemts, O.S.B., *Biblische*

Josephus is content with adding only minor elaborations to the story of the expulsion and the trial and deliverance in the wilderness. The angel of God shows Hagar a spring (as in the flight narrative), and she and her son are assisted by shepherds who attend to their needs. This brief report is then rounded off with Ishmael's descendants listed in the *toledot* of Gen. 25:12-18 (*Ant.* 1.215-221).

Gestalten bei den Kirchenvätern. Abraham (Münster: Aschendorff, 2005), 87-100, 143-52; Grypeou and Spurling, *Book of Genesis,* 259-88.

The Covenant of Circumcision

Grace Abounding, Covenant, and Circumcision in Genesis 17

The practice of circumcising infants or adults is a subject of interest to anthropologists; psychologists, including child psychologists; medical specialists; and feminists, and among the latter are some who characterize circumcision as initiation into a patrilineal lineage, a male bloodline that serves to validate and perpetuate male status in Judaism and other ethnic groups.[1] We must, however, with regret leave this fascinating area of research to others and continue our task of tracing the narrative logic of the Abraham story as it unfolds.

In Jewish tradition Gen. 17 is called *berit milah,* "the covenant of circumcision" (*diathēkē peritomēs* in Acts 7:8), but circumcision is by no means the only theme taken up in this chapter. The consensus is that the chapter belongs to the Priestly source (P), and that it is the one and only revelation made to Abraham in that source. It is also the axis or fulcrum for the Abraham cycle as a whole, situated as it is between the birth of Ishmael (Gen. 16:15-16) and the birth of Isaac (21:1-5), both passages also

---

1. This is not the place to document these studies, but I take the liberty of recommending three essays of fairly recent date that touch in interesting ways on some aspects of current interest: Howard Eilberg-Schwartz, *The Savage in Judaism: An Anthropology of Israelite Religion and Ancient Judaism* (Bloomington and Indianapolis: Indiana University Press, 1990), especially 141-76; Nancy Jay, *Throughout Your Generations Forever: Sacrifice, Religion, and Paternity* (Chicago: University of Chicago Press, 1992); Lawrence A. Hoffman, *Covenant of Blood: Circumcision and Gender in Rabbinic Judaism* (Chicago: University of Chicago Press, 1996).

assigned to the Priestly source.[2] The chapter contains four clearly distinct sections:

1. A vision report in which Yahweh God, who identifies himself as El Shaddai (God Almighty),[3] after exhorting the ninety-nine-year-old Abraham to live blamelessly in the presence of God,[4] announces a perpetual covenant according to which Abram, now to be renamed Abraham, is to be the father of a multitude of nations and their kings and is to have possession of the land in which he is living as an alien (vv. 1-8).

2. The law of circumcision, also promulgated as a covenant (vv. 9-14).

3. The promise to the ninety-year-old Sarai, now to be renamed Sarah, of a child to be named Isaac who will inherit the covenant (vv. 15-22).

4. The circumcision by Abraham of himself, his son Ishmael, and all his household including slaves in obedience to the law promulgated in the second section (vv. 23-27).

This arrangement, in which the theme of Abraham's and Sarah's descendants (vv. 1-8, 15-22) alternates with the law of circumcision and its implementation (vv. 9-14, 23-27) in an *abab* pattern, already strongly suggests that the chapter is a redactional rather than an authorial unit. Furthermore, the abrupt transition between the first and the second of these four sections poses the question: How can a covenant commitment that Abraham will be the ancestor of many nations and their kings, made *unconditionally* to him by Yahweh — El Shaddai — be reconciled with a covenant that inculcates under severe penalties the observance of a practice signifying ethnic self-segregation?[5] Or, in what sense does circumcision

2. An excellent and up-to-date summary of research on the formation and structure of Gen. 17 is in Konrad Schmid, "Judean Identity and Ecumenicity: The Political Theology of the Priestly Document," in *Judah and the Judeans in the Achaemenid Period,* ed. Oded Lipschits, Gary N. Knoppers, and Manfred Oeming (Winona Lake, Ind.: Eisenbrauns, 2011), 3-26.

3. This is the first appearance of this title in Genesis. It is characteristic of the Priestly source (Gen. 17:1; 28:3; 35:11; 48:3; Exod. 6:3), but even more so of Job (thirty-one times) and other late texts (Ruth 1:20-21; Pss. 68:14; 91:1). See E. Axel Knauf, "Shadday," *DDD,* 2nd ed., 749-53.

4. Literally, "walk in my presence and be blameless" *(hithallēk lēpānay wĕhyēh tāmîm).* The same language is used with respect to Enoch (5:22, 24) and Noah (6:9).

5. There is a connection between circumcision and fertility that, in the Levitical legislation, is applied even to fruit trees (Lev. 19:23-25), on which see Schwartz, *The Savage in Judaism,* 146-54, but there is no indication that this was in the mind of whoever drafted

qualify Abraham to be ancestor of many nations? An even more obvious problem is that the legal idiom in which circumcision is mandated in the second section has nothing in common with the language of the vision immediately preceding it. One of the many commentators who have noted this contrast observed that the second section "reads like a stray leaf from the book of Leviticus."[6] The idiom and vocabulary have elements in common with the first section, hence its assignment to P, but the origin of this kind of writing is to be sought in a different milieu from that of the Priestly narrator in the first section, in all likelihood among those members of the temple staff responsible for the drafting of ritual law. We might compare it with the laws governing participation in Passover in Exod. 12:43-49, which also have to do with circumcision. We are therefore justified in testing the hypothesis that the circumcision theme represents a later addition from a temple scribe, probably a priest, who may well have been scandalized that Abraham, practically a centenarian, had not been circumcised.

The distinct origin of the two sections finds additional support in Jacob's vision at Bethel after returning from Paddan-aram in Gen. 35:9-13:

> God (Elohim) appeared once again to Jacob after he returned from Paddan-aram and blessed him. God said to him: "Your name is now Jacob, but you will not be called Jacob any longer; instead, your name will be Israel, Israel is what you will be called." God then said to him, "I am El-Shaddai (God Almighty). Be fruitful and increase. A nation and a company of nations will come from you; kings will issue from you. The land that I gave to Abraham and Isaac I give to you, and I will give the land to your descendants after you." Then God (Elohim) left him.[7]

This incident, also assigned to the Priestly narrative strand (P), has much in common with Gen. 17:1-8 but without the latter's sequel in the circumcision command of 17:9-14; in fact, the circumcision of Jacob is nowhere mentioned. It begins and ends in the same formulaic manner as in Abra-

---

the law in Gen. 17:9-14. The emphasis is on membership of a people, which can include even foreign slaves.

6. John Skinner, *A Critical and Exegetical Commentary on Genesis,* 2nd ed. (Edinburgh: T. & T. Clark, 1930), 293. See also Claus Westermann's observation that 17:9-14 "cannot be part of God's speech because of the utterly impersonal legal style." Westermann, *Genesis 12–36* (Minneapolis: Augsburg, 1985), 264.

7. Literally, "God went up from him," as in 17:22. The rest of 35:13, "in the place where he had spoken with him," was added by dittography; see v. 14.

ham's vision. The introductory statement, "God appeared to Jacob again when he came from Paddan-aram . . . and God said to him" (35:9), corresponds to "Yahweh appeared to Abraham and said to him . . ." (17:1); and its conclusion, "God went up from him (Jacob) at the place where he had spoken with him" (35:13), corresponds to the conclusion of 17:1-8 + 15-22: "When he had finished speaking with Abraham, God went up from him" (17:22). In both addresses the deity identifies himself as El Shaddai; both Abraham and Jacob are given new names; both are to be fruitful and have numerous descendants,[8] including nations and their kings; and the promise of land is repeated. The only significant difference is that, in addition to a "company of nations" (*qehal goyim,* 35:11),[9] like the "multitude of nations" that will acknowledge Abraham as their ancestor (17:4-5), a nation *(goy)* set aside from the others will also issue from Jacob. In the second visionary revelation to Abraham (17:15-22), the descendants are always nations, among which the only great nation mentioned is the one Ishmael will father (17:20), whereas with Jacob the one nation bears the name of its eponymous ancestor. Abram's name change to Abraham internationalizes him; Jacob's name change to Israel makes him the eponymous ancestor of a particular people. The close similarity in style and theme of Jacob's vision with that of Abraham — without the circumcision command — therefore strengthens the suggestion that this important chapter 17 represents a combination of two substantially different ideas about covenant.

The Origins of Circumcision as Covenant and Sign

It must have seemed inconceivable for the pious Israelite of a later day, and more so for a member of the temple personnel, that father Abraham could have entered into a covenant with his God when still uncircumcised. Hence the addition of the circumcision "on the very same day in

8. As Van Seters points out (*Abraham in History and Tradition* [New Haven: Yale University Press, 1975], 283), the combination of the verbal pair *prh* and *rbh* ("be fruitful and multiply," NRSV) may correspond to a liturgical blessing. It is repeated often throughout the ancestral history (Gen. 17:20; 28:3; 35:11; 47:27; 48:4), as the application of the creation command to be fruitful (prolific) and increase (1:22, 28; 9:1, 7).

9. The term *qāhāl* (company, host, assembly) is more often than not used of Israel as a religious and political entity, in keeping with the status of Jacob-Israel as the original ancestor. It can also connote foreign nations, usually hostile, with especial frequency in Ezekiel (17:17; 23:24; 26:7; 27:27; 32:3; 38:4, 7, 15).

which God had spoken to him" (17:23). In that respect, the fulfillment of the command in the fourth section of the chapter is in competition, as an account of *the origins* of circumcision, with the strange passage in which the quick-witted Zipporah saved Moses' life by circumcising him, at least symbolically, before he undertook the mission to set his people free from Egypt (Exod. 4:24-26). As an account of the origins of infant circumcision on the eighth day of life — as mandated in Lev. 12:3 — it is, however, not entirely satisfactory since it had to be accommodated to the chronological schema according to which Ishmael was then thirteen years old, even though his birth is recorded immediately prior to the vision (in Gen. 16:15-16).

This brings us up against the question about the time and circumstances in the history of Israel and early Judaism in which circumcision would have served as a distinguishing ethnic and religious marker of such irreplaceable significance as Gen. 17:9-14 suggests. Throughout the entire historical period Israelites and Judeans practiced circumcision, but so did all their neighbors. Circumcision was the common practice among northwest Semitic peoples, which explains the frequent derogatory use of the term "uncircumcised" *(arelim)* with reference to the non-Semitic Philistines.[10] A point is made in passing, in Jer. 9:25-26, in which Egypt, Judah, Edom, Ammon, Moab, and the desert Arabs are denounced as circumcised only in the flesh and not in the heart. In his capacity as amateur ethnologist, Herodotus is in agreement in reporting that the practice began with Egyptians and Ethiopians and spread to Phoenicians and Syrians of Palestine, which latter group would have included Jews.[11] The fact that Israelites and Judeans shared the practice with their neighbors is consistent with the infrequent reference to circumcision in texts from the pre-Hellenistic period. Apart from Joshua's circumcision ceremony at Gilgal after crossing the Jordan (Josh. 5:2-12), and leaving aside metaphorical circumcision of the heart, lips, or ears,[12] the historical books are silent on the subject. Circumcision is also conspicuous by its absence from the

---

10. Judg. 14:3; 15:18; 1 Sam. 14:6; 17:26, 36; etc. The same pejorative term is used in the catalogue of the uncircumcised and those fated to join them in Sheol (hades) in Ezek. 32:20-32.

11. Herodotus 2.104, cited in Josephus, *C. Ap.* 1.168-171, and *Ant.* 8.262.

12. Jer. 4:4; 9:25-26, cf. Lev. 26:41; Deut. 10:16; 30:6 (circumcision of the heart); Jer. 6:10 (circumcision of the ears, i.e., obedience to the word of God); Exod. 6:12, 30 (circumcision of the lips, i.e., fluent speech). Metaphorical usage would very likely indicate diminished emphasis on the practice itself.

prophetic writings.[13] It is often suggested that the practice would have served as a form of self-segregation among Jewish communities settled in Babylon where circumcision was not the norm, and where there was a fairly high level of interethnicity. Judean expatriates in Babylon who already practiced circumcision would very likely have continued to do so, but evidence is lacking for circumcision as indicative of self-segregation in diasporic Jewish communities, and what limited sources of information we possess, mostly prosopographical, do not favor the view that Babylonian diaspora Jews lived a strictly self-segregating existence.[14] Circumcision is also conspicuously absent from the rigorous application of self-segregating rules and procedures of Ezra, Nehemiah, and the *bene haggolah* (the diaspora assembly) of Babylonian diasporic origin. The same goes for the Aramaic documents from the Jewish colony on the island of Elephantine at the first cataract of the Nile, which do not even mention circumcision.[15]

Add that not even in Deuteronomy, in which covenant *(berit)* is a ruling concept, is circumcision linked to covenant either as practically synonymous or as sign. Circumcision occurs in Deuteronomy only as metaphor;

13. The complaint in Ezek. 44:7 about foreigners "uncircumcised in heart and flesh" profaning the temple by their presence and employment probably refers to the *nĕtînîm* named in the lists in Ezra 2 and Neh. 7, descendants of the Gibeonites condemned to be hewers of wood and drawers of water in the service of the temple (Josh. 9:23, 27). This was therefore a special case. See G. A. Cooke, *A Critical and Exegetical Commentary on the Book of Ezekiel* (Edinburgh: T. & T. Clark, 1936), 479; Walther Zimmerli, *Ezekiel 2: A Commentary on the Book of the Prophet Ezekiel Chapters 25–48* (Philadelphia: Fortress, 1983 [1969]), 454. The uncircumcised and ritually unclean who in Isa. 52:1 will no longer be present in the Jerusalem of the future are foreign conquerors, as is apparent from the context of the saying.

14. Elias J. Bickerman, "The Babylonian Captivity," in *The Cambridge History of Judaism*, vol. 1, *Introduction: The Persian Period*, ed. W. D. Davies and Louis Finkelstein (Cambridge: Cambridge University Press, 1984), 342-58; Ran Zadok, *The Jews in Babylonia during the Chaldean and Achaemenian Periods according to the Babylonian Sources*, Studies in the History of the Jewish People and the Land of Israel 3 (Haifa: Haifa University Press, 1979). Updates on the more recent prosopographical data, including texts from Āl-Yāhūda and Našar in southern Babylonia, in Laurie E. Pearce, "New Evidence for Judeans in Babylonia," in *Judah and the Judeans in the Persian Period,* ed. Oded Lipschits and Manfred Oeming (Winona Lake, Ind.: Eisenbrauns, 2006), 399-411, and in "'Judean': A Special Status in Neo-Babylonian and Achemenid Babylonia?" in *Judah and the Judeans in the Achaemenid Period*, 267-79, both with up-to-date bibliographies.

15. Bezalel Porten holds that circumcision and Sabbath observance would have been required of converts to Judaism; perhaps so, but it is still noteworthy that circumcision is never mentioned in the Elephantine archive. See B. Porten, *Archives from Elephantine* (Berkeley and Los Angeles: University of California Press, 1968), 248-58; Bob Becking, "Yehudite Identity in Elephantine," in *Judah and the Judeans in the Achaemenid Period,* 403-19.

the uncircumcised in heart are those who refuse to heed the admonitions of the Moses who speaks in the book (Deut. 10:16; 30:6). More probably, the link between covenant and circumcision would have originated during the ascendancy of the Zadokite-Aaronite priesthood toward the end of the first or the beginning of the second century of Persian rule.[16]

In the present state of our knowledge, or rather ignorance, a better documented background for circumcision as a mark or sign of ethnic and religious identity comes into view in the mid- or late Persian period, or even in the early Hellenistic period, when Jewish communities were beginning to come into contact with the Greek way of life, including frequenting the baths and the youth center *(ephēbeion)* and attending and participating in athletic activities, both involving nudity. Herodotus (2.104) reports that Phoenicians in touch with Hellas tended to abandon the practice of circumcision, and something similar could be expected among Jews in Judea and beyond. Under the Hellenistic monarchies many Jews, we are told, had recourse to epispasm, the surgical removal of the marks of circumcision.[17] At a later date, the abolition of circumcision among his Jewish subjects was a major goal of Antiochus IV (1 Macc. 1:48, 60-61), in reaction to which it became an essential mark of Jewish identity among the devout, beginning with Mattathias (2:46) and culminating with the coercive imposition of the practice after the conquest of foreign peoples inhabiting territories annexed by the later Hasmoneans.[18] These are later and more extreme developments, but they assume a situation that must have been in place for some time.

The incident reported in Gen. 34 in which Jacob's sons imposed circumcision — disingenuously, it is true — on the inhabitants of Shechem as a condition for intermarriage with a view to creating "one people" *(am ehad,* 34:22) is curiously reminiscent of the Hasmonean practice of coercive circumcision. This is not the place for a detailed analysis of this

16. On the late date for the emergence of the Aaronite priesthood and their relations with the Zadokites, on which admittedly much is obscure, see my "The Judaean Priesthood during the Neo-Babylonian and Achaemenid Periods," *CBQ* 60 (1998): 25-43; "The Mystery of the Missing 'Sons of Aaron,'" in *Exile and Restoration Revisited,* ed. Gary N. Knoppers and Lester L. Grabbe (London and New York: T. & T. Clark, 2009), 65-77.

17. 1 Macc. 1:11-15; 2 Macc. 4:11-17; Josephus, *Ant.* 12.241.

18. Circumcision as a condition for avoiding expulsion from territories temporarily occupied by the Hasmonean princes was imposed on Idumeans by Hyrcanus I (Josephus, *Ant.* 13.257-258) and on Itureans of the Phoenician hinterland by Aristobulus I (*Ant.* 13.318-319).

incident, but it cannot be passed over without comment. All commentators agree on the existence of a number of incongruities in the account. It is assumed that the Hivites of Shechem are uncircumcised, but the fact that a Hivite-Israelite union could have been contemplated puts them in a position vis-à-vis Israelites entirely different from that of the Philistines.[19] The date and background of this story of rape, slaughter, and treachery are obscure. Most commentators claim to identify a strand or redaction later than the conventional sources, but in the present state of our ignorance further precision is impossible.[20]

Returning to the fourfold sectioning of Gen. 17, we may tentatively conclude the following. First, that the circumcising by Abraham of himself and Ishmael (section 4: vv. 23-27) was the original follow-up to the promulgation of the law (section 2: vv. 9-14); the language is the same, and we are told that the implementation of the law took place on the same day (v. 23). Second, that the promise of an heir to Abraham and Sarah was interposed between the promulgation and implementation of the law. The insertion would have been motivated by the need to counter the embarrassing implication that Ishmael entered the covenant, now signified and sealed by circumcision, before Isaac, indeed a year before Isaac was born. In any case, something had to be said at this point, since the initial revelation predicted many descendants for Abram, now Abraham, indeed a whole multitude of nations, at a time when advanced age and a wife sidelined by infertility made such a prospect dubious, to say the least. We shall return to this problematic situation after taking a closer look at the initial revelation and its sequel, dealing with the crucial issue of an heir (sections 1 and 3).

---

19. Even if disingenuous, the reply of the sons of Jacob to Shechem ben Hamor must have at least sounded plausible (34:14-17). Jacob, who plays no part in the proceedings, complains bitterly to his sons after it is all over that "you have brought trouble on me by making me odious to the inhabitants of the land" (34:30).

20. Consult Skinner, *Genesis*, 417-22; Hermann Gunkel, *Genesis* (Macon, Ga.: Mercer University Press, 1997), 357; Westermann, *Genesis 12-36*, 532-45. A late stage of editing, conflating two narrative strands (e.g., in Gerhard von Rad, *Genesis: A Commentary* [London: SCM, 1961 (1956)], 325-30), cannot very well be as late as the Hasmonean dynasts, but it can certainly be Hellenistic. The opinion of Van Seters, *Abraham in History and Tradition*, 150, that it is "a late southern polemic against a paganized 'Samaritan' north," may not be far off the mark.

The Covenant of Grace Abounding

We return, therefore, to the first section, the everlasting covenant made with Abraham. The life story of Abraham moves forward at an uneven pace with abrupt transitions and several large gaps. The century he spent in Canaan covers the period from his arrival at age 75 to his death at 175. A first gap of 11 years after his arrival ends with the birth of Ishmael; then 14 years pass until Isaac is born; then 75 years with only two events of note, the near-death experience of Isaac (22:1-19) and the real death of Sarah at the age of 127 (23:1). Thirty-eight years then elapse before his own death at 175 years (25:7-8). The covenant of grace recorded here (17:1-8, 15-22) occupies a critical position between the birth of Ishmael (16:15-16) and that of Isaac (21:1-3), both beloved sons who are inseparably part of the future presented to Abraham in the vision. During the 13 years that had passed since the birth of Ishmael, this firstborn of Abraham was accepted without challenge as Abraham's heir designate. His status as Abraham's heir was not intended as a temporary measure. Abraham's own acceptance of this situation is apparent from his appeal, made even after the promise that Sarah would bear a child, that Ishmael might be the one to win God's special favor (literally, "to live in God's presence," 17:18). He was, after all, his firstborn son, and Abraham's great affection for him is apparent throughout the cycle. Nothing in this covenant of grace followed by the covenant of circumcision would have changed this situation; Ishmael is still the heir presumptive. It does not call for undue psychologizing to imagine what bond of affection would have been nurtured between father and son during the preceding 13 years, and what a long time it was for Sarah to remain silent in the background.

The vision consists in a declarative statement of the deity identified as Yahweh in the editorial introduction, as Elohim (God) after the initial announcement of a covenant (v. 3), and as El Shaddai in the deity's own self-identification. The only element of interactivity in the vision is Abraham's prostration (literal translation: "he fell on his face") as he prepared to hear the revelation. El Shaddai[21] is the first of several indications that the

---

21. In biblical usage El Shaddai is associated with extreme meteorological phenomena (Ezek. 1:24; 10:5; Job 6:4), divine anger (Job 21:20; 29:5), destruction (Joel 1:15; Job 19:29), and disaster in general (Ruth 1:20-21). It has been explained by way of assonance with the verb *šdd*, "destroy," as in Isa. 13:6 and Joel 1:15, *kĕšōd miššadday yābô'* ("it approaches like destruction from Shaddai"), and in connection with the *šadayîn* (avenging deities or demons?) of the Deir Allah texts. On these texts see Jo Ann Hackett, *The Balaam Text from*

chapter is the work of the priest-scribe, the so-called Priestly source (P). This title occurs in other passages assigned to the same source, including the vision experienced by Jacob at Bethel (35:9-13) and the instructions of Isaac to Jacob as he sends him to Paddan-aram to find a wife among his own extended kinship (28:1-4). The revelation in Exod. 6:2-8 to Moses of Yahweh–El Shaddai, which refers back to the covenant of Gen. 17:1-8, looks like the Priestly (P) version of the revelation to Moses at the burning thornbush in Exod. 3:1-22. The latter took place in the wilderness, but the Priestly version is located in Egypt (Exod. 6:28-29), in keeping with the Priestly belief in Yahweh as a cosmic deity who transcends national, ethnic, and territorial boundaries. This fundamentally important development in the religious history of Israel is represented symbolically in the departure of the *kābôd,* the divine glory, from the temple and its appearance in Babylonia to the priest-prophet Ezekiel in the vision of the mobile chariot throne.[22]

Other linguistic and thematic features either peculiar to or characteristic of this narrative source establish linkage with the P account of the original creation and the new dispensation established in the postdeluge world. The exhortation to Abraham to "live your life in my presence and be blameless" recalls, and is intended to recall, the description of Enoch and Noah, who lived their lives in God's presence (literally "walked with God," Gen. 5:22, 24; 6:9); Noah, in addition, was considered blameless (6:9). The prediction that Abraham would be fruitful and numerous in his progeny (17:6; also 28:3; 35:11) takes up the original creation command to be fruitful and increase (1:28), repeated as a corollary to the covenant established after the waters of the deluge had subsided (9:1, 7). This will help to establish the broader context of Abraham's many auditions and visions. The story of God's relations to the world is a story of failures and disasters followed by new beginnings. This was so with the postdeluge world, and we might think of this revelation to Abraham as a new initiative of God after things went wrong again with the debacle of the first empire ruled by Nimrod and the building of the city and tower of Babel.

Covenant *(berit)* is clearly a dominant concept throughout this entire

---

Deir 'Allā, HSM 31 (Chico, Calif.: Scholars Press, 1980), 85-89, and on the linguistic and cultural background of Shaddai *(šadday),* Knauf, "Shadday," 749-53.

22. The exile of the *kābôd* begins in its movement from the holy of holies (Ezek. 3:12), to the threshold of the temple (9:3), then to the east gate (10:18-19), to the Mount of Olives east of the city (11:22-23), thereafter to be seen in the vision of the chariot-throne by Ezekiel among the Babylonian diaspora (1:4-28).

seventeenth chapter. Impressed because the term *berit* occurs thirteen times in it, Rabbi Ishmael mused how significant circumcision must be that it occasioned thirteen covenants (*b. Ned.* 31b). Our attempt to grasp the meaning of covenant in this text moves in a different direction. The thematic and linguistic link with the first covenant in the archaic period after the deluge, the covenant with the entire animate creation (9:8-17), inaugurates a new dispensation for the postcatastrophe world. It is addressed to Noah and his three sons, but concerns not just the eight members of his family but all surviving living creatures. We might think of it as presaging, in the language of myth, the survivors of the "Great Extinction" at the end of the Mesozoic age 66 million years ago. This Noachide covenant opens with a solemn performative statement, as if to say, "I hereby establish my covenant with you and your descendants" (9:9), and it concludes with a similar, inclusive statement (9:17). We should therefore respect the priest-scribe's precision of language and avoid extrapolating by including the prohibition of blood immediately preceding (9:1-7). That, too, is a distinct statement that should not be interpreted as a stipulation of the covenant that follows.[23]

Unlike the standard bilateral covenant, whether between God and the people, as in Deuteronomy, or between two individuals negotiating an agreement as representatives of their tribes or lineage, like the pact between Laban and Jacob as the latter was leaving Mesopotamia (31:43-54), the archaic covenant is unilateral, a commitment on the part of God given unconditionally. It can therefore be described as a "perpetual covenant," that is, a covenant that neither requires nor allows for periodic reconfirmation. It also includes a sign that guarantees the fulfillment of the commitment made by God and serves also, in biblical terms, to activate God's memory (9:12-16). The only form of revalidation of this commitment as covenant is therefore when God is said to remember his covenant — whether in favor of those caught up in some disaster (8:1), or his people in distress in Egypt (Exod. 2:24; 6:4-5) or in Babylon (Lev. 26:42, 45).

The similarity between the Noachide and Abrahamic covenants is unmistakable. Both are established by God using the same terminology;

---

23. The author of the *Book of Jubilees,* in 6:4-10, and perhaps also Josephus conflate the two passages. Josephus relates how Noah, afraid that God might inundate the earth on a yearly basis, interceded for humanity. In response to his prayers, God declared a truce and promised never to repeat the catastrophic deluge, but exhorted Noah and his family to refrain from shedding blood (*Ant.* 1.96-103).

both are made with a patriarch as representative of his descendants after him; and, most importantly, both are perpetual covenants (Gen. 9:16; 17:7, 13, 19) confirmed by a sign (9:12-17; 17:17-21). Within the Priestly theology of Israel's history these are the only covenants, since there is no P version of the Sinai covenant. What happened according to P is that Israel arrived at Sinai (Exod. 19:1-2a) and Moses went up the mountain alone into the numinous cloud concealing the divine effulgence (24:15b-18a), where he received detailed instructions for the establishment of the wilderness sanctuary and its cult (chaps. 25-31). The instructions were then carried out (chaps. 35-40), and Israel departed processionally from Sinai (Num. 10:11-36). The command to observe Sabbath as a perpetual covenant is misleading. There is nothing in this strand resembling the two *certain* Priestly covenant texts. Sabbath is a sign pointing to creation as the rainbow is a sign of re-creation, and the circumcised organ is a sign of a relationship already in existence. Apart from this, there is no explanation as to how Sabbath is or could be considered a covenant. If the priest-scribe had wished to present a covenant analogous to the covenants of Gen. 9 and Gen. 17:1-8, both of them promissory and unconditional, we would have been left in no doubt about it.

The theological originality and unique character of the Priestly understanding of covenant are therefore apparent even though these priest-scribes use the same term *(berit)* together with some of the associated language in speaking of covenant. To summarize: in the P covenant there are no stipulations contingent on the observance of which God makes a responsive commitment. The P covenant is therefore unilateral, a disposition arising out of the absolute freedom of God. It is also indefectible, an "everlasting covenant" that, unlike the standard Deuteronomic model, neither requires nor allows for periodic renewal. It is therefore in its essence not attached to the promulgation and observance of laws.[24] Finally, it is moved back into the archaic period, with the focus on Noah and Abraham, precisely to give this key concept an international and universal resonance. Abraham is to be father to many nations, a promise repeated three times in the initial revelation, and this internationalizing

24. The P narrative generally, but not invariably, uses the term *'ēdūt* (translated "testimony" or, more problematically, "covenant"), often in the expression *lûhōt hā'ēdūt* ("the tablets of the testimony/covenant"), for example, throughout the seven instructions in Exod. 25:1–31:18. Given the well-known precision of language in P, this term may have been employed to free up the other term, *běrît,* for the special purpose it serves for the Priestly writers.

of him is given symbolic expression in the change of name from Abram to Abraham.[25]

A Son for Sarah

This third communication from God to Abraham in this chapter (17:15-22) is under the same rubric of covenant as the one immediately preceding (17:9-14), but the subject matter is completely different. Any attempt to explain how this third section of the chapter fits in must be tentative and provisional, but one approach might proceed as follows. Genesis 17:1-8, the initial communication, holds out the prospect of nations and kings among Abraham's descendants but says nothing about the immediate and absolutely essential problem of an heir. The presumption would therefore still be in favor of Ishmael, especially since in the prevailing circumstances he was, according to legal precedent, the son and heir, and had been for thirteen years. However, this promise of a future rich in blessing would have seemed incredible and scandalous to many of the Priestly persuasion, deriving as it did from an ancestor and his son as yet uncircumcised. Hence the addition of the circumcision law in 17:9-14, couched in traditional legal form unusual for a vision (cf. Exod. 12:43-49 in connection with Passover). Abraham, at any rate, promptly obeyed the law by circumcising himself at age ninety-nine, painfully no doubt, after which he circumcised his son, age thirteen (Gen. 17:23-27), and all male members of his household, including slaves. The command and its implementation clearly belong together. At some point, however, a further communication to Abraham announced that Sarah would bear a child after all, and in confirmation of this new status her name was changed from Sarai to Sarah by divine fiat, which once again altered the predicted course of events (17:15-22). This decisive intervention of the deity in favor of Sarah and Isaac was inserted between the promulgation of the circumcision law in vv. 9-14 and its execution in vv. 23-27 in order to interpose the announcement of the birth of Isaac before the circumcision of Ishmael, as if to make a point about precedence. The actual legal situation at issue here, in which the original wife happens to give birth to a son after the birth of a son to the surrogate wife,

---

25. In Gen. 17:5 the new name *'abrāhām* is explained by not very convincing assonance with *'ab-hămôn,* "father of a multitude (of nations)," in spite of which the point is clear.

and the further question whether that son would still have precedence after thirteen years, remains unclear; and the present circumstances are, in any case, unusual, to say the least.

While the announcement about Sarah's prospects is accommodated to the themes and language of the initial vision to Abraham in 17:1-8, there is good reason to read it as a Priestly reworking of the announcement of a miraculous birth in the following chapter (18:9-15). At this point we must anticipate briefly. Practically all commentators agree that Gen. 18 is a combination of two themes. The principal and much the longer narrative theme is the mission of angel-messengers to Sodom to inquire into a judicial plea for redress from the city, followed by the outcome of the investigation (18:1-8, 16, 20–19:38). The subsidiary theme, about Sarah and her prospects (18:9-15), was suggested by the presence of Sarah in the women's tent when the visitors arrived (18:6). The close affinity between 18:9-15 and 17:15-22, in spite of the marked difference in style and tone, is clearly in evidence. The theme is identical: Sarah, no longer Sarai, will have a son, and this will happen in a year's time.[26] Isaac is prefigured once again for the discerning Hebrew-language reader or hearer by Sarah's incredulous laughter (18:12-15), as by Abraham's laughter in the Priestly version (17:17).[27] The interior monologue of both is expressed in the form of rhetorical questions (17:17; 18:12-13), while Sarah's comment about the prospect of sexual pleasure in advanced old age, and the author's perhaps not entirely serious comment about the menopausal Sarah, at the same time illustrate the difference in tone and sensitivity between the two versions.

As with Abraham, so with Sarah, the name change indicates a new direction into the future. Abraham is to be the ancestor of "a multitude of nations" (17:4-6); Sarah is to have a son after all, and she is to be the mother

26. That the name Sarah appears throughout 18:9-15 does not call into question the dependence of 17:15-22 on 18:9-15; it is simply due to the final editing and arrangement of the episodes. In both versions where Abraham is addressed initially, it is emphasized that Sarah is his wife (17:15; 18:9). The time predicted for the birth of Isaac is expressed in similar terms: *lammô'ēd hazzeh*, "at this time/season next year," 17:21; cf. *lammô'ēd*, "at the set time," 18:14, and *kā'ēt ḥayyâ*, "at the due time," 18:10. It seems to have been familiar practice to announce or predict the birth of a child to take place a year after conception; see 1 Sam. 1:20 and especially 2 Kgs. 4:16-17 for the idiomatic language used (Elisha addressing the Shunammite woman).

27. Much more is made of Sarah's laughing than of Abraham's. Abraham's insistence on Ishmael ("If only Ishmael might enjoy your special favor!," literally, "If only Ishmael might live in your presence" [17:18]) would seem to imply that not only did he not believe the announcement that Sarah would give him a son, but he did not want to believe it.

of nations, and "kings of peoples" will be counted among her descendants (17:16; cf. 17:4-6). What this means can best be conjectured by reference to the role of nations and their kings in the later sections of the book of Isaiah (primarily chaps. 40–66), especially where Zion, the new Jerusalem, is being addressed, often represented as an ideal female figure. In Isa. 60–62 the seer promises that "nations will come to your light, kings to the radiance of your dawn" (60:3; also 60:11, 16; 62:2). You will have numerous offspring (60:22), with whom God will make a perpetual covenant, and they will be recognized by all as blessed (61:8-9). They will be enriched with the wealth of nations (60:5-7, 9, 11) and will possess the land (60:21; 61:7). Especially interesting is the promise of a new name:

> Nations will see your vindication,
> all kings will witness your glory.
> You will be called by a new name
> that Yahweh himself will bestow. (62:2)

These three chapters provide only the more obvious indications that the *Urvater* Abraham and the *Urmutter* Sarah are somewhere in the background of these later sections of the book of Isaiah. What they imply for our understanding of the origin and development of the narrative traditions about them — whether already in place or in process of formation — awaits fuller clarification.

Ishmael

Abraham's reaction to the voice announcing that he will have a son with Sarah was outwardly the same as when he received the earlier revelation: he made a deep obeisance in acknowledgment of the message. The real state of his mind and emotions was, however, revealed by the sour laughter of incredulity and the rhetorical questions he put to himself:[28]

> Can a son be born to a man who is a hundred years old?
> Can Sarah, ninety years old, bear a child?

28. Literally, "he said in his heart." The verb *'āmar,* for speaking, can also do service for thinking. The verb *ḥāšab,* "think" in modern Hebrew, has the somewhat different meaning of calculate, reckon, estimate in classical Hebrew.

This is the laughter of disbelief. What he felt like saying may have been something like, "What do you mean? I *have* a son! This fine sturdy teenager here! He is the only son I have, and I love him!" What he actually said was, literally translated, "If only Ishmael might live in your presence!" To live in God's presence is to have God's approval, to enjoy God's special favor. A psalmist, for example, ends his prayer with the assurance that God is well pleased with him, has upheld him, and has set him in God's presence forever (Ps. 41:13). In the present context, Abraham is saying more than this; he is in effect pleading that Ishmael may be the one through whom the promises will be fulfilled, as is clear from his response, which simply repeats the message.[29]

This reply is followed by a second oracle about Ishmael and the descendants who will bear his name, following on the pronouncement of the angel-messenger in the wilderness to Hagar (Gen. 16:11-12). Both play on the name Ishmael, a typical West-Semitic formation meaning "God (El) has heard (heeded, listened to) your prayer," that is, the prayer for the child whose birth is being celebrated. Ishmael is already blessed by God.[30] Like the first parents (1:28) and the first of the new race after the catastrophe (9:1, 7), he will be fruitful and have numerous descendants (17:20). He will be the ancestor of twelve "princes," meaning tribal leaders or sheiks, like the leaders of the Israelite tribes, also twelve in number (e.g., Num. 2:3-29). He personifies the "great nation" that will issue from him, a promise repeated by the angel-messenger after the expulsion into the wilderness (Gen. 21:18) and shared with Abraham (12:2) and Jacob (46:3; Deut. 26:5).

What is said here about Ishmael provides one more illustration of the skillful combination in the Abraham cycle of ethnology and biography, of the history and mores of families, ancient at the time of composition, with the realistic and at times moving account of real individuals struggling with

---

29. Schmid, "Judean Identity and Ecumenicity," 20-26, argues that for Ishmael to "live in God's presence" would entail a special cultic relationship, beginning with access to the wilderness sanctuary *(miškān),* which, however, is destined to be the privilege of Isaac and his descendants alone. The phrase *lipnê YHWH* can have a cultic connotation, but not exclusively so; Hosea anticipates that if the people return to YHWH, they will live "in his presence" *(lĕpānâw),* with no suggestion of a cultic sense, and the Gadites assure Moses that they will cross over into Canaan armed and "in the presence of YHWH" *(lipnê YHWH)* in a military context (Num. 32:32). There is no suggestion that Ishmael ever aspired to priestly or cultic employment. The sense is closer to the initial injunction to Abraham to "walk" in God's presence, implying the enjoyment of God's special favor (Gen. 17:1; also 24:40; 48:15).

30. *Bēraktî,* past tense, as REB, not future, as NRSV.

real problems and trying to direct their lives in a good direction. Ishmael stands for the Arab peoples in general and the twelvefold Ishmaelite tribal confederacy listed in the second *toledot* unit in Gen. 25:12-18 in particular. Their lifestyle, briefly and vividly described by the angel-messenger in the wilderness, is his (16:12). They were known as expert bowmen in hunting and warfare, and so was he (1 Chr. 5:19; Isa. 21:17; cf. Gen. 21:20). His destiny is played out in tense relationship to Abraham's other beloved son as, already within the biblical period, and for long afterward, were the destinies of his descendants with those of Isaac's.[31] We shall return to this central theme of the two sons in chapter 8.

Filling In the Gaps

The repetition of the word for "covenant" thirteen times in Gen. 17 led some rabbinic scholars to conclude that circumcision was the subject of thirteen covenants and therefore transcendentally important, even more so than Sabbath.[32] On the basis of a rather forced interpretation of the word *berit* (covenant) in Jer. 33:25, it was even argued that, if it were not for circumcision, God would not have created the world (*m. Ned.* 3:11). The fact that Abraham was ninety-nine years old and had still not been circumcised served for some to explain the injunction at the beginning of the chapter that he was to be blameless, taking it as a mild reproach, a gentle reminder to get himself circumcised. On this subject there is some unappealing discussion about foreskins — when, how, and by whom they are to be removed. The foreskin is a physical defect that must be got rid of if one is to be blameless (*Gen. Rab.* 46:1, 4 on Gen. 17:1), though why the thought of a design defect in God's good creation did not give the rabbinic author of this opinion pause is not clear. Fearing that it would be a barrier between himself and the rest of the world, Abraham was at first reluctant to circumcise himself, so he consulted with his friends Mamre, Eshcol, and Aner. Two of his friends very reasonably advised against it in consideration of his advanced years, but Mamre urged him to go through with

---

31. At the time when the Abraham cycle was attaining its final form, or shortly afterward, the Qedarite Arabs, descendants of the second son of Ishmael according to Gen. 25:14, had displaced the Ishmaelites and occupied much of the Transjordanian region and southern Palestine. On the history of the Ishmaelites, see E. Axel Knauf, *Ishmael,* 2nd ed., ADPV (Wiesbaden: Harrassowitz, 1989), and "Ishmaelites," in *ABD* 3:513-20.

32. *b. Ned.* 31b; *b. Šabb.* 132a; etc.

it in gratitude for the great privileges God had bestowed on him (*Ag. Ber.* 19:39). And so the ceremony was performed on Yom Kippur as atonement for Israel (*Pirqe R. El.* 28), or perhaps on Shavuot in the third month, the festival that celebrated the covenant for the Qumran sectarians and those to whom the *Book of Jubilees* was addressed (*Jub.* 15:1).[33]

The circumcision of Abraham also provided the occasion for noting specific provisions of the law. The rite may be performed only by one already circumcised (*b. Avod. Zar.* 26b, 27a). The father must circumcise his son, but if this is impossible then another circumcised person may perform the rite. Failing that, one must do it oneself (*b. Qidd.* 29a). If the child is born circumcised, an incision is to be made and a drop of blood drawn, so that the mark of the covenant may be in the flesh (*y. Šabb.* 17a, with reference to Gen. 7:13).

The early stages of this standardization of the circumcision law can be found in the ritual legislation in Gen. 17:9-14, Exod. 12:43-49, and Lev. 12:3. Apart from that, the biblical texts evince a low level of interest in the rite, as we have seen. Ben Sira's eulogy on Abraham is longer and more enthusiastic than the perfunctory notices about Isaac and Jacob that follow. God has sworn that Abraham will be ancestor to many nations by an oath certified in his flesh, and he will bring blessing on these nations (Sir. 44:19-21). Some decades later, the situation changed dramatically, and for the worse. The persecution of his Jewish subjects by Antiochus IV (175-164 B.C.), and the proscription of their traditional ritual practices, resulted in circumcision becoming a hallmark and test of faith.[34] The author of the *Book of Jubilees,* writing about the middle of the second century B.C., was well aware that not all resisted the allure of Hellenistic culture (*Jub.* 15:33-34). As a rite signifying self-segregation from what was considered a corrupt way of life, circumcision is therefore highly regarded in this work. It even extends into the heavenly sphere since angels are created circumcised —

---

33. Other references in Louis Ginzberg, *The Legends of the Jews,* vol. 1 (Philadelphia: Jewish Publication Society of America, 1961), 239-40; Dirk U. Rottzoll, *Rabbinischer Kommentar zum Buch Genesis* (Berlin: De Gruyter, 1994), 241-60. Several of these traditions about circumcision are reproduced in chapter 3 of Maimonides' "Laws concerning Blessings"; see Isadore Twersky, *A Maimonides Reader* (New York: Behrman, 1972), 99-100.

34. 1 Macc. 1:41-50, 60-64; 2 Macc. 6:7-11; 4 Macc. 4:25. On the practice of epispasm, the surgical removal or concealment of circumcision, see 1 Macc. 1:15; *Assumption of Moses* 8:3; 1 Cor. 7:18. On circumcision in the Greco-Roman world in general, see Emil Schürer, *The History of the Jewish People in the Age of Jesus Christ,* vol. 1, rev. and ed. G. Vermes and F. Millar (Edinburgh: T. & T. Clark, 1973), 148-49, 337-40.

how, it is not said — a condition that enables them to share in the liturgies of worshipers on earth. Circumcision is also, apparently, apotropaic. It was Mastema, chief of demons, not Yahweh, who not only tempted Abraham to kill Isaac (*Jub.* 17:15-18:13) but also attacked Moses on his way to Egypt, and would have killed him if his quick-witted wife Zipporah had not there and then circumcised him (Exod. 4:24-26; in *Jub.* 48:2-3).

Josephus's brief summary of Gen. 17 (*Ant.* 1.191-193) identifies the nations and kings among Abraham's descendants (vv. 4-6) as referring to the history of the Israelite and Jewish people. In his estimate of the land as reaching from Sidon to Egypt, Josephus probably had the Hasmonean principate in mind. The institution of circumcision was to prevent Abraham's descendants from mixing with other peoples, but for further information on the rite the reader is referred to his treatise *On Customs and Causes,* apparently never completed.

After the parting of the ways between the first Christians and the parent body, it was inevitable that early Christian writers would understand circumcision analogically, as spiritual purification, following on the metaphorical use of the rite in biblical texts.[35] An early example is the reinterpretation of Jewish ritual, including circumcision and the food laws, in the *Epistle of Barnabas,* written sometime between the two revolts against Rome.[36] Much of the early Christian material belongs to the homiletic genre, adapted therefore to the understanding of ordinary folk, many of whom would have been illiterate. Solutions to possibly problematic matters in the liturgical readings would generally find a moralizing, spiritual, or allegorical interpretation. Abraham's incredibly advanced age served to exemplify his endurance in faith and virtue as well as the power of God to create new life (Chrysostom). His name change, signifying an inner transformation, could take place only after he had left behind his father's house in search of spiritual enlightenment, an observation of Origen *(Homily on Genesis 3:3),* drawing on his reading of Philo's treatise *On the Migration of Abraham.*[37] For Ambrose, circumcision on the eighth day somehow

35. Lev. 26:41; Deut. 10:16; 30:6; Jer. 4:4; 9:24-25.

36. Michael W. Holmes, *The Apostolic Fathers,* 3rd ed. (Grand Rapids: Baker, 2007), 407-10.

37. On circumcision as an issue in the canonical early Christian texts and early Christianity in general, see Mark Sheridan, *Ancient Christian Commentary on Scripture: Old Testament II; Genesis 12-50* (Downers Grove, Ill.: InterVarsity, 2002), 50-57; Theresia Heither, O.S.B., and Christiana Reemts, O.S.B., *Biblische Gestalten bei den Kirchenvätern. Abraham* (Münster: Aschendorff, 2005), 101-15.

could prefigure the resurrection of Jesus on the eighth day, understood as inclusive of the previous week. In the early decades of the Christian movement, however, circumcision was abandoned only after a period of fierce polemic, with Paul, Barnabas, and the Antiochian church at the center of the dispute. Today, only the Christians of Ethiopia continue the practice, circumcising their children before baptism, between the third and eighth day after birth.

• 6 •

Abraham Entertains Guests,
Sodom Is Destroyed, Lot Rescued

Abraham Puts Together a Meal for Three Guests

With chapters 18 and 19 we encounter another example of the Abrahamic cycle as an assemblage of mostly brief narrative pieces that nevertheless results in a genuine literary production with its own plot and at times vivid characterization. Several distinct and overlapping themes are combined in these two chapters. The first has Abraham entertaining three unanticipated visitors at Mamre (18:1-15). This apparently chance encounter leads, as so often in the Abraham cycle, to unforeseen developments: in this case, the prediction of a son and the mission of angel-messengers to investigate the outcry from Sodom and take action. The departure of two of the three visitors for Sodom provides the occasion for Abraham to plead for the righteous caught up in the doom of an unrighteous city, and for the salvation of the city itself. Abraham's plea comes too late, and the fiery doom of the city provides the occasion for one more rescue of the hapless Lot (19:1-14). Lot, finally, takes to the hills, inadvertently becomes the ancestor of the Transjordanian Moabites and Ammonites (19:15-38), and disappears at last from the narrative.

To see how this complex of narrative themes fits into the Abraham cycle as a whole, we need to backtrack to the early days in Canaan. It begins with Lot's arrival from Harran with Abraham his uncle (12:4-5); his separation from Abraham and decision to settle in Sodom, a wealthy and corrupt city (13:2-13); and his rescue in the War of the Nine Kings (14:12-16). This sequence of episodes led Hermann Gunkel, in his famous commentary on Genesis written more than a century ago (1901), to conclude that the complex of texts featuring Lot together with Abraham formed the nucleus of the Abraham cycle prior to the addition of the Priestly narrative strand.[1] This starting point for further investigation was adopted with modifications by a number of scholars, prominently Rolf Rendtorff and Erhard Blum.[2] Lot, however, is not quite so central a character as Gunkel made him out to be. He fits into the plot of the Abraham cycle as a foil to Abraham in moral character but also, and more significantly, as the first in a series of expedients arising out of the infertility of Sarah, followed by the obscure Eliezer, the recourse to a surrogate wife, and finally the climactic appearance on the scene of Ishmael. The allusion to Lot's decision not only to disqualify himself as Abraham's heir apparent but also to choose to live in Sodom (13:2-13) is simply a dramatic anticipation of events that, according to the schematic chronology of the cycle, took place about a quarter of a century later. This reading makes better sense than the hypothesis that the texts featuring Lot formed the original nucleus of the Abraham story, which leaves unanswered the question why this original nucleus was later pulled apart.

The account of the unanticipated visit and Abraham's hospitable reception of the visitors reads as follows (18:1-8):

> Yahweh appeared to him (Abraham) at the oaks of Mamre while he was seated at the entrance to the tent in the heat of the day. When he looked up he saw three men standing near him. No sooner had he seen than he hurried from the tent opening to meet them. Bowing low to the ground, he said, "Sir, if I find favor with you, do not pass by your servant. Let some water be brought so you can bathe your feet and rest under the tree. Let me fetch a morsel of food so you can refresh yourselves; then you can continue on the journey which brought you to your servant." They replied, "Very well, do as you say." So Abraham hurried to the tent, to Sarah, and told her, "Quick, take three measures of fine flour, knead it, and make some cakes." Then Abraham ran to the herd, picked out a fine, tender calf and gave it to a slave who quickly

---

1. The texts in question are Gen. 12:1-8; 13:1-18; 18:1-16a; 19:1-28, 30-38. Hermann Gunkel, *Genesis* (Macon, Ga.: Mercer University Press, 1997), 158-61; Ger. *Genesis*, 6th ed. (Göttingen: Vandenhoeck & Ruprecht, 1964), 159-62.

2. Rolf Rendtorff, *Das Überlieferungsgeschichtliche Problem des Pentateuch*, BZAW 147 (Berlin and New York: De Gruyter, 1977), 34-35; Eng. *The Problem of the Process of Transmission in the Pentateuch*, JSOTSup 89 (Sheffield: JSOT, 1990), 48-52; Erhard Blum, *Die Komposition der Vätergeschichte*, WMANT 57 (Neukirchen-Vluyn: Neukirchener Verlag, 1984), 273-86.

dressed it. He then took curds and milk with the calf that had been dressed, and set it before them. He waited on them under the tree while they ate.

The identity of the visitors who suddenly appear in front of Abraham's tent in the blazing Palestinian midday sun, apparently out of nowhere, is complicated by the shift between singular and plural address that cannot be reproduced in normal English. They are identified as men on their first appearance and again as they prepare to depart (vv. 2, 16). Abraham invites them to bathe their feet and rest; he addresses them and they answer, he puts food before them ("a morsel of food"!) and serves them, and, in the course of the meal, or after eating, they inquire about Sarah (v. 9). At the same time, Abraham addresses one of them politely as "Sir" *(adon),* and the announcement of the birth of a son to Sarah is made by one only (v. 10), later identified as Yahweh (vv. 13-14). Then, finally, only two "men" leave for Sodom and arrive at their destination (18:16; 19:1), while Yahweh stays behind with Abraham, converses with him, and then leaves (18:16-33).

It is certainly not the case that the three somehow represent Yahweh God, nor that Abraham recognized the central figure as the deity with two angel-messengers in attendance, along the lines of the Trinitarian interpretation of some early Christian writers: *tres vidit et unum adoravit* ("he saw three and worshiped One"). Where the plural is used, all three are addressed and spoken about in the same way without differentiation. The interpretation of the scene offered by Gunkel still seems satisfactory. He argued that the episode has taken over an old topic of divine beings, often three, coming to earth, and conferring favors on their host, including the great favor of the birth of a child, as a reward for a hospitable reception. The motif was familiar to the Greeks: "Even the blessed gods in the image of wandering strangers, assuming any form, traverse lands and cities so that they may see both the sin and the piety of mortals" (*Odyssey* 17.485-487).[3] Something similar is attested in early Christianity: "Do not neglect to show hospitality; for by doing so some have entertained angels unawares" (Heb. 13:2). The motif is also frequently encountered in Christian legends connected, for example, with Saint Christopher. The example from early antiquity presented by Gunkel, and often repeated in the exegetical catena, is recorded in Ovid's *Fasti:* the visit of Zeus, Poseidon, and Hermes to Hurieus, a childless peasant in Boeotia, on whom they bestow the gift of a son, to

---

3. Gunkel, *Genesis,* 192-200 (Ger. 193-201).

be named Orion.[4] A Late Bronze Age Ugaritic text about Aqhat, originally childless, has some features in common with Gen. 18:1-9. The hero, seated at the gate of a city, looks up and sees the artificer god Kothar-Hasis approaching, has his wife prepare food and drink for the divine visitor, and receives in exchange for his hospitality a magical bow and arrows. In this version, however, there is only one supernatural being, who is recognized at once as such by Aqhat.[5] What is peculiar in the Genesis case is that the visitors are recognized as no ordinary men only when they reveal that they know the identity of Sarah without having seen her (v. 9), not unlike the angel-messenger encountered by Hagar in the wilderness (16:8).

The combination of singular and plural address, the problem of the three and the one, can therefore be explained as the adoption and sanitization of an old pagan narrative theme by introducing Yahweh as one of the three. It is also possible that two distinct narrative themes have been combined. The first is the mission of two angel-messengers who pass by Mamre on their way to Sodom (18:20-21). The second is the announcement of a son for Sarah (18:10-15). In between, the narrative is in the plural with the sole exception of v. 3, addressed to one of the three, namely, Yahweh, as recognized by the translator of the Septuagint. The link between these two themes comes with the inquiry of the visitors about Sarah, and Abraham's answer: "They asked him, 'Where is your wife Sarah?' and he replied, 'There, in the tent'" (18:9).

A feature of the narrative motif of heavenly beings visiting incognito is that the visit is often a test, and that passing the test by a gracious and hospitable reception of the visitor or visitors is rewarded with a gift, often the gift of a child to a childless pair. This is the case with the childless woman from Shunem in northern Palestine who provided hospitality for Elisha, the "man of God." Elisha rewarded her with the promise that she would give birth to a child within a year; she reacted with incredulity, but it nevertheless turned out as foretold (2 Kgs. 4:11-17). Abraham was hospitable almost to a fault. He is deferential to the visitors and speaks respectfully to them; as old as he is, he rushes around in order not to keep them waiting, and attends them during the meal. Abraham's hospitable

---

4. Gunkel, *Genesis,* 192-93 (Ger. 193-95); John Skinner, *A Critical and Exegetical Commentary on Genesis,* 2nd ed. (Edinburgh: T. & T. Clark, 1930), 302; Gerhard von Rad, *Genesis: A Commentary* (London: SCM, 1961 [1956]), 200; Claus Westermann, *Genesis 12–36* (Minneapolis: Augsburg, 1985), 275.

5. For the text see *ANET* 151, and Michael David Coogan, *Stories from Ancient Canaan* (Philadelphia: Westminster, 1978), 35-36.

reception of his guests is rewarded by the announcement of a child to be born to Sarah within the year; this is another example, therefore, of the skillful combination of distinct narrative themes into a basically coherent and compelling story. It contrasts not so much with Lot's reception of his two visitors, which is at least adequate and is modeled on that of Abraham, as with the abominable treatment by the men of Sodom of visitors so ill-advised as to make a stopover in their city.

Yahweh Soliloquizes

The soliloquy or inner musings of Yahweh (Gen. 18:16-22) linking the visit and the meal with the dialogue between Abraham and Yahweh read as follows:

> The men set out from there and looked down toward Sodom, while Abraham accompanied them to set them on their way. Then Yahweh thought to himself: "Can I conceal from Abraham what I am about to do, seeing that Abraham is to become a great and mighty nation, and all the nations of the earth are to receive blessing through him? I have singled him out that he may charge his sons and his family after him to keep to the way ordained by Yahweh, doing what is righteous and just, so that Yahweh may bring to pass with regard to Abraham what he has promised him."
>
> Yahweh thought: "How great is the outcry over Sodom and how very grave is their sin! I shall go down to see whether their actions justify the plea[6] that has come to me. I mean to find out."
>
> When the men turned and left for Sodom, Abraham remained standing before Yahweh.[7]

In terms of its narrative logic, the passage presents the reader with some problems. First, Abraham sees the two angel-messengers on their

---

6. In context, there is a distinction, but one not entirely consistent in usage, between *zĕʿāqâ* ("outcry," v. 20) and *ṣĕʿāqâ* ("plea," v. 21) since the latter is a quasi-judicial term meaning an appeal for redress after suffering serious injustice, as in the following examples: the Israelites in Egypt seek redress against their unjust taskmasters (Exod. 3:7); the resident alien makes his appeal against the violation of his rights (Exod. 22:25).

7. *Tiqqun sopherim* ("correction of the scribes") for an original "YHWH remained standing before Abraham" — after the two angel-messengers had left. A reverential correction since the inferior usually stands before the superior.

way (v. 16), but at the conclusion of the soliloquy we are told that they left by themselves and Abraham remained behind. Second, it is clear from Abraham's opening plea that the decision to destroy had already been made (v. 23), yet we are told that Yahweh had not yet determined the extent of the city's moral depravity (vv. 20-21). Third, Yahweh intends to respond to the plea for justice, but from whom would it come? There were not ten righteous people in the city. Lot and his family added up to six (he, his wife, two daughters, and two sons-in-law), but would Lot, who chose to live in this corrupt city, have been the one to address the plea to Yahweh? The thrust of the action is, notwithstanding, clear enough. Since the narrator had no interest in the journey itself, a long journey from Mamre/Hebron to Sodom, somewhere north or south of the Dead Sea — we notice that actual journeys are hardly ever described in this type of narrative — the space between the departure and the arrival of the emissaries is filled in with the deliberations of Yahweh, now for a time alone (vv. 17-21). The return of Abraham from performing his final act of hospitality, in setting the travelers on their way, provided the occasion for the dialogue between Abraham and Yahweh about the fate of the doomed city and its inhabitants (vv. 23-33).

The interior monologue of Yahweh serves the purpose of summarizing the two themes combined in the chapter: the promise of a son to Abraham and Sarah (vv. 17-19) and the fate of Sodom and its inhabitants (vv. 20-21). As for the first, Abraham has already heard about the "great nation" theme and the worldwide effects of the blessing, but much had happened since these promises were first uttered in Harran (12:1-3), most recently and significantly the very natural incredulity of the two principals. In both wording and substance, what is revealed is not a mere repetition. What Abraham is to become is now "a great and mighty nation," a more emphatic expression characteristic of the Deuteronomists;[8] and the language of passing on to sons and descendants the charge of observing "the way of Yahweh" is at home in the same milieu.[9] What, however, is most striking about these musings is that the fulfillment of the promises is now conditional on the observance of "the way of Yahweh," namely, the practice

8. See especially Deut. 9:14; 26:5. The adjective *'āṣûm* (mighty) occurs more often with reference to peoples and nations in Deuteronomy than in any other context.

9. For the verb *swh* ("command," "charge") with *derek YHWH*, *darkê YHWH* ("the way/ways of YHWH"), see Deut. 9:12; 11:12. The emphasis on *ṣĕdāqâ ûmišpāt* ("righteousness and justice"), more often in the reverse order, is also very much part of the moral universe of the Deuteronomists.

of righteousness and justice in dealing with others. This, too, is characteristically Deuteronomistic; witness the frequent exhortation to observe the law "in order that you may live long on the land which Yahweh your God is giving you," thus clearly indicating the conditional nature of the territorial promise.[10] This was the harsh lesson learned finally at the cost of the fall of the two kingdoms followed by exile.

As for the second theme, Yahweh contemplated the outcry, in this context the cry of anger, grief, and distress from the oppressed and exploited in the Cities of the Plain. The internal deliberations of Yahweh are therefore reminiscent of the Tower of Babel story in which, on learning of the intentions of the builders, and conscious that "nothing they propose to do will now be beyond their reach," Yahweh proposed to go down and see for himself. It would have been unnecessary to add that, for Sodom, this task had been confided to the two angel-messengers, at that time on their way to fulfill their mission. We are not told that Abraham was privy to these deliberations, but he must have sensed that time was fast running out for Sodom, and therefore for Lot his nephew, who had taken up residence there. Hence his pleading for the doomed city.

Abraham Pleads for the Doomed City[11]

The dialogue between Abraham and Yahweh, a passage unique in Genesis and perhaps in the entire Hebrew Bible, should first be read in its entirety:

> Abraham approached and said, "Will you really sweep away the righteous together with the wicked?[12] What if there are fifty righteous people in the city, would you still sweep it away rather than pardon the place for the sake of the fifty righteous people in it? Far be it from you to act in this manner, to kill the righteous with the wicked, so that the righteous are treated in the same way as the wicked! Far be it from you! Should not the Judge of all the earth do what is just?" "If I find fifty righteous people in the city," Yahweh replied, "I will pardon the entire place for their sake." Abraham replied, "I am presuming

10. See also Deut. 4:1; 5:33; 8:1; 30:19.

11. The discussion that follows draws on my article "Abraham and the Righteous of Sodom," *JJS* 33, nos. 1-2 (1982): 119-32; the issue entailed essays in honor of Yigael Yadin.

12. One could also translate *ṣaddîq* and *rāšāʿ* as "innocent" and "guilty" respectively, but the qualification in this case is more generalized.

to speak to the Lord, I who am but dust and ashes: What if there are five short of the fifty righteous, will you destroy the city for the lack of five?" He answered, "I will not destroy it if I find forty-five there." Once again he spoke to him, "What if forty are found there?" and Yahweh answered, "For the sake of forty I will not do it." Abraham then said, "Let not my lord be angry if I speak again; what if thirty are found there?" "I will not do it if I find thirty there," he replied. Abraham said, "I am presuming to speak to the Lord; what if twenty can be found there?" "I will not destroy for the sake of twenty," he replied. "Let not my lord be angry; let me speak one more time," said Abraham. "What if ten can be found there?" Yahweh replied, "For the sake of ten I will not destroy."

When he had finished speaking with Abraham, Yahweh went away, and Abraham returned to his place.

The distinctive character of the dialogue between God and Abraham has greatly complicated the search for its literary origins. Earlier commentators made valiant efforts to fit it into the classical four-source hypothesis,[13] but what complicates this attempt is its theoretical and programmatic character, for which nothing comparable exists in Genesis. The closest parallels, and the best clue to the date and original location of the dialogue, are those disputations and moral *exempla* in the book of Ezekiel, of a theoretical and didactic nature in the manner of case law, dealing with issues of the moral responsibility of the individual, the rejection of intergenerational moral accountability, the question whether the righteous can influence the fate of the unrighteous, and the moral character of the God of Israel, in other words, the issue of theodicy.[14] Such questions called most insistently

13. Von Rad, *Genesis*, 199, 209-10: Yahwistic in general, though not part of the ancient narrative; Otto Eissfeldt, *The Old Testament: An Introduction* (Oxford: Blackwell, 1956), 194: all of chaps. 18 and 19 belong to his *Laienquelle* (L) incorporated in J; R. Kilian, *Die vorpriesterlichen Abrahamsüberlieferungen* (Bonn: Peter Hanstein, 1966), 96-189: the basic J stratum of chaps. 18–19 is in the singular, the parts in the plural correspond to J's *Vorlage*; John Van Seters, *Abraham in History and Tradition* (New Haven: Yale University Press, 1975), 214-15, 313: part of the larger episodic unit 18:1b-9, 15–19:38, from the Yahwist at work in the exilic period or shortly afterward; Martin Noth, *A History of Pentateuchal Traditions* (Englewood Cliffs, N.J.: Prentice-Hall, 1972 [1948]), 238: it stems from J writing as a theologian, not from an interpolator.

14. Ezek. 14:12-23; 18:1-32; 33:10-20. As early as Wellhausen, *Die Komposition des Hexateuchs und der historischen Bücher des Alten Testaments* (Berlin: De Gruyter, 1876), 25-36, Gen. 18:23-33 was recognized as a late addition to the narrative; see also Skinner,

for answers in the aftermath of the fall of Jerusalem and destruction of the temple in 586 B.C. There was no question as to where the ultimate responsibility for this massive disaster lay. A probably contemporary poet laments that "Yahweh determined to lay in ruins the wall of daughter Zion. . . . He did not hold back from destroying" (Lam. 2:8). Amos asks rhetorically, "If disaster strikes a city, is it not the work of Yahweh?" to which a later scribe, writing in the postdisaster period, has added the explanatory and exculpatory gloss that "surely Yahweh God does nothing without revealing his design to his servants the prophets" (Amos 3:6-7). In other words, you, the people, were warned about the consequences of your conduct, so the responsibility lies with you, not with your God.[15] Also to be considered is the prophetic condemnation of Jerusalem as a figurative Sodom, paradigm of moral corruption according to proverbial usage by then well established. Isaiah, himself a Jerusalemite, directs his threats against the rulers of Jerusalem/Sodom (Isa. 1:10); Jeremiah reviles contemporary prophets as comparable to the inhabitants of the same cities (Jer. 23:14); and in Ezekiel's extended allegory of the three sisters — Samaria, Jerusalem, and Sodom — Jerusalem is the most corrupt of the three (Ezek. 16:43-58). This last passage is of particular interest in specifying the conduct that led to the destruction of Sodom: pride, abundance, and prosperity coexisting with neglect of the poor and needy (Ezek. 16:49-50).

The magnitude of the disaster of 586 B.C. called into question widely shared assumptions about the character of the God of traditional religion, and also traditional ideas about corporate identity and moral responsibility. An ancient formulation represents Yahweh as a God who "visits the iniquity of the parents upon the children and upon their children's children to the third and fourth generation" (Exod. 34:7; Num. 14:18). The qualification "of those who reject me," added at the conclusion of this formulation in the Decalogue (Exod. 20:5; Deut. 5:9), introduced a more reflective approach to both the ethical character of the deity and the moral responsibility of the individual. This would then be inscribed as a legal principle: "Parents shall not be put to death for their children, nor children for their parents; each one shall be put to death for his own sin" (Deut.

Genesis, 304-5 ("the product of a more reflective age than that in which the ancient legends originated"); Gunkel, *Genesis,* 202-5; Westermann, *Genesis 12–36,* 286-87.

15. On the Amos passage, see, in addition to the commentaries, my *A History of Prophecy in Israel,* 2nd ed. (Louisville: Westminster John Knox, 1996), 75. The expression "his servants the prophets" is standard in the Deuteronomistic History (1 Kgs. 14:18; 15:29; 18:36; 2 Kgs. 9:7, 36: 10:10; 14:25; 17:13, 23; 21:10; 24:2).

24:16); it was put into practice by King Amaziah of Judah, who executed his father's murderers but not their children with them (2 Kgs. 14:6). The rejection of intergenerational moral accountability is stated in a more formal and scholastic form in Ezekiel's paradigm case of three generations: a father who is righteous, his son who is vicious and morally unprincipled, and his grandson who rejects his father's example and chooses to observe the laws given by God (Ezek. 18:1-20).[16] The conclusion is that each will be judged on his own account without reference to antecedents; only the one who sins will die. Hence the charge that the victims and the survivors of the disaster of 586 B.C. were punished for the sins of their ancestors is refuted, and the righteousness of Yahweh God in dealing with people is vindicated (18:1-4, 25-29).

If this, then, is the environment that elicited the composition of the dialogue in Gen. 18, how are we to understand the issue it addresses? It is evident from Abraham's opening question that the decision to destroy the city had already been made, though it remains unclear how Abraham came to know this. No doubt with Lot and his family in mind, he makes the reasonable assumption that there must be some righteous people in Sodom, or any other city for that matter. Neither partner in the dialogue seems to have taken account of the children in the city, who may be presumed to be innocent,[17] though that should not seem so strange to us today who are familiar with the fate of children as "collateral damage" in wars and acts of violence around the world. On this assumption, then, Abraham concluded that Yahweh God must spare the city, since otherwise he would be making no distinction between the righteous and the reprobate. Unless this distinction is made, the destruction of the city would be an immoral act, a conclusion Abraham states in the strongest terms (v. 25), though not as strong as the midrash on the dialogue or, for that matter, the book of Job. In his agony of despair Job blurts out: "It is all one; therefore I say, he destroys both the blameless and the wicked. When disaster brings sudden death, he mocks at the calamity of the innocent. . . . If it is not he, who then is it?" (Job 9:22-23). In commenting on the expression *halilah lekah* ("far be it from you!" Gen. 18:25), one midrash has Abraham placing the accusation directed against God in the mouths of future generations

---

16. Walther Zimmerli, *Ezekiel 1* (Philadelphia: Fortress, 1979), 374-77.

17. Perhaps some awareness of this problem may be reflected in the description of the crowd besieging Lot's house as *minna'ar wĕ'ad-zāqēn* ("both young and old," 19:4) and *miqqāton wĕ'ad-gādôl* (literally, "both small and big," 19:11).

who, if justice is not done, will conclude that "this is his *métier,* destroying the generations in the measure of cruelty. He destroyed the generation of Enosh, the generation of the deluge, and that of the dispersion of the nations. He never leaves off his trade."[18] The issue is therefore the morality of an act, namely, the destruction of a city and its inhabitants, which, while visiting just punishment on the reprobate majority, inflicts suffering and death on an innocent minority.

The dialogue could therefore have served as a test case in the debates about moral accountability going on in the period immediately preceding and following the disaster of 586 B.C. Jeremiah's invitation to his hearers to search Jerusalem for one just and truthful person so that Yahweh God might pardon the city (Jer. 5:1), though doubtless hyperbolic, addresses the same issue as the Genesis dialogue. More convincing, since set out in a more formal and didactic manner, is Ezekiel's test case of a country and city, for example, Judah and Jerusalem, over which Yahweh God stretches out his hand to destroy. The paradigm is presented, for greater emphasis, in four panels corresponding to the four agents of disaster: famine, wild animals, invasion and occupation represented by the sword, and pestilence. The lesson is that even if Noah, Daniel, and Job, figures of legendary righteousness and wisdom in the archaic period, were present in that land or city, they would save only themselves by their righteousness, and not even their sons and daughters (Ezek. 14:12-20).[19] The righteous Job of the Bible likewise lost his sons and daughters, and though he was given another family at the end, those who had died in the disasters at the beginning stayed dead. The righteous Noah, who survived the great deluge, was more fortunate in that his sons and daughters survived with him, and in the holocaust of Sodom, Lot's daughters also survived. His sons-in-law would have done so if they had not ignored the warning given them, and his wife, too, but for her backward glance after leaving the city.

Yahweh God must therefore not destroy the city if it involves destroying any righteous people in it. But then the question of critical mass arises:

---

18. *Tanhuma Vayyera* 10. The same interpretation occurs, with variations, in other midrashim and in Rashi's comment on the same verse.

19. On this issue in Ezekiel, see Walther Eichrodt, *Ezekiel: A Commentary* (Philadelphia: Westminster, 1970), 129-34, 185-91; Zimmerli, *Ezekiel 1,* 310-16; Paul Joyce, "Ezekiel and Individual Responsibility," in *Ezekiel and His Book: Textual and Literary Criticism and Their Interrelation,* ed. J. Lust (Leuven: University Press; Leuven: Peeters, 1986), 317-21; F. L. Hossfeld, "Die Tempelvision Ez 8–11 im Licht unterschiedlicher methodische Zugänge," in *Ezekiel and His Book,* 159-60.

How many righteous would it take to save the city? The issue is not identical with Ezekiel's test case of the land in which Noah, Daniel, and Job save only themselves, since in that instance there is no question of the city being saved by their presence in it. The situation in Gen. 18:23-33 is closer to the great deluge, in which the focus is on the salvation of Noah and his family, eight in all, though in that instance there was no one to plead or intercede for the salvation of the rest of humanity. Abraham's countdown from fifty to ten reflects the knowledge that Lot and his family, six in all, were in the city and that Abraham would be concerned for their safety, but if this had been his only concern, he would not have started the countdown at fifty. The fate of the entire city and its population was hanging in the balance.

As for the numbers, fifty and ten seem to have been the smallest military and judicial subunits at some stages in the history of Israel, so they could have provided convenient limits for the countdown.[20] Perhaps, then, ten was taken to be the smallest significant functional and visible social group.

A final observation. The dialogue is often described in terms of bargaining, but it would perhaps be more appropriate to speak of it as a unique form of intercession for the doomed city. Intercession is a prophetic function, and we have already seen Abraham interceding on behalf of Abimelech and his womenfolk (Gen. 20:7, 17). But intercession is not always successful, as it was not here. Jeremiah was forbidden to intercede for Jerusalem (Jer. 14:11-12), and was assured that Yahweh God would not even heed Moses and Samuel, were those masters of intercessory prayer to pray alongside him (15:1-4).[21] So it was here, and all that remained was, once again, to rescue Lot from the consequences of his own folly.

---

20. Moses is advised by his father-in-law to divide the people into units of a thousand, a hundred, fifty, and ten for legal and judicial purposes (Exod. 18:21, 25; cf. Deut. 1:15), somewhat analogous to the Anglo-Saxon "hundreds," and fifty appears to have been the basic military unity (1 Sam. 8:12; 2 Sam. 15:1; 1 Kgs. 1:5). Ludwig Schmidt, *De Deo. Studien zur Literarkritik und Theologie des Buches Jona, des Gesprächs zwischen Abraham und Jahwe in Gen. 18.22ff und von Hi 1* (Berlin: De Gruyter, 1976), 151-56, pointed to the same organizational features but added that in Gen. 18:23-33 fifty stood for the typical household and ten for the smallest unit within a city — for which the evidence is less clear.

21. Moses pleaded for the people after the apostasy of the Gilded Calf (Exod. 32:11-14), which resulted in Yahweh God "repenting," that is, changing his mind, as he would do after proclaiming through the prophet Jonah the destruction of Nineveh (Jonah 3:10). Moses also had to intercede for the stubborn and obstreperous Israelites in the wilderness (Num. 14:13-25). The pleading of Moses and Aaron for the people after the "rebellion" of Dathan and Abiram is especially instructive since, like Abraham, they question the exercise of divine

The Destruction of Sodom and Rescue of Lot

With the exception of Abraham's visit to the site of the destruction at the end of the account, the only contribution of the priest-scribe to this narrative, the action takes place over the space of one evening and the following morning. The story is told economically, vividly, and with lively dialogue (Gen. 19:1-29).

In the evening, when the two angel-messengers arrived at Sodom, Lot was sitting at the city gate. As soon as he saw them, he got up to meet them. Bowing low to the ground, he said, "Pray, sirs, turn aside to the house of your servant. Bathe your feet, pass the night here, then you can rise early and be on your way." "No," they replied. "We will spend the night in the city square." But Lot prevailed on them, so they turned aside and entered his house. He prepared a festive meal for them, baked unleavened cakes, and they ate.

Before they retired for the night, the men of the city, the men of Sodom, all the people without exception, all the males both young and old, surrounded the house. They called out to Lot, "Where are the men who came to stay with you tonight? Bring them out so that we can get to know them!" Lot went out to them in the doorway, closing the door after him. "I beg of you, my brothers," he said, "do not do this evil deed. I have two daughters who are virgins. Let me bring them out to you and you can do to them as you please. Just do not do anything to these men since they have come under the shelter of my roof." "Get out of the way," they replied. "This fellow came here as a resident alien; is he now to set himself up as a judge? We will deal with you worse than with them!" They crowded around Lot and came close to breaking down the door. The men inside reached out and brought Lot into the house with them and shut the door. Moreover, they struck the men at the entrance of the house, both old and young, with blindness, so they gave up trying to find the door. The men then said to Lot, "Have you anyone else here — a son-in-law, sons and daughters, or anyone in the city belonging to you? Get them out of here. We are about to destroy this place since their outcry has increased in the presence of Yahweh. He has therefore sent us to destroy the city." So Lot went out

---

justice in applying the practice of collective punishment: "If one man sins, will you be angry with the entire congregation?" (Num. 16:20-22).

and spoke to his sons-in-law who were to marry his daughters: "Come on, get out of here, for Yahweh is about to destroy the city." But to his sons-in-law he seemed to be speaking in jest.

As soon as it was dawn, the angel-messengers spoke urgently to Lot, "Quick, take your wife and your two daughters who are here and leave, or you will be swept away in the punishment of the city." But Lot lingered, so the men grabbed him by the hand, and took his wife and two daughters by the hand. Since Yahweh had spared him, they brought him out and left him outside the city. While they were doing so they told him, "Flee for your life! Don't look behind you! Don't stay anywhere in the Plain! Flee to the hills or you may be swept away!" But Lot replied, "Oh no, my lords! Your servant is in your debt; you have shown me great benevolence in saving my life, but I cannot flee to the hills lest the disaster overtake me and I lose my life. Look, this city here is close enough for me to reach it quickly; it is just a little place. Let me take refuge there — is it not a little place? — so that I may save my life." One of them said to him, "I grant you this request also. I will not overthrow the city of which you speak. Flee there quickly, for I can do nothing until you arrive there." (That is how the city got the name Zoar.)[22] By the time Lot arrived at Zoar the sun had risen over the land.

Then it was that Yahweh rained down on Sodom and Gomorrah brimstone and fire from the sky. He destroyed those cities, the entire Plain, together with all the inhabitants of the cities and anything growing out of the ground. But Lot's wife looked back and she was turned into a column of rock salt. Abraham went early in the morning to the place where he had stood in the presence of Yahweh. Looking down over Sodom and Gomorrah and the entire extent of the Plain, he saw thick smoke rising from the earth like the smoke from a kiln.

Thus it came about that when God destroyed the cities of the Plain, God remembered Abraham and rescued Lot from the disaster when the cities in which he had been living were overthrown.

The arrival of the two angel-messengers, their reception by Lot, the attack of the male population on Lot and his guests, the rescue and destruction of the city and its inhabitants — all this was prepared for in the previous ep-

---

22. A popular etymology of the name of the settlement, *ṣôʿar,* from the verbal stem *ṣ'r,* "to be small" (Jer. 30:19; Zech. 13:7; Job 14:21).

isode. The two who set out after the midday meal arrived in Sodom in time for an evening meal, though hardly on the same day, unless by some kind of supernatural transport system. They are identified as angel-messengers on their arrival and encounter with Lot, and again when the destruction is about to take place (19:1, 15). Elsewhere, however, they are simply men as far as Lot and the men of Sodom are concerned. They inform Lot that their mission is to destroy Sodom on account of the outcry that has reached Yahweh (18:20-21), yet only one of them repeats the information (19:21). This may be taken to reflect the uncertainty about "the one and the three problem" in the previous chapter. In any event, the two act as emissaries and agents on behalf of Yahweh, as the final summary states (19:24-25).

In addition to the question of divine agency, there is some dubiety about the extent of the punishment. The mission of the two emissaries is the destruction of Sodom only, since the primary focus is on the rescue of Lot and his daughters, and Sodom was the city in which he chose to settle (13:12-13). In the conclusion and summary of the account, however, Sodom and Gomorrah are destroyed together with other cities and the entire plain (19:24-28),[23] and the same two cities are mentioned together in Yahweh's soliloquy (18:20-21).[24] When this is taken into account, together with the absence of angelic agents of destruction in 19:24-28, this brief passage, 19:24-28, could have been added as a summary at a later date. It is followed by another, and final, résumé from the hand of the priest-scribe (19:29), reminding the reader that the rescue of Lot is the central theme of the incident, and that it came about for the sake of Abraham rather than Lot. The addition, like God remembering Noah during the great deluge (8:1),[25] was no doubt suggested by the absence of Abraham from the ac-

---

23. "Plain" is a somewhat misleading translation of *kikkār,* which more frequently refers to something round — a coin, disk, or orb. This translation word derives from 1 Kgs. 7:46 = 2 Chr. 4:17, *kikkār hayardēn,* "the plain of the Jordan," which probably refers to the Rift Valley; or perhaps Deut. 34:3, where the *kikkār* is identified as *biqʻat yĕrēḥô,* "the valley of Jericho."

24. The "Cities of the Plain" form a pentapolis (Sodom, Gomorrah, Admah, Zeboiim, Zoar) only in the late War of the Nine Kings (Gen. 14:2-8). This came about by the addition of Zoar to the other four, as in Gen. 10:19 (the Table of Nations) and Deut. 29:23, certainly postexilic. An earlier stage would have been the addition of Admah and Zeboiim, only in Hos. 11:8, to Sodom and Gomorrah listed frequently in prophetic texts as paradigms of corruption or destruction or both (Amos 4:11; Zeph. 2:9; Isa. 1:9-10; 13:19; Jer. 23:14; 49:18; 50:40).

25. On the theme of God remembering in the Priestly source (P), see also Gen. 9:15-16; Exod. 2:24; 6:5; Lev. 26:42, 45.

count of the rescue and destruction. What is clear, at any rate, is that the corruption and destruction of Sodom, or of Sodom, Gomorrah, and the *kikkār,* is an independent tradition, one that originally had nothing to do with Abraham but has been used to explicate and carry forward the role of Lot in relation to Abraham.

Lot's reception of the two visitors is modeled on Abraham's reception of the three who suddenly appeared at his tent (18:1-8). Abraham was seated at the entrance to his tent, but given the urban environment of the present scene, Lot is in the plaza or open space at the city gate. Like Abraham, he rises to meet the visitors, makes a profound obeisance, offers water to wash their feet, and puts on a good meal. Since it is now evening, he offers hospitality for the night, as was de rigueur among desert tribes at that time. Different reasons have been given for why they at first declined the offer. Of these, the simplest and most accessible is that visitors customarily waited in the city square until the city offered hospitality in the person of one of its citizens. In the story about the crime of the city of Gibeah, to which we shall return, a Levite, anxious to reach home with his concubine, declined her father's invitation to spend yet another night in his house. En route, they arrived in the Benjaminite city of Gibeah and waited in the city square until someone took them in (Judg. 19:10-21). Lot's two visitors therefore simply assumed that this was the way one could expect hospitality in a strange city, but Lot prevailed on them to accept his hospitality, and eventually they did so.

The parallels between what happened in Sodom and what happened in Gibeah, Saul's city, with the Levite and his female companion, are not limited to the offer of hospitality and suggest dependence of one episode on the other. As the couple of weary travelers were resting in the town square of Gibeah, an old man, coming in from the country, came upon them and gave them hospitality in his house. At this point events took a bad turn:

> While they were having a good time, the men of the city, a depraved lot, surrounded the house and started pounding on the door. They shouted to the old man, the owner of the house, "Bring out the man who has just come to your house so we can get to know him!" The owner of the house went outside to them and said to them, "No, my brothers, I beseech you, don't do such a wicked deed, now that this man has come into my house. Do not commit this outrage. Here is my daughter, a virgin, and the man's concubine; let me bring them out to

you. Abuse them and do to them what you please, but against this man do not commit this outrage." When the men refused to listen to him, the Levite took his concubine and thrust her out to them. They raped and abused her all night until the morning, letting her go only when dawn began to break. At daybreak, the woman came and collapsed at the entrance of the man's house where her master was, and lay there until it was light. (Judg. 19:22-26)

This account, which differs in its structure and essence from the Sodom episode only in its dreadful outcome, seems to have served as a model for portraying the moral depravity of the men of Sodom.[26] There has been much discussion on the nature of the intended criminal act and, more generally, the criminality of the male population of Sodom. Violation of the sacred duty of hospitality is emphasized by Lot (Gen. 19:8), though this in no way mitigates the grievous offense of offering his daughters to the sex-crazed crowd, any more than the shameful treatment by the Levite of his female companion could ever be justified (Judg. 19:25-30).[27] It is typical of Lot as portrayed throughout the Abraham cycle that at no point does he appear to recognize the two "men" for what they are, and of what they were capable, not even after they strike the aggressors with blindness. Apart from that, we are left in no doubt about the intentions of the men of Sodom, no less than about their counterparts in Gibeah. Homosexual rape is clearly intended, though the offer of Lot's daughters signals Lot's awareness of a more indiscriminate lasciviousness.[28] And since the sexual

26. The background of the crime of Gibeah and the war against Benjamin in Judg. 19–21 is Judean-Benjaminite hostility during the neo-Babylonian and early Persian periods; on which see my "Benjamin Traditions Read in the Early Persian Period," in *Judah and the Judeans in the Persian Period,* ed. Oded Lipschits and Manfred Oeming (Winona Lake, Ind.: Eisenbrauns, 2006), 638-43. On the chronological priority of the Judges narrative, see Julius Wellhausen, *Prolegomena to the History of Ancient Israel* (New York: Meridian, 1957), 235-37; Westermann, *Genesis 12–26,* 300, who, however, assigns the Judges narrative to his prestate Yahwist source. For Gunkel, *Genesis,* 215 (Ger. 216-17), on the other hand, Judg. 19:22-26 imitates Gen. 19:1-29; somewhat similarly George Foot Moore, *A Critical and Exegetical Commentary on Judges* (Edinburgh: T. & T. Clark, 1895), 417.

27. We are left wondering why only the Levite's woman companion and not the virgin daughter of the householder was subjected to this abominable treatment.

28. The verb *yāda',* "know" (here "get to know"), has a broad range of meanings and uses, including as a euphemism for intercourse or sexual activity in general. Such usage is common in other Semitic languages, e.g., Arabic *('arafa)* and Ugaritic *(yd'),* and is attested elsewhere in biblical texts (e.g., Gen. 4:1; Judg. 19:25; 1 Sam. 1:19; 1 Kgs. 1:4). For more in-

abuse of strangers constitutes a particularly heinous and gross violation of hospitality, there is no need to choose between the two explanations.

Once this crisis is past, the angel-messengers begin to prepare for the final act by rescuing Lot and his household, no easy task as it turned out. They announce the imminent destruction of the city on account of the outcry referred to earlier (Gen. 18:20-21).[29] Nonchalant like their father-in-law, the two sons-in-law do not take the warning seriously and perish in the conflagration. The narrative logic of the story, however, required their elimination in anticipation of and preparation for the scene in the cave with Lot and his daughters, still virgins, and their complaint of the absence of potential husbands (19:31). At dawn on the following morning the warnings become more insistent. Lot, still lingering, has to be hustled out of the city and told to leave the *kikkār* and take to the hills. What happens next is not entirely clear. Lot asks permission to take refuge in a nearby settlement named Zoar rather than in the hills; the permission is granted by his minders, no doubt by now thoroughly exasperated; and he arrives there by sunrise (19:18-23). Shortly afterward, however, he leaves Zoar and settles in a cave in the hills (19:30), thus eventually obeying the original instruction. The sequence of events would be clearer if we were to read the intervening dialogue about Zoar and its outcome (19:18-23) as an insertion.[30] The command to flee to the hills (19:17) would then be read as preparation for the incident involving Lot and his daughters in the cave in the hills immediately after the destruction (19:30b-38).

---

formation on this verb, see G. J. Botterweck, "ידע, *yāda*," *TDOT* 5:448-81, especially 460, 464; W. Schottroff, "ידע, *yd'*," *TLOT* 2:508-21, especially 515. Attempts to avoid the sexual connotation involve large-scale neglect of context and the Gibeah parallel; for a recent example, see Scott Morschauser, " 'Hospitality,' Hostiles and Hostages," *JSOT* 27 (2003): 461-85. According to Morschauser, the entire (male) population of Sodom, engaged in trying to break down the door, only wanted to ascertain from Lot, a kind of immigration officer, why the men had come to the city; to which Lot responded by offering his two daughters as hostages for the visitors' good standing.

29. The outcry from Sodom (*ṣa'ăqātām*) would more naturally be a cry of distress, like the cry of the Egyptians after the death of the firstborn (Exod. 11:6; 12:30), or a plea for redress, like the cry of the oppressed Israelites in Egypt (Exod. 3:7, 9), but the problem then is to know from whom the cry could have come. The ancient versions are not helpful on this point. LXX and Vulgate have the same word, *kraugē* and *clamor* respectively, here and in 18:20 and 18:21. The narrative is less than clear at this point.

30. As proposed by Westermann, *Genesis 12–26*, 303. Exceptionally, only one angel-interlocutor is involved, and the high level of interest in the etymology of Zoar does not make a good fit with the pace and urgency of the narrative at this point.

Lot, His Daughters, and the Ethnogenesis of Moab and Ammon

Destruction by fire and brimstone or sulfur (19:24), of which the annihi-
lation of the Cities of the Plain served as a paradigm,[31] became a standard
expression of divine punishment of the reprobate.[32] Since the following
scene in the cave called for the absence of not only Lot's designated sons-
in-law but also his wife, this requirement was satisfied when the unnamed
wife looked behind and was turned into a column of salt rock (19:26). In
the narrative context, her punishment could be explained by her disobe-
dience to the prohibition of looking behind issued earlier that morning
(19:17). In reality, however, it corresponds to an ancient taboo familiar
to classical scholars and others from the myth of Orpheus and Eurydice,
combined with widespread stories of petrification of a kind familiar from
Medusa and the Gorgons of Greek mythology.[33] It was no doubt inevitable
that this one verse would also serve as a fanciful etiology for one or another
physical feature of the landscape around the Dead Sea — a column of rock
salt — which might, with imagination and a little good will, assume the
form of a female figure and therefore be associated with Lot's wife.[34]

The final scene depicts Abraham looking down over the smoking
ruins and the many dead, the end of that world. It might serve as a parallel
panel in a diptych with Noah removing the covering of the ark and viewing
the land from which the water was receding, and from which every living
thing had been blotted out (Gen. 7:23; 8:13). The same scene is presented,
with greater poignancy, in *Gilgamesh* (11:131-137), with Utnapishtim, Noah's Mesopotamian counterpart, looking out over the postdisaster world:

> The sea grew quiet, the storm abated, the flood ceased.
> I opened a window and light fell upon my face.
> I looked upon the sea, all was silence,
> and all mankind had turned to clay. . . .
> I bowed my head, sat down, and wept,
> my tears ran down my face.

The episode in the cave reads as follows (Gen. 19:30-38):

31. Cf. Deut. 29:22-23; Isa. 1:9; Jer. 49:18; 50:40; Amos 4:11; Zeph. 2:9.

32. Cf. Isa. 30:33; 34:9; Ezek. 38:22; Ps. 11:6.

33. Other examples in Gunkel, *Genesis,* 211-12 (Ger. 213).

34. One illustration can be seen in *IDB* 3:163; a more up-to-date selection can be
consulted in Wikipedia under "Lot's Wife."

Lot went up from Zoar into the hill country with his two daughters and settled there, living with them in a certain cave. The elder daughter said to the younger, "Our father is old, and there is no man left on earth to consort with us in the way of all the world. Let us, then, get our father drunk with wine and lie with him to preserve issue with our father." So that night they plied their father with wine. The elder came and lay with him, and he had no idea as to when she lay down or got up. The next day, the elder sister said to the younger, "Last night I lay with my father. Let us ply him with wine again tonight, then you go and lie with him in order to preserve issue with our father." That night also they plied their father with wine. The younger sister went and lay with him, and he had no idea as to when she lay down or got up. Thus both of Lot's daughters came to be pregnant by their father. The elder gave birth to a son and called him Moab.[35] Today he is still considered the ancestor of the Moabites. The younger also gave birth to a son and called him Ben-Ammi. Today he is still considered the ancestor of the Ammonites.

This episode, originally a distinct unit, is one of the many building blocks that make up the Abraham cycle, even though Abraham is not even mentioned in it. It is at the same time a sequel to the destruction of Sodom, prepared for by the elimination of Lot's wife and the husbands of the two daughters, leaving father and daughters the last ones alive. It is a spare story, quickly told using repetitive language that somehow adds to its effect. It fits into the larger picture by virtue of its genealogical character revealed in the conception and birth of the ancestors of the Transjordanian Moabites and Ammonites. To appreciate this we must begin not with Abraham but with Terah, since Lot and his Moabite and Ammonite descendants are traced back to Terah's third son, Haran, in the same way that Arameans originated with Terah's second son, Nahor (11:27). This is part of the wider world of the Abraham cycle, and the ancestral history in general. Abraham, the first son, and his Israelite and Arabian descendants are part of that world.

Terah, tenth in line from Noah, established linkage with the archaic world long before Israel came into existence. The fiery end of Sodom can

---

35. The LXX adds "saying, 'from my father'"; Hebrew, *mē'ābî*, suggesting *mô'ābî*, "Moabite" by assonance. Likewise, in the following verse, the LXX reads ". . . she called him Amman, son of my kinsman," corresponding to Hebrew *ben-'ammî*.

be read, and perhaps was intended to be read, as replicating on a smaller scale the watery end of the ancient world from which Noah was rescued as Lot was from Sodom. Noah's drunkenness (9:20-27) has its counterpart in the present episode, and the statement of the elder sister, that there was no man left alive on earth outside their cave, should be taken on face value. This is the view of those commentators who commend the courage and piety of the sisters in fulfilling, in the only way available to them, the creation command to increase and multiply, convinced that they and their father were the only survivors of a disaster of cosmic proportions.[36] By the time Moabites and Ammonites were considered hostile enough to be excluded *in perpetuum* from membership in the Israelite assembly (Deut. 23:4-7),[37] the scene in the cave would have been interpreted as an account of tainted origins. In any case, there is no justification for us today to interpret the proposal of the two young women as grossly improper. In this respect rabbinic midrash is on surer ground than some contemporary exegetes.

Filling In the Gaps

It is hardly surprising that these texts, which leave so much unsaid, give rise to so many questions, some of obvious importance for understanding the narrative, others of more marginal interest. As an example of the latter, we might wish to know why Abraham was sitting at the entrance of his tent[38] at midday, the time of greatest heat, rather than working, or attending to family business, or resting in the tent. Rabbinic commentators noted that the visit occurred immediately after his circumcision, perhaps on the same day (Gen. 17:23-27), and he would have been in pain, given his advanced age.[39] As for the identity of the visitors, Jewish commentators tended to distinguish the appearance of God in 18:1 from the three mentioned in the following verse. These were angels, in fact, the three archangels: Michael

---

36. *Gen. Rab.* 51:8; Josephus, *Ant.* 1.205; Philo, *Questions and Answers on Genesis* 4.56.

37. For evidence of hostility, see especially Deut. 32:32; Isa. 15–16; Jer. 48:26-30; Ezek. 25:8. Moab was famous as producer and exporter of wine, and the Judean poet makes a mock lament for the devastated vineyards of Sibmah, apparently the Napa Valley of Moab (Isa. 16:8-11). This, too, could have influenced the way the story of Moabite origins was interpreted.

38. Josephus transfers the scene to an urban setting, with Abraham seated at the entrance to his courtyard (*Ant.* 1.196).

39. *b. B. Mesi'a* 86b; *Tg. Yer.* and *Tg. Ps.-J.* on Gen. 18:1.

to announce the birth of a son to Sarah, Gabriel to destroy Sodom, and Raphael either to rescue Lot or to heal Abraham (*b. B. Mesi'a* 86b; *b. Yoma* 37a). Not surprisingly, early Christian commentators, for example, Caesarius of Arles, read the visit as a foreshadowing of the Trinity,[40] while according to Josephus, one of the visitors had the mission of announcing the news of the birth to Sarah, and the other two were sent to destroy Sodom (*Ant.* 1.198). Another problem, which emerges occasionally in biblical and postbiblical texts (Judg. 13:16; Tob. 12:19), is to explain how angels can eat and drink, as they are said to do on this occasion (Gen. 18:8). Josephus, Philo, and the Targumists content themselves with saying that they only appeared to eat.[41] Some rabbinic commentators could not resist commenting on the menu. Passing over the fact that the meal was decidedly nonkosher, one commentator "improved" the text by having Abraham slaughter three calves rather than just one since he wished to serve the delicacy of calf's tongue with mustard to each of his guests (*b. B. Mesi'a* 86b).

Leaving aside these exegetical trivia, we note that, on the subject of God's deliberations after the departure of the guests, a question arose about the source of the plea for redress that had come up to God from Sodom (18:21). As it turned out, there were less than ten righteous people in the city, and perhaps none except Lot and his family members, or at least his daughters, and we would not expect Lot to address such a plea to God. The rabbinic commentators' ingenuity was equal to the task of creating appropriate scenarios to resolve the question. A young girl in Sodom, apprehended distributing food to the poor, was smeared head to foot in honey, exposed, and stung to death by bees and wasps (*b. Sanh.* 109b). Another invention is attributed to R. Levi, a third-generation Amora (*Gen. Rab.* 49:6; *b. Sanh.* 109a-b). On meeting a companion at the city well whose family was starving to death, another girl filled her own bucket with flour and gave it to the other girl. On hearing this, the inhabitants of Sodom seized her and condemned her to death by burning. The story concludes as follows: "The Holy One (blessed be He!) said, 'the sentence passed on this girl does not permit me to remain silent.' Therefore the Scripture does not say 'according to their plea' *(hakkesa'aqatam)* but 'according to her plea' *(hakkesa'aqatah),* namely, that of the girl." This young girl, therefore,

---

40. Sermon 83.4, in Mark Sheridan, *Ancient Christian Commentary on Scripture: Old Testament II; Genesis 12–50* (Downers Grove, Ill.: InterVarsity, 2002), 66.

41. Josephus, *Ant.* 1.197; Philo, *On Abraham* 11.7-18; *Tg. Neof.* and *Tg. Yer.* on Gen. 18:8; also *Gen. Rab.* 48:18.

enters the story courtesy of the feminine pronominal suffix, which originally referred to the city, cities being regarded as feminine. In due course this young girl will be given the name Pelitit ("Survivor") and will be identified as a daughter of Lot.

The dialogue between God and Abraham over the fate of the city is, understandably, the subject of a great deal of commentary. One of the most striking features of the midrash on Gen. 18:23-33 is the presentation of divine judgment on Sodom in the form of a forensic process. The plea for justice (18:20) leads to a judicial investigation (18:21). The articles of indictment against Sodom emphasize oppression of the poor, unequal distribution of wealth, and neglect of the basic norms of justice, charity, and hospitality to foreigners. Just procedures call for a counsel for the defense, a *senigor* (from the Greek *sunēgoros*), which is the office assigned to Abraham.[42] In that capacity, he was prepared to go from fifty directly to ten but was instructed by the judge to do it by degrees to assure a fair trial (*Gen. Rab.* 49:14). There remained, however, the problem that, with God as judge, a judicial appeal seems to be ruled out: "When you proposed to judge your world, you delivered it into the hands of two, Remus and Romulus, so that if one wished to do something his counterpart could veto him. But you, since there is no one who can veto you, will you not judge justly?"[43] There is here and throughout the history of the interpretation of this passage the expectation that actions attributed to God, however mysterious in their operations, will manifest standards of justice no less than those to which the best of humanity can aspire.

The emphasis is therefore primarily on the fate of the righteous few caught up in divine judgment of the unrighteous many, but the issue can be posed differently: Can the presence of the few righteous influence the fate of the unrighteous, and if so, at what critical mass? For those who started out from Gen. 18:22-33, for example, the third-century rabbinic sage Joshua ben Levi, the requisite number was fifty (*Gen. Rab.* 49:9). This led to the conviction that the world is maintained through the righteousness of the fifty. Alternatively, the world must never lack thirty righteous ones like Abraham, a calculation based, by gematria, on the numerical value of the word *yihyeh* in the phrase "Abraham shall surely become *(hayo yihyeh)* a great and mighty nation" (Gen. 18:18).[44] The most common number, how-

---

42. *Tanhuma Yelammedenu Vayyera* 9:13.
43. *Gen. Rab.* 49:9; cf. *Midrash Haggadol Bereshit* 1:314.
44. y + h + y + h = 10 + 5 + 10 + 5 = 30.

ever, is thirty-six, the *lamed vavniks* of Jewish lore, based on the sequence of the two letters *lamed* and *vav* (numerically thirty and six) in Isa. 30:18.[45] This idea, less amenable to critical scrutiny, has haunted Jewish thinking throughout the ages, from the earliest of the rabbinic sages to André Schwarz-Bart's *Le Dernier des Justes*.

On the sins of Sodom, something has already been said.[46] The character of Lot, at this juncture of his checkered career, is variously assessed. For some early Christian writers (2 Pet. 2:6-8 and *1 Clement* 11.1), he was the one righteous person in Sodom and was rescued on account of his piety and hospitality to strangers. The assessment of the Qur'an (37:132-34) is equally positive. Other early Christian theologians and moralists, who took a dim view of the incest in the cave, made a somewhat halfhearted attempt to exonerate him from blame.[47] A novel approach is taken in the *Alphabet of Ben Sira* (#268), according to which Lot was righteous but, sadly, not a Torah scholar like Abraham. But for many commentators Lot stood in contrast to the incomparable Abraham and was rescued from the doomed city only on account of Abraham.

45. The numerical value of the letters *lamed* and *vav (lô)* in the last phrase of Isa. 30:18 (*'ašrê kol-ḥôkê lô*, "Blessed are all those who wait for him," that is, God), is thirty-six, hence the reading "Blessed are all those who wait for the Thirty-Six." As Gershom Scholem points out, the real origin of this tradition lies elsewhere, probably in astronomical speculations. See his *The Messianic Idea in Judaism* (New York: Schocken Books, 1971), 251-56.

46. For further documentation, see Louis Ginzberg, *The Legends of the Jews,* vol. 1 (Philadelphia: Jewish Publication Society of America, 1961), 245-50.

47. Origen and Irenaeus, cited in Sheridan, *Ancient Christian Commentary,* 80-81.

7

In the Land of Moriah

Early Encounters

The story of the binding and near sacrifice of Isaac by Abraham (Gen. 22:1-19), often referred to as the Aqedah, a Hebrew word meaning "binding," is doubtless one of the most controversial texts in the Hebrew Bible. Yet in the earliest stages of commentary on, or allusion to, the Abraham story, it was not experienced as particularly prominent or problematic. In the writing about Abraham, the emphasis tended to be on covenant, oath, and promise, therefore on Gen. 15 and 17 rather than on chapter 22. It comes up in no other Hebrew Bible text, and is clearly outside of, and later than, the core P narrative encountered in earlier chapters. The trial inflicted on Job that, like Abraham's trial, turned out all right in the end, at least for Job (Job 1–2; 42:7-17), invited comparison with the Aqedah, but the invitation was not taken up until the author of *Jubilees* produced a decidedly sinister rereading of Gen. 22 involving the Satan (Mastema) as a leading player (*Jub.* 17–18), on which more will be said later.

In other respects, however, the scene played out in the land of Moriah provided strength and encouragement in times of crisis. Abraham's survival of the test by demonstrating his trust in the God who had guided him up to that point was a not uncommon theme in prayers, sermons, and speeches during the Hellenistic period. In his brief encomium on Abraham, Ben Sira praised him in that "when tested he proved to be faithful" (Sir. 44:20), and some years later Mattathias, father of the Maccabee brothers, exhorted his sons on his deathbed to bear in mind how Abraham was found faithful when tested (1 Macc. 2:52). Under the rule of the Hellenistic monarchies and the allure of a culture with which Palestinian Jews had previously been only sporadically acquainted, the story came to serve quite naturally as a source of inspiration. This was a testing time, and not all passed the test. With the prohibition of Jewish religious practices by Antiochus IV Epiphanes (175-164 B.C.), we have the beginnings of a martyr cult that resulted in a new genre, martyrology, also well developed in the early centuries of Christianity. This had the effect that, in appealing for inspiration to the Aqedah, emphasis was placed as much on Isaac as on Abraham, since Isaac was the one faced with death. One of the first examples is the gruesome description of the martyrdom of a mother and her seven sons (2 Macc. 7:1-42; 4 Macc. 8–18). The mother recalled how, during his lifetime, her husband read Bible stories to his children, including the story of the sacrifice of Isaac (4 Macc. 18:10-12). When the persecution and the time for resisting the tyrant arrived, she imitated Abraham in refusing to be swayed by the intense feeling she had for her children (14:20). As they were undergoing atrocious tortures, the seven martyr-brothers were encouraged by their mother to recall the example of Isaac, who submitted willingly to death (16:20), and the brothers themselves encouraged each other. In a later retrospective, probably from the reign of John Hyrcanus I (135-104 B.C.), Judith, heroine of the book named for her, made a similar appeal when reminding the elders of Bethulia, then under siege, that God was testing them as he had tested both Abraham and Isaac (Jdt. 8:26). The Wisdom of Solomon makes a similar point, in its own very different idiom, about the righteous Abraham sustained by wisdom in the face of the compassion he felt for his child (Wis. 10:5).

In his treatise *On Abraham* (167-207), Philo praises the greatness of Abraham on account of his willingness to sacrifice his son, and Isaac's virtue, beyond his years, in accepting death at his father's hands. He takes issue with those "quarrelsome critics" who belittled Abraham's virtue. After all, they were saying, fathers often send their sons into battle, both Greeks and barbarians sacrifice their children to their gods, and in India widows throw themselves on the pyres of their husbands. Philo responds with the assertion that they did this either through fear or because of pressure from higher powers, whereas Abraham and his son accepted death as a free and loving tribute to God. To this he adds his own allegory on the name Isaac *(yiṣḥaq)*, as signifying not ordinary laughter but participation in the joy of God.[1] In his usual anodyne fashion, Josephus has God motivating Abraham

---

1. The verbal stem *shq,* "laugh," is the assumed derivation of the name. See also Gen. 17:17; 18:12-13; 21:6.

to obey by reminding him of all the benefits he has received, and Abraham passes it on by reminding Isaac of all the care lavished on his upbringing — in the circumstances, a rather inadequate motivation, one would think. To further reduce the tension, God reassures Abraham that it was not a craving for blood that led to the command to sacrifice.[2]

While some medieval schoolmen, Thomas Aquinas and Philip the Chancellor in particular, found the Aqedah philosophically and ethically challenging,[3] it was only in the Enlightenment that its problematic nature came into full and open view. Immanuel Kant's judgment in *The Dispute between the Philosophical and Theological Faculties* is well known: "Abraham at God's command was going to slaughter his own son — the poor child in his ignorance even carried the wood. Abraham should have said to this supposed divine voice: 'that I am not to kill my beloved son is quite certain; that you who appear to me are God, I am not certain, nor can I ever be, even if the voice thunders from the sky.' "[4] No commentary can hope to come up with an adequate answer to Kant's complaint; but perhaps by means of a deeper working through the narrative in its successive stages, we may come to a better and more sympathetic understanding of the underlying issues. That, at any rate, is what we now propose to attempt.

The Command

The one who issues the command (Gen. 22:1-2), and in whose name Abraham prepares to obey it, is identified simply as God, the Deity *(ha-'elohim);* the personal name of the God of Israel appears only with the intervention of the angel-messenger of Yahweh and in the name of the sanctuary where the sacrifice is to take place (vv. 11, 15). These names and designations are insufficient to justify the common practice of assigning this incident, and the narrative block consisting of chapters 20–22, of which it is a part, to

2. *Ant.* 1.222-236, on which see Louis H. Feldman, "Josephus' Version of the Binding of Isaac," in *SBL Seminar Papers,* ed. Kent H. Richards (Chico, Calif.: Scholars Press, 1982), 113-28.

3. Emily Arndt, *Demanding Attention: The Hebrew Bible as a Source for Christian Ethics* (Grand Rapids: Eerdmans, 2011).

4. Cited from Claus Westermann, *Genesis 12–36* (Minneapolis: Augsburg, 1985), 354. See Emil L. Fackenheim, "Abraham and the Kantians," in Westermann, *Encounters between Judaism and Modern Philosophy: A Preface to Future Jewish Thought* (New York: Basic Books, 1973), 31-77.

a putative Elohistic source; and this practice is almost certainly mistaken when that source is dated to the ninth or eighth century B.C.[5] The more general designation *elohim,* rather than Yahweh, is well represented in biblical texts of acknowledged late date, for example, Job 1–2, Proverbs, and Jonah, which have nothing to do with the conventional Pentateuchal source criticism.[6] The name Yahweh occurs only with the introduction of the "angel-messenger of Yahweh," last encountered by Hagar in the previous chapter, and the name of the holy place (22:11, 14, 15).

We are thrust at once into the problematic nature of the episode in the first sentence: "Sometime later God put Abraham to the test." Let us be clear, in the first place, that testing is not the same as tempting, though the language is at times confusing. The Old Greek version translates the Hebrew verb for "putting to the test" *(nissa')* with *epeirazen,* and the Vulgate translates with *tentavit.* Both of these verbs *(peirazein, tentare)* occur respectively in the Greek and Latin versions of the temptation of Jesus in the wilderness (Matt. 4:1), and in the second-last petition of the Lord's Prayer, "lead us not into temptation," in the traditional rendering.[7] But the biblical God does not tempt, and where elsewhere in biblical texts God puts people to the test, as with the people of Israel in the wilderness, the testing does not seem to be much of a test at all. More of a challenge are the nations left in Canaan to test the mettle of the invading Israelites (Judg. 2:22; 3:1, 4), and yet more problematic is the idea that false prophecy is permitted by God as a test of Israel's faith (Deut. 13:3). But when, in the prophet Micaiah's vision of the heavenly throne room, he hears Yahweh

---

5. On the Elohist (E) of the classical documentary theory, see Otto Eissfeldt, *The Old Testament: An Introduction* (Oxford: Blackwell, 1956), 200-204; Ger. *Einleitung in das Alte Testament* (1934), 238-42; Martin Noth, *A History of Pentateuchal Traditions* (Englewood Cliffs, N.J.: Prentice-Hall, 1972 [1948]), 35-41, 263-74; more recently Hans-Christoph Schmitt, "Die Erzählung von der Versuchung Abrahams Gen 22, 1-19 und das Problem einer Theologie der elohistischen Pentateuchtexts," *BN* 34 (1986): 82-109; Ronald Hendel, *The Book of Genesis: A Biography* (Princeton: Princeton University Press, 2013), 234.

6. Timo Veijola, "Das Opfer des Abraham-Paradigma des Glaubens aus dem nachexilischen Zeitalter," *ZTK* 85 (1988): 129-64; Timo Veijola, "Abraham und Hiob. Das literarische und theologische Verhältnis von Gen 22 und des Hiob-Novelle," in *Vergegenwärtigung des Alten Testaments: Beiträge zur biblischen Hermeneutik. FS für Rudolph Smend zum 70. Geburtstag,* ed. Christoph Bultmann et al. (Göttingen: Vandenhoeck & Ruprecht, 2002), 127-44.

7. It is somewhat strange that this translation has gone unchallenged, since we tend to think of God permitting temptation but not leading us into it. The *peirasmos* in question is better understood as either the eschatological testing time or a testing or challenge beyond our moral capacity, including the testing time of death.

asking for volunteers to entice King Ahab to go to Ramoth-gilead where he foresees that he will fight and be killed (1 Kgs. 22:19-23), the line between testing and inciting seems to have become very thin.

The testing of Job is on a more catastrophic scale than that of the Aqedah, but the two have features in common. The environment is similar; both Job and Abraham are figures of immemorial antiquity living among the people of the east; they are wealthy and, withal, exemplary in righteousness and piety; and they are ready to intercede with God on behalf of others (Job 42:8-9; Gen. 20:7). When sorely tried, both confess to being but dust and ashes yet insist that God also must act justly (Job 42:6; Gen. 18:27). But what sets the disasters afflicting Job apart is the role of the Satan, who is permitted by God to persecute this righteous man to test whether he will continue to be faithful to God or follow his wife's advice and "curse God and die" (Job 2:9). The trials of Job therefore proceed more from a wager than as a straightforward putting to the test.[8] Reading Job 1–2 together with Gen. 22 led to a new and sinister version of the incident in the *Book of Jubilees.* Prince Mastema, another name for the Satan of Job 1–2, makes a proposal to the Lord God. Since Abraham loves Isaac more than anything or anyone else, God should command him to sacrifice his son in order to be certain that Abraham would remain faithful in all afflictions. Since Abraham has already been tried six times and passed the test, God knows he would pass this seventh and last test also. He therefore gives Abraham the command, and it comes about as anticipated.[9]

Returning to the biblical account: Abraham is given three commands: take your son, go to the land of Moriah, and sacrifice him as a burnt offering. The first of these is qualified in three ways: your only one, whom you love, who is Isaac. Isaac must be named because the author

8. Sara Japhet, "The Trial of Abraham and the Test of Job: How Do They Differ?" *Hen.* 16 (1994): 153-72; Hans Strauss, "Zu Gen 22 und dem erzählenden Rahmen des Hiobbuches (Hiob 1,1-2,10 und 42,7-17," in *Verbindungslinien. FS für Werner H. Schmidt zum 65. Geburtstag,* ed. A. Graupner et al. (Neukirchen-Vluyn: Neukirchener Verlag, 2000), 377-83.

9. *Jub.* 17:15-18, partially reproduced in 4Q225 (4QPseudo-Jubilees). See Florentino García Martínez, "The Sacrifice of Isaac in 4Q225," in *The Sacrifice of Isaac: The Aqedah (Genesis 22) and Its Interpretations,* ed. Ed Noort and Eibert Tigchelaar, Themes in Biblical Narrative 4 (Leiden: Brill, 2002), 44-57. *Jubilees* has seven trials of Abraham, but more commonly there are ten, with the Aqedah as the last and most grievous. See Shalom Spiegel, *The Last Trial: On the Legends and Lore of the Command to Abraham to Offer Isaac as a Sacrifice,* translated with an introduction by Judah Goldin (Woodstock, Vt.: Jewish Lights Publishing, 1993; original New York: Schocken Books, 1969).

knows that there is another beloved son, Ishmael, who was Abraham's only child for thirteen years. The loss of an only child is more grievous than the loss of the firstborn, and a greater source of sorrow and mourning.[10] We recall the sacrifice of the unnamed daughter of Jephthah, his only child, and the lamenting that continued for years (Judg. 11:34-40). The author of Chronicles reports that Jeremiah wrote a lament for King Josiah, the only son of his predecessor Amon, struck down in the prime of life, and all the rhapsodists male and female were still lamenting his death at the time of writing (2 Chr. 35:24-25). Use of the term *bekor* (firstborn) may have been considered inadvisable in any case, either because it raised the troubling question of Ishmael, biologically the "womb opener," or because it could have conjured up the idea of a sacrifice of the firstborn offered to the underworld deity Molech.

Moriah, the destination of Abraham's journey, is known only from 2 Chr. 3:1, where it is the site on which Solomon built the temple, now Haram esh-Sharif, the Temple Mount in Jerusalem. Since the author of Chronicles associates the site with David rather than with Abraham, it is unlikely that he is drawing on the Aqedah; and on the assumption that Gen. 22:1-19 antedates the composition of Chronicles, Moriah probably replaced an original name now lost.[11] The substitution of the original name with Moriah would have been another way, following on Abraham's encounter with Melchizedek, of associating Abraham with Jerusalem and its temple. It could also have been suggested by the identification of Mount Moriah with the threshing floor of Ornan (Araunah in 2 Sam. 24:18), where an angel-messenger from Yahweh encountered David and where David built an altar and sacrificed, with Araunah providing the wood and the sacrificial animal (2 Sam. 24:15-25). Hence the journey to the mountain in the land of Moriah was, in effect, a pilgrimage to a holy site, like Elijah's pilgrimage to Horeb the mountain of God, except a lot shorter (1 Kgs. 19:8-9).[12]

---

10. On the mourning for the death of an only child, the most grievous of all bereavements, see Jer. 6:26; Amos 8:10; Zech. 12:10.

11. The uncertainty about Abraham's destination is reflected in the early versions. The Syriac Peshitta has "the land of the Amorites," LXX "the highland country" *(eis tēn gēn tēn hupsēlēn),* and the Vulgate "the land of vision" *(terra visionis).* None of the hypotheses explaining "the land of Moriah" with reference to *môreh* (teacher) or *môrāh* (fear, awe) has gained much support.

12. Consistent with the threefold repetition of the term *māqôm* (vv. 3, 9, 14) for Abraham's destination, a common epithet for a shrine or temple; compare Jacob's visit to Bethel

The Journey

The journey, described after the manner of a pilgrimage to a hilltop shrine to pay respects to the local numen, is soon under way (Gen. 22:3-8). Early in the morning Abraham first splits the wood needed for the burnt offering — the order of activities seems somewhat confused — saddles his donkey, and assembles his small party: himself, Isaac, two attendants who are perhaps slaves, and one donkey for the first two days. In the first of Kierkegaard's four versions of the command and journey, both Abraham and Isaac ride off on donkeys with Sarah watching them leave from the window of their house.[13] We are perhaps meant to recall that other, much longer journey from Harran to Canaan: there is the same peremptory command (*lek-leka,* "Go!"), an expression used only in these two places (12:1; 22:2); the same prompt, obedient response; and the same initial uncertainty about the destination ("the land I will show you," 12:1; "one of the mountains I shall show you," 22:2). Abraham's obedience to the voice of his God is certainly emphasized, but we recall previous occasions when he hesitated, sought reassurances, expressed doubt, or asked questions (15:8; 17:17-18), and we may wonder why on this most critical and wrenching occasion he said nothing.

The silence during the journey is oppressive. Abraham's silence is understandable, for what can a father on his way to killing his own son have to say to him? "And so they went, both of them together, the one to bind, the other to be bound, the one to slaughter, the other to be slaughtered" (*Gen. Rab.* 56:4). But Isaac also has nothing to say until they come within sight of the shrine. This narrative element, the silence, the impression of traveling through a vacuum, finds expression in Erich Auerbach's classic reading of the episode set off against Homeric epic style, here exemplified in the return of Odysseus to Ithaca and his recognition by Eurycleia, his old nurse: "Thus the journey is like a silent progress through the indeterminate and the contingent, a holding of the breath, a process which has no present, which is inserted, like a blank duration, between what has passed and what lies ahead, and which yet is measured: three days!"[14] The

---

where *māqôm* occurs six times with reference to the sanctuary there (Gen. 28:10-22), and the Jerusalem temple described frequently in Deuteronomy as "the place *(māqôm)* that Yahweh your God will choose" (Deut. 12:14, 18; 14:23, 25; etc.).

13. See the prelude to his panegyric on Abraham in *"Fear and Trembling" and "The Sickness unto Death,"* trans. Walter Lowrie (Princeton: Princeton University Press, 1941), 27.

14. From the essay "Odysseus' Scar," in *Mimesis: The Representation of Reality in West-*

silence is broken on the morning of the third day. Abraham instructs the attendants: "Stay here with the donkey; the boy and I will go on ahead, worship, and come back to you." As befits a visit to a holy place, especially one on a hilltop, the rest of the journey must be on foot. Abraham loads the wood on to "the boy"; he himself carries the more dangerous equipment, the flint for the fire and the knife; and they continue on their way.

The sharing of responsibility for carrying the equipment necessary for the sacrifice — wood, fire, and a knife[15] — raises the question about the age of the intended victim, a question that has exercised artists in different media throughout the centuries. We might compare, for example, the painting of Jacob Jordaens the Elder in the Brera, Milan, in which Isaac is a young but well-developed adult, with Gustave Doré's black-and-white illustration in which Isaac is a subadult, or with Domenichino's rendering of him in the Prado, Madrid, in which he is a young boy. In Rembrandt van Rijn's painting of 1635 and his black-and-white sketches, Isaac is a teenage boy, in keeping with early Jewish and Christian representations, for example, in Dura-Europos, in the Beth-Alpha synagogue mosaic, and in the Roman catacombs. In Abraham's instructions to his attendants, Isaac is referred to as a *na'ar*, a term often translated "youth" or "boy," as here, but quite indeterminate about age, being used for all stages from infancy to mature adulthood. The last time we heard about Isaac, in the previous chapter (21:8), he was being weaned. So if he is here assigned the task of carrying enough wood for the fire, several years must have passed. By that time Abraham would have been well into his second century (see 21:5).

Questions have also been raised about Abraham's instructions to the attendants to await the return of both himself and his son (22:5). Some have wondered whether he had, from the first, known that he was not to go through with the command to sacrifice his son or, alternatively, whether he had made up his mind to go through the motions without consummating the sacrifice.[16] But to read it in this way is to reduce it to a trite and uninter-

ern Literature, trans. Willard R. Trask (Princeton: Princeton University Press, 1953; first published in German, 1946), 10.

15. The rare word for "knife," *ma'ăkelet,* occurs only here (22:6, 10); in Judg. 19:29, the incident in which the Levite from Benjamin cuts up his concubine, raped and murdered by the men of Gibeah; and in Prov. 30:14, where it is a metaphor for carving up and devouring the poor and needy (cf. Mic. 3:2-3). The root *'kl* (eat) therefore suggests either a knife used for culinary purposes or a butcher's cleaver.

16. Jon D. Levenson, *Inheriting Abraham: The Legacy of the Patriarch in Judaism,*

esting episode stripped of its tragic urgency and suspense. It is enough to conclude that the attendants were not to know the real goal of the journey and should not be present at the sacrifice, and were therefore not told that Abraham alone would be returning.

The silence between Abraham and his son is broken only when the last part of the journey gets under way on the morning of the third day, a conventional temporal expression that can indicate that the time of preparation for an important event has come to an end and the critical point has been or is about to be reached. The exchange between son and father is typical of the narration as a whole: not a word too many; much suspense, much left unspoken:

> Isaac: My father?
> Abraham: What is it, my son?
> Isaac: Here are the fire and the wood, but where is the lamb for the sacrifice?
> Abraham: God will provide himself with a lamb for the sacrifice, my son.

Note that Isaac mentions the fire and wood but not the knife, perhaps because Abraham kept it hidden until the moment came to make use of it. After that exchange, there would be no more use for words, and so they continued on their way in silence until they arrived at the shrine.

The Sacrifice

The account of the sacrifice (22:9-14) is stripped down to the essentials. There are no embellishments and there is no authorial comment: they arrive, Abraham builds the altar, arranges the wood on it, binds Isaac, and places him on the wood. The critical juncture is reached as Abraham takes the knife to plunge it into his son's body. As Luther says in a sermon on the Aqedah, "If God had blinked, Isaac would have been dead."[17] But at that moment Abraham hears once again the voice coming from somewhere

---

Christianity, and Islam (Princeton and Oxford: Princeton University Press, 2012), 73, suggests another possibility, that Abraham plans to supplicate God to call off the sacrifice, which however would presumably have resulted in the return of both Abraham and Isaac to the attendants.

17. The citation, the authenticity of which is not guaranteed, is from the second act of John Osborne's play *Luther*.

above him and speaking, as always, in the name of the God he has come to know: "Abraham, Abraham.[18] . . . Do not raise your hand against the boy or do anything to him, for now I know that you fear God and that you have not withheld your son, your only son, from me."

The first thing Abraham does on reaching the hilltop shrine is build an altar. Sacrifice requires an altar, as the Hebrew word for "altar" (*mizbeah,* from the verb *zbh,* "sacrifice") indicates. Since his arrival in Canaan, Abraham has had good practice at building altars, beginning at Shechem (12:7), then at Bethel (12:8; 13:4), and finally at Mamre (13:18). But this is the first time he is told to go to such a place in order to sacrifice. Like these other shrines, the one to which Abraham leads Isaac would have been consecrated to a local deity, and, like others visited by the patriarchs, including Isaac's altar at Beersheba (26:25) and Jacob's at Bethel (28:10-22; 35:1-7), the shrine is taken over for the cult of Yahweh.

We are given no information about the location of the sanctuary where Isaac was to be sacrificed except that it was a two-to-three-day donkey ride from Beersheba, in the land of Moriah, and on a mountain. The account of the attempted and aborted sacrifice itself conforms with only minor modifications to the ritual ordinance for the performance of the burnt offering *(ola)* in Lev. 1:3-9, which can be summarized as follows: The sacrificer begins by laying his hand on the head of the victim, an initial action not recorded of Abraham but quite likely performed, and perhaps alluded to obliquely in the angel-messenger's injunction to Abraham not to lay his hand on the boy, implying not to go ahead with the sacrifice (22:12). After the victim is slaughtered, it is to be cut up and placed on the fire on which the wood has been arranged (with the verb *arak,* as in 22:9). The ordinance does not specify binding the victim; the verb *'qd* in 22:9, which gives us the title *aqedat yishaq,* "the Binding of Isaac," occurs only here in the Hebrew Bible, but the same verb is used in rabbinic texts for the binding of the sacrificial animal's legs.[19] Though formulated only in the time of the Second Temple, these procedures, followed faithfully by Abraham, were no doubt much more ancient.

---

18. Apart from 15:1, "Abram, I am your shield . . . ," the voice addresses Abraham by name only in this episode: it does so once at the beginning (22:1) and, with more urgency by repeating the name, at this critical point, the climax of the narrative.

19. *b. Sanh.* 54a; on which see Nahum Sarna, *The JPS Torah Commentary: Genesis* (Philadelphia: Jewish Publication Society, 1989), 361.

The Second Intervention of the Angel-Messenger

The angel-messenger addresses Abraham a second time (22:15-18), here too in the name and person of Yahweh, once again expressing approval of Abraham's willingness to sacrifice his son, and in the same words as the first time: "You have not withheld your son, your only son, from me."[20] There is broad agreement that this second intervention is an appendix added to the basic narrative, which ended with Abraham's naming of the sanctuary and his return to Beersheba (22:1-14, 19).[21] If this is so, the scribe responsible for the insertion may have wished to contextualize the event more adequately by introducing the promise theme with which the Abraham story begins in 12:1-3, and doing so in the most ample terms. The promise is reinforced with an oath sworn by Yahweh's own self, a formulation found only here and in the prayer of Moses after the apostasy of the Golden Calf (Exod. 32:13).[22] Both of these texts link the promise of descendants as numerous as the stars of heaven with the theme of the land. In Gen. 22:15-18 the demographic promise, hyperbolically expressed as a people as numerous as the stars in heaven or the grains of sand on the seashore,[23] is in the foreground, and the territorial promise is expressed obliquely by the assurance that Abraham's descendants will "possess the gate of their enemies," meaning that they will occupy their enemies' territory, including the cities. This most comprehensively formulated promise is crowned with the repetition of the assurance given Abraham before leaving Mesopotamia, that all the nations of the earth will wish to be blessed as Abraham and his descendants were blessed. The fulfillment of these blessings, however, is contingent on Abraham's obedience to this most recent command from God. The language in which this is expressed is that of the book of Deuteronomy, in which the conditionality of the

---

20. "From me" *(mimměnnî)* is absent from MT but supplied by the LXX, the Samaritan Pentateuch, the Vulgate, the Syriac, and Targums.

21. Following on early commentators including Wellhausen and Dillmann, this conclusion is accepted by, *inter alios*, Hermann Gunkel, *Genesis* (Macon, Ga.: Mercer University Press, 1997), 236; Gerhard von Rad, *Genesis: A Commentary* (London: SCM, 1961 [1956]), 237-38; Claus Westermann, *Genesis 12–36* (Minneapolis: Augsburg, 1985), 363-64. See also Levenson, *Inheriting Abraham*, 83-84. Walter Moberly, "The Earliest Commentary on the Akedah," *VT* 38 (1988): 302-22, assigns a more precise function to this addition.

22. A similar formulation, but without reference to the ancestral promises, occurs in Amos 6:8; Jer. 22:5; 49:13; and Isa. 45:23.

23. Gen. 15:5; 32:12; Exod. 32:13; Deut. 1:10; 10:22.

promises is repeatedly emphasized. This is clearly an important point for the author of this addition to the Aqedah.

Abraham's Sacrifice and the Practice of Human Sacrifice

The biblical texts leave little room for doubt that human sacrifice, especially the sacrifice of children, was practiced at certain times, in certain places, and in certain circumstances in ancient Israel.[24] In the first place, the legal, prophetic, and narrative materials attest, by way of denunciation, the practice of the crematory sacrifice of children to the chthonic deity Molech. This "passing through the fire" is attested in Phoenicia, Carthage, and Carthaginian colonies around the western Mediterranean, and is condemned in Deuteronomy and the Holiness Code as a Canaanite import.[25] Two Judean kings, Ahaz and Manasseh, sacrificed their sons in this way (2 Kgs. 16:3; 21:6), probably on the ritual platform called the *tophet* in the Valley of Hinnom (Gehenna) on the southern edge of the city, which was destroyed by the reforming king Josiah (2 Kgs. 23:10). These indications, reinforced by the denunciations of the practice in Jeremiah and Ezekiel,[26] suggest that the practice may have been largely confined to Jerusalem and the royal court. But the practice has no bearing on Abraham's sacrifice; it was a different phenomenon. Sacrifice to Molech was confined neither to the firstborn nor to males, and there was no provision for animal substitution.[27]

The sacrifice of a son or daughter in a critical situation of extreme need is also attested in many parts of the ancient world, including Israel, but this too has no direct relevance for Abraham's sacrifice, which is not

24. Roland de Vaux, O.P., made a vigorous attempt to demonstrate that, apart from sacrifices offered to Molech (*molk* sacrifices), which he held were practiced only in Jerusalem and only for a limited period of time, human sacrifice was unknown in ancient Israel, a minimalist view not widely accepted. See his *Ancient Israel: Its Life and Institutions*, trans. John McHugh (London: Darton, Longman and Todd, 1961), 441-46; Roland de Vaux, O.P., *Studies in Old Testament Sacrifice* (Cardiff: University of Wales Press, 1964), 52-90.

25. Lev. 18:21; 20:2-5; Deut. 12:31; 18:10.

26. Jer. 7:31-32; 19:5-6; Ezek. 16:20-21; 20:30-31.

27. John Day, *Molech: A God of Human Sacrifice in the Old Testament* (Cambridge: Cambridge University Press, 1989); John Day, *Yahweh and the Gods and Goddesses of Canaan* (Sheffield: Sheffield Academic Press, 2000), 209-16; George C. Heider, *The Cult of Molek: A Reassessment*, JSOTSup 43 (Sheffield: JSOT Press, 1985); George C. Heider, "Molech," in *DDD* 581-85.

presented as a reaction to a critical situation. Mesha, king of Moab, unable to break out of a city besieged by Edomites and Israelites, sacrificed his firstborn son and eventual heir as a burnt offering on the city wall, which, we are told, brought the siege to an end as far as the Israelites were concerned (2 Kgs. 3:26-27). The warlord Jephthah made a vow that, if he defeated the Ammonite army and returned victorious, he would sacrifice the first person to come out of his house to greet him on his return. Tragically, this turned out to be his daughter, his only child, who was sacrificed after a two-month delay (Judg. 11:30-40). Parallels to both of these instances have been cited from neighboring regions. The unnamed young daughter of Jephthah has been proposed as the Hebrew counterpart to Iphigenia, sacrificed to the goddess Artemis by her father Agamemnon, who was anxiously waiting with the fleet in Aulis for a favorable wind to set sail for Troy. In one version, Agamemnon vowed to offer Artemis the most beautiful person born that year in his kingdom, who happened to be Iphigenia. In another version, however, she was replaced as sacrificial victim by a hind, as Isaac was by a ram.[28]

It is understandable that the biblical texts, redacted at a time when human sacrifice was no longer countenanced, should contain no laws requiring it. But what we do have is the statement, often repeated, that the first male child belongs in a special way to the deity and therefore, to avoid being made over to the deity as a sacrificial offering, must be "redeemed," that is, replaced by a surrogate, normally an animal. A law in the so-called Covenant Code states unambiguously, in the name of Yahweh, that "the firstborn of your sons you must give me" (Exod. 22:29b). The same requirement applies to domestic animals, oxen and sheep, which are to be sacrificially offered to Yahweh on the eighth day after birth (Exod. 22:30). The demand is repeated in an instruction addressed to Moses in Exod. 13:1-2, assigned by some to the Priestly source, according to which every "womb opener," human and animal, is to be offered to Yahweh.[29] A codicil to this prescription in Exod. 13:11-16, following on the command to celebrate the Feast of Unleavened Bread as a memorial of the exodus from Egypt (13:3-10), states that the prescription applies only to male humans and animals, and adds that the firstborn of humans are to be redeemed,

28. Jan N. Bremmer, "Sacrificing a Child in Ancient Greece: The Case of Iphigenia," in *The Sacrifice of Isaac: The Aqedah (Genesis 22) and Its Interpretations*, 21-43.

29. "Womb opener" is an attempt to render the technical term *peṭer-reḥem* or, in one instance *piṭrâ* (Num. 8:16), related to the verb *pṭr*, meaning to open, release, set free, and synonymous with *bĕkôr*, "firstborn" (Exod. 34:19-20; Num. 3:12; 18:15; Ezek. 20:26).

but does not say how this is to be done. Among domestic animals, only the donkey, a ritually unclean animal and therefore unsuitable for sacrifice, is to be redeemed. The law ends by providing a historical origin for the practice in the last of the ten plagues inflicted on Egypt, the killing of the firstborn of the Egyptians, both human and animal. The death of the Egyptian firstborn led to the rapid departure of the Israelites from Egypt, followed immediately by the promulgation of the law of the firstborn (13:1-2): "Consecrate to me all the firstborn. Whatever first opens the womb among the Israelites, of human beings and animals, is mine." The timing of this promulgation, repeated after the apostasy of the Golden Calf (34:19-20), raises interesting questions about the relation between the redemption by substitution of the firstborn and the redemptive event of the exodus from Egypt celebrated in the Festival of Unleavened Bread and Passover. The connection is stated explicitly in an additional comment, Deuteronomistic in language and theme, on this first promulgation (13:15-16): "When Pharaoh stubbornly refused to let us go, Yahweh killed every firstborn in the land of Egypt, human and animal. That is why I sacrifice to Yahweh every male that opens the womb, but every firstborn of my sons I redeem."

Like other deities in the ancient Near East and the Mediterranean world, therefore, the Israelite God had a special claim on the firstborn of animals and human beings. In the normal course of events, the claim would be acknowledged by the ritual killing of the firstborn unless redeemed by substituting a domestic animal, though this form of substitution is not explicitly stated in the references to the practice listed earlier. In late ritual legislation, Levitical ordination played a role in this process. As Yahweh's special possession, the Levites served as substitutes for the sacrificial offering of the firstborn (Num. 3:11-13; 8:14-18). This substitutionary system was further regulated on a numerical, one-to-one basis; one Levitical ordination redeems one firstborn. But since the number of firstborn Israelites (22,273) exceeded the number of Levites (22,000), those families without a Levitical counterpart were subject to a fine of five shekels, payable into the temple treasury (Num. 3:46-51; 18:16). The ancient law was maintained but "rationalized" on a monetary basis to the benefit of the temple and its personnel.

With these arrangements we are at a considerable distance from the original emotional and religious impulse behind the practice and Abraham's obedience to the command to sacrifice his son. What is more interesting, but also more difficult to define, is the relationship between the law of the sacrifice and redemption of the firstborn on the one hand and the more familiar religious institutions of Passover and circumcision on the other. In the book of Exodus, Yahweh commands Moses in peremptory fashion to bring the message to Pharaoh that "Israel is my firstborn son. I tell you, let my son go to worship me. Should you refuse to let him go I shall kill your firstborn sons" (4:22-23). But then, on the way to fulfilling this commission accompanied by his wife and son, Moses encounters Yahweh, who is prepared to kill him. This eventuality is avoided by the quick-witted Zipporah, his wife, who circumcises their son and touches Moses' genitals with the foreskin (4:24-26). Contact with the blood of the circumcision saved Moses' life, as the blood of the slaughtered Passover sacrifice, daubed on their doorposts and lintels, saved the Israelites in Egypt from sharing the fate of the Egyptian firstborn. Whatever else it is, therefore, circumcision is an apotropaic rite, a way of cheating death. We already know that it was to be performed on the eighth day after the birth of the child (Gen. 17:12, 23; 21:4), and it was considered essential for participation in Passover (Exod. 12:43-49). The eighth day is also the day appointed for the sacrifice of firstborn animals (Exod. 22:29). The biblical texts are more reticent on the procedures involved in the substitutionary rite for a human firstborn and the precise time when it is to take place, but the time appointed for the redemption of an animal could also have served for a human firstborn, and this would be the eighth day, the day on which circumcision is to take place.

As we read on in Exodus, we see that the Passover ritual (12:1-28) is clamped between the announcement of the tenth plague, the killing of the Egyptian firstborn of humans and animals (11:1-10), and its execution (12:29-32). There follow detailed rulings about who may and who may not participate in Passover, but in all cases circumcision is the essential requirement (12:43-49). Then, on the day of departure from Egypt, the day of the exodus, the law about the consecration to Yahweh of the firstborn of animals and human beings is promulgated together with the requirement to redeem the firstborn of Israelites (13:1-2, 11-16). This close connection between the spring Festival of Unleavened Bread–Passover, with its overtones of blood as both dangerous and redemptive, and the redemption of the firstborn of Israel is present wherever the law of the firstborn is mentioned. In Exod. 34:19-20 it follows immediately on the ritual for the Feast of Unleavened Bread; in the late legislation in Numbers (Num. 3:11-13; 8:14-18), it originates with the death of the Egyptian firstborn; and in Deut. 15:19-23, it is followed immediately by the Passover ritual. This, then, is the rich fund of belief, tradition, and custom that underlies and gives added resonance to the account of what happened in the land of Moriah.

Isaac's Sacrifice and the Death of Jesus

We comment briefly here on the proposed parallel between Isaac's sacrifice and the death of Jesus as sacrificial. Apart from the triadic formula (Abraham, Isaac, Jacob), Isaac's name is not of frequent occurrence in the New Testament. The deacon Stephen mentions his birth and circumcision on the eighth day (Acts 7:8), and in his letter to the Romans Paul somewhat paradoxically uses descent through Isaac to demonstrate that the true Israel consists in "children of the promise" rather than those who claim physical descent (Rom. 9:6-10; also Gal. 4:28). In his catalogue of those in Israel's past who lived by faith, the author of Hebrews assigns the most prominent place to Abraham, the supreme example of whose faith was his willingness to sacrifice his only son through whom the promises were to be fulfilled. He reckoned that God had the power even to raise the dead to life, and, figuratively, Abraham did receive his son back (Heb. 11:17-19).[30] For James, on the contrary, Abraham's sacrifice of Isaac illustrates the need for faith to be demonstrated and confirmed in action (Jas. 2:21-24).

These are the only explicit references to the sacrifice of Isaac in the New Testament, but it was practically inevitable that the death of Jesus understood in sacrificial terms would sooner or later be seen to be prefigured in the sacrifice of Isaac, especially in view of the Passover associations of the sufferings and death of Jesus, explicitly stated in Paul's reminder to the Corinthian Christians that "Christ our paschal lamb has been sacrificed" (1 Cor. 5:7; cf. Exod. 12:1-13), as also in the Gospel accounts of events leading to the death of Jesus.[31] The Aqedah itself has such strong "paschal" associations that it might be considered a sort of dramatization of the Passover festival even without the many midrashic elaborations and amplifications it has acquired over the centuries. The idea of sacrifice is at

---

30. "Figuratively" (NRSV) translates *en parabolē,* which may reflect the midrashic idea that Isaac did in fact die and was resurrected (e.g., *Pirqe R. El.* 31:3). This midrash is not, however, attested in the pre-Christian period. More probably, it is an anticipation of the eschatological resurrection of the dead, as proposed by Harold W. Attridge, *The Epistle to the Hebrews,* Hermeneia (Philadelphia: Fortress, 1989), 333-35.

31. Matt. 26:1-2, 17-19; Mark 14:1-2, 12-16; Luke 22:1-2, 7-15; John 13:1; 18:28, 39-40.

the heart of Passover, more fully described as "the Passover sacrifice to the Lord" (Exod. 12:27). The sacrificial victim is a lamb, the same animal whose absence puzzled Isaac on the way to Moriah (Gen. 22:7). Passover is intimately associated with ancient patterns of violent death, propitiation, atonement, and redemption. The law for the celebration of Passover in Exod. 12:1-28 is bracketed by the announcement of the death of the Egyptian firstborn, which precedes it (11:1-10), and the actual death of the firstborn, which immediately follows (12:29-32). This literary complex is then closely linked with the law of the offering and redemption by substitution of the firstborn, the "womb opener," following the command: "Sacrifice to Yahweh every male that first opens the womb, but every firstborn of my sons I redeem" (13:15). This is essentially what happened with Abraham and Isaac in the land of Moriah.

The close association between Passover and the sacrificial offering of the firstborn of Abraham was not lost on the author of *Jubilees* (17:5–18:19), who dates the sacrifice of Isaac to the twelfth day of Nisan, the first month of the liturgical year, the month in which Passover is celebrated. Since the journey to the site in the land of Moriah took three days, the actual sacrifice would then coincide exactly with the date for Passover between the evening of the fourteenth and the evening of the fifteenth of Nisan (*Jub.* 17:15; 18:3; cf. Exod 12:1, 6). The author goes on to say that after returning to Beersheba, Abraham celebrated the festival every year for seven days (*Jub.* 18:18-19), in obedience to the biblical ordinance for the Feast of Unleavened Bread (*Jub.* 18:18-19; cf. Exod. 12:14-20). The connection is reinforced by identifying the mountain in the land of Moriah with Mount Zion, site of the future temple (*Jub.* 18:13).[32]

Sacrifice involves bloodshed, and the shedding of blood can release powerful forces either for disaster or for well-being. Blood can atone: "The life of the living creature is the blood, and I have appointed it for making atonement" (Lev. 17:11). The blood of the Passover lamb is also apotropaic. Daubed on the doorposts and lintels of the houses of the Israelites in Egypt, it spared them the devastating visit of the Destroying Angel (Exod. 12:7, 17, 22-23). *Genesis Rabbah* affirms that the blood of the sacrificed ram substituted for Isaac's blood, and thus provided assurance that a sacrifice had taken place (*Gen. Rab.* 56:9). Other rabbinic commentators

---

32. *Jub.* 18:12-13; Josephus, *Ant.* 1.226. Also frequently in the Aramaic Targums. See Roger Le Déaut, *La Nuit Pascale* (Rome: Pontifical Biblical Institute, 1963), 161-63; Geza Vermes, *Scripture and Tradition in Judaism,* 2nd ed. (Leiden: Brill, 1973), 193-227.

go further in asserting that Isaac's blood must have been shed in some measure. *Liber antiquitatum biblicarum* asserts that Israel's election was due to Isaac's blood (18:5-6), and the commentary on Exodus attributed to Rabbi Ishmael identifies the blood on the Israelite houses in Egypt as the blood of Isaac (*Mekilta de Rabbi Ishmael* on Exod. 12:13, 23).

But there is no direct and explicit link between the sacrifice of Isaac as a redemptive act and the sacrificial death of Jesus, much less — given the uncertain dating of most of the midrashic texts referred to — between the blood of Isaac and the redemptive and atoning blood of Jesus.[33] There are, however, intimations and verbal cues suggesting that the sacrifice of Isaac is somewhere in the background where the New Testament attempts to express the meaning of the death of Jesus, especially where it does so in connection with the Passover sacrifice. Paul reminds the Christian communities in Rome that God "did not withhold his own son but gave him up for us all" (Rom. 8:32). This language brings to mind the words addressed to Abraham after the sacrifice of the ram: "Because you have not withheld your son, your only son, I shall bless you abundantly" (Gen. 22:16).[34] In the Johannine circle the designation, often translated "only-begotten" *(monogenēs)*, expresses the intensity and intimacy of relationship between a parent and an only child, between Abraham and Isaac, between God the Father and Jesus.[35] Jesus as the paschal "lamb of God" (John 1:29, 36; 1 Pet.

33. The case for the late, that is, post-Christian date for the haggadic elaborations on Gen. 22:1-19, especially its presentation as a vicariously atoning sacrifice, was made forcefully by Philip R. Davies and Bruce D. Chilton, "The Aqedah: A Revised Tradition History," *CBQ* 40, no. 4 (1978): 514-46. The authors' thesis was subject to detailed criticism by Alan F. Segal, "'He Who Did Not Spare His Own Son . . .': Jesus, Paul, and the Akedah," in *From Jesus to Paul: Studies in Honour of F. W. Beare,* ed. P. Richardson and J. C. Hurd (Waterloo, Ontario: Wilfrid Laurier University Press, 1984), 169-84; C. T. R. Hayward, "The Present State of Research into the Targumic Account of the Sacrifice of Isaac," *JJS* 32 (1981): 127-50; C. T. R. Hayward, "The Sacrifice of Isaac and Jewish Polemic against Christianity," *CBQ* 52, no. 2 (1990): 292-306. These criticisms seem justified at least to the extent that some of the haggadic material in the midrash and Targums would have contained older oral and liturgical tradition.

34. The verb corresponding to "withhold," *epheisato,* is the same verb as in Gen. 22:16 LXX *(epheisō);* "his own son" corresponds to "beloved son" (Gen. 22:2), while also suggesting an intertextual link with the Isaian Servant, especially in view of the verb *paradidōmi* ("give up," "hand over"), with reference to God "giving up" the Servant as an expiation for sin in the last of the four Servant passages (Isa 53:5, 12).

35. John 1:14, 18; 3:16, 18; 1 John 4:9. *Monogenēs* and *agapētos* (beloved) seem at times to be practically synonymous: *agapētos* occurs in the account of the baptism of Jesus with its background in the first of the four Servant passages (Matt. 3:17 and parallels; also 2 Pet.

1:19) could likewise have brought to mind Isaac's perplexity on the way to the sacrifice about the missing lamb (Gen. 22:7-8), as also the Isaian Servant of the Lord who was led like a lamb to the slaughter (Acts 8:32; cf. Isa 53:7-8). In some important respects, therefore, these early Christian texts may be read as within the same intertextual reality as the sacrifice of Isaac.

Questions Remain

The near sacrifice of Isaac was not quite the end of the Abraham life story. The next event recorded is the death of Sarah, which leads to the negotiations for the outright purchase of a burial plot and arrangements for a suitable marriage for the son he almost sacrificed. According to Gen. 25:1-6, there was even time for Abraham to remarry and beget six more children before his death and aggregation to the great kinship fellowship of the living and the dead in what was now patrimonial domain. Here also, in these closing scenes, there is the discrepancy noted earlier between the sense of time passing as we read the sequence of scenes and events and the schematic time to which everything must conform, especially the life span of Abraham. Since Abraham was 100 years old at the birth of Isaac, and died at age 175 (25:7), while Isaac married Rebekah at age 40 (25:20), Abraham would, schematically speaking, have been 140 at that time, with 35 years yet to live. Sarah, meanwhile, who died at 127 (23:1), passed away 3 years before her son's marriage. After what happened in the land of Moriah, all this was anticlimactic. The sacrifice on the mountain was the turning point, the *peripateia,* of the Abraham story in its final form, which implies that the drama of divine election would be continued in the life story of Isaac.

As we come to the end of our reading of the Aqedah, we will no doubt have our own lists of questions still unanswered and problems still unresolved. The lists would probably contain some or all of the following, and no doubt other questions as well: How could the God of Abraham command the death of a child or condone human sacrifice? How could Abraham, who had pleaded, questioned, and sought reassurances on previous occasions, have obeyed such a command without hesitation? Why was Abraham commanded to carry out the sacrifice at a certain holy site some

---

1:17; cf. Isa. 42:1-4). At the beginning of the Aqedah passage in the LXX version, Abraham is told to "take your beloved son whom you love," whereas MT has "your only son (yĕḥîdkā) whom you love."

distance from where he and his son were living? What is the relationship, if any, between the endangering of Ishmael and that of Isaac recounted in immediate succession? Why is Sarah not a witness to the anticipated death of her son? Why do we hear of the return from the mountain shrine of Abraham alone, without Isaac?

The first of these questions has attracted more discussion and commentary and generated more perplexity than the rest: How could the God of Abraham, Isaac, and Jacob command Abraham to kill his son, and how could he demand that the firstborn male be turned over to him in commemoration of the mass slaughter of Egyptian children (Exod. 12:30; 13:11-16)? Some would answer with Hannah at Shiloh that God is the one who both kills and gives life (1 Sam. 2:6). He is the Lord of Life and Death; his ways are beyond human calculation. But whatever answer we come up with, it may be well to bear in mind that what we have before us is not some directly transmitted information about the nature of God but, in the first place, a text that, like all texts, calls for interpretation. We do not know with any precision when Gen. 22:1-19 was composed, but it was surely at a time when human sacrifice was no longer an accepted ritual practice.

A remarkable statement of the prophet Ezekiel, made in the course of a retrospective on the history of Israel, suggests that the practice of child sacrifice, embedded in the idea of substitutionary redemption, was problematic from early times (Ezek. 20:25-26): "I gave them statutes that were not good and ordinances by which they could not have life; and I defiled them through their gifts in making them offer up all their firstborn, that I might horrify them." The reference is to the law according to which all the firstborn, animal and human, are to be dedicated to Yahweh by sacrifice. The statute or ordinance that is not good and does not lead to life is Exod. 13:12: "You must set aside for Yahweh all that opens the womb." The author of the Aqedah is therefore envisaging a time in the distant past, before the exodus and the death of the Egyptian firstborn, therefore before the introduction of the practice of "redeeming" the firstborn with an animal surrogate, when this type of sacrifice, far from being morally problematic, was considered a uniquely heroic act of piety and devotion. In other words, he would have chosen the most extreme example he could imagine in order to put the final mark of authenticity on Abraham's faith in God and trust in God's word. We could illustrate the point by comparison with the list of offerings to God on a scale of increasingly hyperbolic extremity in a passage from the prophet Micah (6:6-7):

What shall I bring when I come before the Lord,
when I bow before God on high?
Shall I come into his presence with burnt offerings,
with calves a year old?
Will the Lord be pleased with thousands of rams,
ten thousand rivers of oil?
Should I give my firstborn for my transgression,
my child for the sin I have committed?

The answer is clearly in the negative, since the prophet goes on to say that what the Lord really wishes from us is to act justly, be loyal and loving, and walk humbly with our God (6:8). For the author of the Aqedah, the God whom Abraham obeyed without hesitation was not thirsty for the blood of children. Ambiguities remain, but we do well to recall that the God who commanded Abraham to sacrifice Isaac was the same God who intervened to prevent him from doing so.

8

Abraham's Other Beloved Son

Abraham's Locations and Relocations

The Aqedah, the emotionally tense story of the near sacrifice of Isaac, is by far the most familiar episode in the Abraham story and, as such, has been groaning for centuries under the weight of commentary from theologians, philosophers, artists, literati in general, and of course, biblical scholars. One result of the massive attention the Aqedah has received, and continues to receive, is the tendency to isolate it from its literary context in the Abraham cycle. And since context is an essential factor in the interpretation of texts, a new line of inquiry might start out from the immediate *literary* context of Gen. 22:1-19. One notable aspect of that narrative is the absence of the spatial dimension, a sense of location. Abraham is to go to a mountain that will be pointed out to him, later identified only as "the mountain of Yahweh" (22:2, 14). The destination of the journey is first described only as "a place" *(māqôm)* with the unusual name "Yahweh will provide" *(YHWH yireh)*. This "place" is situated in "the land of Moriah" (22:2), the location of which is not disclosed. It is only when the dramatic events in this topographically arcane location are concluded and Abraham, unaccompanied by Isaac, has rejoined his servants and returned to Beersheba, where he continues to live, that we have a reference to a known location, a place on the map (22:19): "Abraham then went back to his men, and together they returned to Beersheba; and there Abraham remained."

This piece of information is our point of departure. It matches what we are told about Abraham's movements immediately prior to the call to sacrifice his son — identified in the opening revelation as his only son, as if Ishmael did not exist. There is broad agreement that Gen. 20–21 contain a combination of two narratives: the first (20:1-18; 21:22-34) deals with re-lations between Abraham and Abimelech, elsewhere identified as a Philis-tine king (26:1, 8); the second (21:1-21) records the birth, circumcision, and weaning of Isaac, during the celebration of which event something went badly wrong, resulting in the expulsion of Hagar and her son Ishmael into the wilderness. This second of the two narrative strands, with its climax in the last-minute rescue of Hagar and Ishmael from death by exposure, dis-cussed in chapter 4 above, resulted in the juxtaposition of two near-death experiences: the first, that of Ishmael, in the presence of his mother and the absence of his father; the second, that of Isaac, in the presence of his father and the absence of his mother. We, the readers, are left to speculate as to what connection there might be between the two incidents, and to draw out the significance of this perhaps not entirely coincidental juxtaposition.

The first of the two strands, recording the strained but courteous negotiations between Abraham and Abimelech dealing with access to and ownership of wells, concludes with Abraham setting up as a resident alien in Beersheba in the Negev, a place sanctified by a cult center consecrated to El Olam, God Eternal (21:32-34). Since this is the last residence of Abra-ham to be mentioned before the sacrifice in the land of Moriah, it was from Beersheba in the Negev that Abraham departed after hearing the voice, and to Beersheba that he returned and continued to live after the sacrifice.

This new and, as it turned out, final relocation of Abraham calls for further scrutiny. To go back to the beginning of the story: After Lot chose to move outside the limits of the Promised Land, thereby disqualifying himself as heir designate to Abraham, Abraham remained in sole pos-session of the land and the future was left open (13:14-18). Only then is Abraham told to "walk through the length and breadth of the land." This walking was not for the purpose of exercise; the "walkabout" (with verb *hithallek*) corresponds to a traditionally sanctioned way of affirming a claim to the land traversed, a practice not confined to that place and that time. At that point Abraham settled by the oak (terebinth?) of Mamre at Hebron, where he built an altar (13:17-18).[1] From this point on, Hebron, or Mamre close by, became Abraham's home insofar as he had a home. It was there that he heard the news of Lot's further troubles during the War of the Nine Kings (14:13), and it was there that he entertained the three visitors (18:1).

---

1. MT has the plural, "oaks," probably to disguise the "pagan" practice of venerating certain trees considered in some respect numinous or used for divination. Compare the oak at Shechem (Gen. 12:6; Judg. 9:6), at Tabor (1 Sam. 10:3), and at Zaanannim (Josh. 19:33).

Its unique importance as patrimonial domain is confirmed by its choice as the burial site for himself, his wife, and his descendants (23:1-20). Mamre near Hebron therefore remained Abraham's residence until he moved into the Negev, as recorded in Gen. 20:1: "Abraham journeyed by stages from there into the Negev, and settled between Kadesh and Shur."

We are not given a reason for this move into the Negev, but we may note the following coincidences. After her first expulsion, Hagar, pregnant with Ishmael, encountered the angel-messenger near "the spring on the way to Shur" (16:7), near a holy well known as *Bĕʾēr Lahai Roʾî,* "The well of the Living One who provides for me," situated between Kadesh and Bered (16:14). It was shortly afterward that Abraham settled between Kadesh and Shur in the southern Negev or northern Sinai, living as a resident alien in Gerar (20:1).[2] In the course of the second expulsion of Hagar, now accompanied by Ishmael, she and her son had their near-death experience in the wilderness of Beersheba (21:14), and shortly afterward Abraham took up residence in Beersheba and stayed there a long time — "many days," we are told (21:32-34). Sarah, meanwhile, has disappeared from sight. After contemptuously insisting that Hagar, "this slave woman," be sent out into the wilderness together with her son, which she must have known could lead to their deaths (21:8-14), and indeed would have but for supernatural intervention, we hear no more of her until her own death at the age of 127 (23:1-2). She is not even mentioned in the account of her son's near sacrifice, a circumstance that has given rise to a great deal of speculation in the commentary tradition. A rabbinic tradition holds that Abraham told her that he was just taking Isaac to study Torah at the famous school of Shem, otherwise known as Melchizedek. A more sinister explanation, however, has it that she died of shock after Satan brought her the false news that Abraham had slaughtered her son.[3]

---

2. Kadesh is probably Kedesh, a settlement in the same region as Beersheba (Josh. 15:23), rather than Kadesh Barnea (Num. 20:1-21; Deut. 1:2; etc.). Shur as a settlement is unknown, but there is a wilderness of Shur (Exod. 15:22), and the term applies to a line or wall *(šûr)* of forts defending the approaches to Egypt from the northern Sinai (Gen. 16:7). Ishmaelite Arabs controlled the region from Havila to Shur, which faced Egypt (Gen. 25:18), and which, in the time of Saul and David, was occupied by Amalekites (1 Sam. 15:7; 27:8). Gerar may be on or near the site of Tel Haror, about twenty-five kilometers southeast of Gaza, or perhaps Tell Abu Hurēre in the northwest Negev; see Eliezer D. Oren, "Gerar (Place)," in *ABD* 2:989-91; Isaac Gilead, "Gerar," in *NEAEHL* 2 (1993), 469-10. In any case, it is represented in these Genesis texts as the principal territory of Abimelech, a Philistine city-king, in close association with (onetime) Philistine Gaza.

3. *Pirke de Rav Kahana* 26:3. In addition to the commentaries, see Sebastian Brock, "Genesis 22: Where Was Sarah?" *Exp.T.* 96 (1984): 14-17.

At any rate, she died at Kiriath-arba, the old name for Hebron, where presumably she had been living. We are told that Abraham *came* to mourn her, the implication being that he came from somewhere other than Kiriath-arba, and that therefore he was not with her when she died.[4]

Perhaps, then, as we retrace Abraham's movements, we may suggest that the relocation from Hebron/Mamre to the Negev was dictated by Abraham's attachment to Hagar, acknowledged by those Jewish commentators who identified her with Keturah, whom Abraham married (or remarried) after Sarah's death, and who gave him, aged at least 137, six more sons.[5] The attachment to Ishmael was no less strong. Ishmael was, after all, his firstborn son, and for the fourteen years prior to the birth of Isaac he had been accepted without demur as heir to Abraham and to the promises. This solution to the problem of an heir was countenanced by legal precedent, acknowledged by all parties, and was not intended as a temporary measure. Fourteen years is quite a long time, certainly long enough for the establishment of the close bond between Abraham and Ishmael to which the Abraham story attests. Even after hearing the voice telling him that the impossible will happen and he will have a son by Sarah, rather than reacting with enthusiasm, Abraham expostulates and pleads that Ishmael may be the favored one. Then again, Abraham felt obliged to accede to Sarah's ill-tempered insistence that "this slave woman" be driven out into the wilderness; yet we are told that "the matter was very distressing to Abraham on account of his son" (21:11). The pathos of Abraham's situation, and much of the emotion generated by the cycle as a whole, arises from the tension between Abraham's affection for Ishmael, his firstborn, and the imperative of obeying the voice that was guiding him in a direction he had not himself chosen.

Abraham's move into the Negev after Hagar's first expulsion, followed by his relocation to Beersheba after Hagar's wandering in the wilderness of Beersheba together with her son after the second expulsion (21:14), suggests the further possibility that the sacrifice, the location of

---

4. The more commonly accepted translation "went in," "entered" for *wayyābō'*, as in NRSV and REB, assumes that Abraham was there with her in Hebron, but that is not what the narrative so far leads us to conclude. We would also expect to be told that Abraham entered a place where the funerary rituals took place, a "house of mourning" (*bêt 'ēbel*, Qoh. 7:2, 4), as Jeremiah was forbidden to "enter the house of mourning," the *bêt marzēaḥ* (Jer. 16:5).

5. *Gen. Rab.* 61:4; *Tg. Yer.* on Gen. 25:1. The tradition was familiar to Jerome, as we see from his commentary on the passage.

which is left so obscure, took place in the same region, no more than a three-day donkey ride from Beersheba. On the first occasion, Hagar's rescue happened at a holy place associated with a well (16:7-12), and a well was also at hand during the second expulsion (21:19). Wells are often sites of pilgrimage and worship, like the well and the cult center at Beersheba itself (21:33; cf. 26:25). Hagar called the well near which her encounter with the angel-messenger took place "the well of the Living One who provides for me" (16:14). In like manner, Abraham called the place where the sacrifice took place "God (Elohim) will provide" (22:14).[6] In both instances the name is related to a favor or gift received: in one instance by Hagar and her son Ishmael, in the other by Abraham and his son Isaac. The same idea, that the sacrifice of Isaac took place on the site of Hagar and Ishmael's salvation, may have occurred to the author of *Jubilees*. According to this retelling of the story, Abraham's dismissal of Hagar and Ishmael at the insistence of Sarah was Abraham's sixth trial, followed by the command to sacrifice Isaac, the seventh and last (*Jub.* 17:17-18). The *Jubilees* version locates a well at the site of the sacrifice of Isaac (18:4),[7] and has Abraham placing the wood on Isaac's shoulder — a detail not in the biblical account — as he placed the provisions for the journey on Hagar's shoulder before her expulsion (17:8).

The Setting Aside of the Firstborn

Throughout the ancestral story, these often intense human relations, whether of attraction or aversion, are played out within a larger social reality defined in terms of genealogy, inheritance, relations of affinity and consanguinity, and descent rules. The entire ancestral history is driven by considerations of genealogy and descent. We need mention only one major theme, the repeated disavowal of the status of the firstborn, the "womb opener,"[8] together with the blessings that traditionally came with the birth of the firstborn. The opening of the womb by the firstborn is one of those basic physical realities that underlay the functioning and survival

6. MT reads *YHWH yir'eh,* but *'ĕlohîm* is more consistent with the naming of God in the passage as a whole (vv. 1, 3, 8, 9, 12) and is supported by a small fragment from Qumran cave 4 (4QGen-Exod^a at Gen. 22:14).

7. The well also features in 4Q225 frag. 2, col. I 13 (4QPseudo-Jubilees).

8. Translating the more technical term *peṭer reḥem* for the firstborn of humans and animals (Exod. 13:12; 34:19; Num. 3:12; 18:15; Ezek. 20:26).

of traditional societies, in this and many other times and places, societies most of which moved on the father-son axis.

Yet in spite of the primordiality and fundamental importance of the firstborn, the story of the ancestors is the story of the deliberate and repeated thwarting of the natural processes by which intergenerational continuity and the ongoing life of the group were sustained. Ishmael is the firstborn of Hagar and Abraham but is displaced by the miraculous birth of a child to a ninety-year-old woman. Esau is the firstborn of Rebekah and Isaac but is displaced by the deceit and trickery of his twin, aided and abetted by his mother. Reuben is the firstborn of Jacob yet loses out to Judah on account of a sexual misdemeanor. Manasseh is the firstborn of Joseph but is replaced by Ephraim following an apparently arbitrary decision of the grandfather Jacob. Like ethnic myths and legends of origins all over the world, the story of Abraham, Isaac, and Jacob is ethnogenesis designed to sustain the identity and destiny of the ethnic group within which it came into existence. And as with the myths and legends of origins of other peoples, questions of historical accuracy are of secondary importance.

The disavowal of Ishmael's status as firstborn is related in the narrative usually referred to as "the covenant of circumcision" *(berit mila)* in Gen. 17, which we have seen to be a redactional rather than an authorial unity. This text is in several respects the most important juncture in the entire Abraham story, situated as it is between the notices of the birth of Abraham's two beloved sons: Ishmael in 16:4, 15-16; Isaac 14 years later in 21:1-7, since Abraham was 86 years old at the birth of Ishmael (16:16) and 100 at the birth of Isaac (21:5). To recapitulate briefly: In a vision, Abram, now renamed Abraham, receives a covenanted promise that he is to be ancestor to many nations and their rulers, and his descendants will have living space in the land of Canaan (17:1-8). There follows the law of circumcision as a sign of the covenant already offered and accepted (17:9-14). So far, then, there has been no mention of Ishmael, at this point 13 years old (16:16; 17:24-25), but given that he was Abraham's firstborn and only son, it was understood that the promises should be realized in the first place through him and his descendants. Once circumcised by Abraham on the same day as the promulgation of the law, he is, so to speak, inscribed in the indefectible covenant of grace and promise (17:23-27). If this is so, the announcement of a son to Sarai, soon to be Sarah, was at some point inserted between promulgation and implementation. The insertion complicates the picture in one obvious respect, by creating the troubling impression that, on one and the same day, the God who spoke to Abraham made an indefectible promise to him of posterity through his son Ishmael and then, later in the day, revised it in favor of another son, and one not yet born. However Abraham's request that Ishmael might live in God's presence is interpreted (17:18), the original commitment made to Abraham and his 13-year old son, ratified and sealed by their acceptance of the promise and circumcision, is modified but not abrogated. Abraham's plaintive request has been heard (17:20). Ishmael is still recipient of blessing and inheritor of the promise made to Abraham. He remains within the covenant into which he entered a year before Isaac.

Ishmael, Ancestor of Arab Peoples

In the book of Genesis, genealogy is the modality in which history unfolds. In a sense, genealogy generates the historical narrative; hence the structural significance of the ancestral *toledot* discussed earlier. It is self-evident that this historical narrative comes to us as the ethnography of one people, the one within which it came into existence, the group identity, cohesion, and self-esteem of which it serves to maintain. In its final form, however, with the inclusion of Terah and his family, by extending the genealogical chain backward from Jacob, it takes in a much broader range. Beginning with Terah in the ninth generation after the catastrophe of the deluge, and Abraham his son in the tenth generation, it not only allowed the inclusion of Moabites, Ammonites, Arameans, and Arabs within the genealogical schema but also placed the ethnography of Israel in the broader, we might say international, context of the sons of Noah, the "families of nations" descended from Shem, Noah's first son, listed in the so-called Table of Nations (Gen. 10), and the postdiluvial world in general. The eight characters to whom we are introduced at the beginning of the Terahite narrative cycle — Terah, Abraham, Nahor, Haran, Sarah, Lot, Milcah, Iscah — correspond to the eight survivors of the great deluge — Noah, his wife, his three sons, and their wives — on whom the future of the human race depended. The Abrahamic blessing and covenant correspond to the blessing of Noah and his family after the subsidence of the flood water, confirmed by an indefectible covenant (*berit olam,* Gen. 9:8-17) on which the new dispensation in the postdisaster world rested. The call to Abraham to undertake a journey, spoken after a long silence, therefore signifies a new initiative on behalf not just of Israel but of all humanity.

Ishmael is an important part of this broader genealogical perspective as eponym of Ishmaelite Arabs and, eventually, Arab peoples as a whole and, from the seventh century, Muslims. The significance for his descendants of the role assigned to him in the story of Abraham is acknowledged by assigning him his own place in the ancestral pentad, the second of the five *toledot,* following immediately after the notice of Abraham's death (25:12-18). This shortest of the five ancestral *toledot* units is intermediate between Abraham and Isaac just as the *toledot* of Esau, ancestor of the Edomites (also Arabs), is intermediate between Isaac and Jacob (36:1-43). The title of the Ishmaelite list has been expanded to remind the reader that Ishmael is the son of Hagar the Egyptian. Like the Aramean list (22:20-24), the list of Arab descendants of Keturah (25:1-6), the Israelite tribal complex, and examples further afield including the amphictyonic federations in Greece, principally those of Delphi and Anthela, the Ishmaelite list has twelve members. These twelve are designated *nesi'im,* usually translated "princes," but more realistically "sheiks," each one of whose names represents a people *('umma;* cf. Arabic *ummat),* thus reproducing the same structure as the Midianite Arabs whom they displaced.[9]

In terms of real history, the Ishmaelite Arabs succeeded the Midianites as the dominant presence east of the Jordan and on both sides of the Gulf of Aqaba. Midian is listed as one of the descendants of Keturah, whom Abraham is said to have married when he was 137, and who gave him six more children (25:1-6). Keturah is unknown as a personal name, but is practically identical with Hebrew *qetorah* or *qetoreth,* "incense," an aromatic gum indigenous to southern Arabia and in great demand for both secular and religious use. We might give her the sobriquet "Lady Incense." Her "sons" are in effect Arabian tribal units and subunits. Midian, the most important name in the list, represents the Midianite tribal confederacy, much in evidence during the formation of Israel and neighboring small states on both sides of the Jordan. Riding camels and recognizable by their golden earrings (Judg. 8:24-26), they ranged far and wide,[10] reaching the height of their power and influence in the latter decades of the Late Bronze Age, and gradually fading from the record during the period of Assyrian

---

9. On the twelve-tribal structure, see Martin Noth, *Das System der zwölf Stämme Israels* (Stuttgart: Kohlhammer, 1930); Martin Noth, *The History of Israel,* 2nd ed. (London: A. & C. Black, 1959), 87-88; Norman K. Gottwald, *The Tribes of Yahweh: A Sociology of the Religion of Liberated Israel* (Maryknoll, N.Y.: Orbis, 1979), 352-56. Edomite and Horite clans were probably organized in the same way, but this conclusion calls for some textual adjustments in Gen. 36:9-30.

10. Gen. 37:28, 36; Num. 22:4-7; 25:6-9; Judg. 6–8; 1 Kgs. 11:18.

ascendancy.[11] Their Ishmaelite successors were equally well known to the inhabitants of Palestine and Syria from the time of Assyrian rule. During the two centuries of Persian rule (539-332 B.C.), and for long afterward under the Hellenistic monarchies, the inhabitants of the province of Judah, and Palestine in general, would have been in fairly close contact with Arab peoples. By that time Qedarite Arabs, represented by the second son in the Ishmaelite genealogy (Gen. 25:13), were encroaching on Edomite territory both east and west of the Rift Valley, eventually becoming the dominant presence in the north Arabian peninsula, much of the Transjordanian region, and west of the Arava from southern Palestine to the borders of Egypt. Geshem the Arab, ruler of the Qedarite tribal federation, was a thorn in Nehemiah's side during his governorship of the Persian province of Judah in the mid–fifth century B.C. (Neh. 2:19; 6:1-9). However, there are indications that relations between Jews in the province of Judah *(yehud medinta')* and Arabs on its southern border were by no means invariably hostile. Onomastic evidence on inscribed ostraca from Idumea, dated to the late fourth century B.C., presupposes a fairly high level of interethnicity involving Judeans and several other ethnic groups, including Arabs, which reminds us that the self-segregation promoted by Ezra and Nehemiah was by no means universally successful. Imperfectly known as it is, this situation in the Judean borderlands has a fair claim to be the environment that the author or authors of these lists had in mind.[12]

11. Ernst Axel Knauf, *Midian,* ADPV (Wiesbaden: Harrassowitz, 1988); Ernst Axel Knauf, "Midianites and Ishmaelites," in *Midian, Moab, and Edom,* ed. John F. A. Sawyer and David J. A. Clines (Sheffield: JSOT, 1983), 147-62. On the Midianite-Kenite hypothesis, see my "The Midianite-Kenite Hypothesis and the Origins of Judah," *JSOT* 33 (2008): 131-53.

12. On the Ishmaelites in general, see Ernst Axel Knauf, *Ismael,* 2nd ed. (Wiesbaden: Harrassowitz, 1989); Ernst Axel Knauf, "Ishmaelites," in *ABD* 3:513-20. On the population of Idumea, see Amos Kloner and Ian Stern, "Idumaea in the Late Persian Period," in *Judah and the Judeans in the Fourth Century B.C.E.,* ed. Oded Lipschits, Gary N. Knoppers, and Rainer Albertz (Winona Lake, Ind.: Eisenbrauns, 2007), 139-44; on the Idumean ostraca, see André Lemaire, "Populations et territoires de la Palestine à l'époque perse," *Transeuphratène* 3 (1990): 31-74; André Lemaire, "New Aramaic Ostraca from Idumaea and Their Historical Interpretation," in *Judah and the Judeans in the Persian Period,* ed. Oded Lipschits and Manfred Oeming (Winona Lake, Ind.: Eisenbrauns, 2006), 413-56. Lemaire's claim in this essay (pp. 419-20), that the bulk of the ancestral traditions must have been written down before the fall of Jerusalem, since Mamre/Hebron and Beersheba, frequented by Abraham and Isaac respectively (actually both by Abraham), were outside Judah and occupied mostly by Edomites and (other) Arabs, ignores the possibility that the patriarchs were associated with these places precisely for that reason, in order to stake a claim on them as Abraham did at Shechem on entering Canaan.

The last contribution to the Ishmaelite list is the notice of Ishmael's death at the age of 137, outliving Abraham by 48 and Sarah by 76 years. Nothing more is heard about the long-suffering Hagar after we left her in the desert giving her son, close to death, a drink of water (Gen. 21:19).

To complete the Terahite genealogy, something had to be said about the descendants of Nahor, the second son, ancestor of the Arameans (22:20-24). The Aramean list was fitted in toward the end of the Abraham narrative cycle, no doubt as a prelude to the account of Isaac's marriage with Rebekah, granddaughter of Nahor and Milcah, named in the list. This brief genealogy contains the names of eight sons of Nahor with Milcah, his primary wife, and four with Reumah, his wife of lower status.[13] It thereby conforms to the familiar twelvefold tribal organization, the eight sons of Milcah representing the core lineages, and the four of Reumah the more peripheral units. Several of the names in the list occur only here in the Hebrew Bible,[14] but some of those that occur elsewhere witness to the well-attested close association between Arameans and Arabs. Uz, the firstborn, occurs in the long list of Esau's Edomite (therefore Arabian) descendants (Gen. 36:28), and the land of Uz, site of Job's misfortunes (Job 1:1), was inhabited by Edomites (Lam. 4:21). Buz, the second name, is listed with Dedan and Tema, important caravan oases in northwest Arabia (Jer. 25:23). Chesed, one of the eight *hapax legomena* names in the list, may be related to the *kasdim,* sometimes mistranslated as "Chaldeans," but more probably a marauding Arabian tribe that contributed to Job's misfortunes and, in real time, to those of the kingdom of Judah in the final phase of its existence (Job 1:17; 2 Kgs. 24:2).[15] Interestingly, Nabonidus, last of the neo-Babylonian rulers, very probably an Aramean from the region of Aram-naharaim and a devotee of the god Sin worshiped in the same region, left Babylon and set up a second capital in the famous oasis

13. The term corresponding to "wife of lower status," *pilleges̆,* is a non-Semitic word, perhaps related to Greek *pallax* and Latin *pellex,* usually translated "concubine" or, less commonly, "secondary wife." In addition to Reumah, the same term is applied to Bilhah and Zilpah, maidservants of Rachel and Leah respectively (Gen. 35:25-26), and to the faithful Rizpah, Saul's companion, who protected the bodies of his murdered sons from the birds of prey (2 Sam. 3:7; 21:7-14). David had several of these lower-status wives, and Solomon had three hundred (1 Kgs. 11:3) or, according to another count, only eighty (Cant. 6:8).

14. Chesed, Hazo, Pildash, Jidlaph, Tebah, Gaham, Tahash, Reumah.

15. A suggestion of John Skinner, *A Critical and Exegetical Commentary on Genesis,* 2nd ed. (Edinburgh: T. & T. Clark, 1930), 333.

of Taima (Teman) in northwest Arabia, where he resided for at least a decade.[16]

Filling In the Gaps

In some strands of rabbinic exegetical tradition Ishmael is depicted as a reprobate, in others as a former reprobate who becomes a model penitent. Somewhat curiously, he is never mentioned in biblical texts — including the New Testament — outside of Genesis and the dependent summary in 1 Chronicles (1:28-31), though the name is attached to distinguished Judean officials (2 Chr. 19:11; 23:1), a priest contemporary with Ezra (Ezra 10:22), and a member of the royal Judean family (2 Kgs. 25; Jer. 40–41). The name also belongs to at least three rabbis: Ishmael ben Elisha, the famous Tanna, contemporary of the great Hillel; Ishmael ben Phoebus; and Ishmael ben Yose; this at least demonstrates that it could not have been a name of opprobrium. He is held in great honor in Islam as patriarch, defender of monotheistic faith and restorer, together with his father Abraham, of the sacred Kaaba in Mecca (Qur'an 2:127-29). He is also considered a prophet (Qur'an 19:54), an ancestor of Muhammad, and father to Muslims, at least those of Arabian descent. It is also Ishmael rather than Isaac who is offered to God as a sacrifice, though his name does not appear in the account of that episode in the Qur'an (37:100-107).

The fulfillment of the "great nation" theme with respect to Ishmael (Gen. 17:20) is fully acknowledged in early commentary on his role in the Abraham cycle. For Josephus, the fame of his descendants was spread far and wide. He tells us that Ishmael's descendants occupied a vast territory from the Euphrates to the Red Sea and called it Nabatene (Nabatea), a name familiar in Josephus's own day (*Ant.* 1.220-221). In connection with the offspring of Abraham and Keturah, Josephus adds that their sons and grandsons were sent out to found colonies *(apoikiai)* throughout the east country (Gen. 25:6). They occupied Troglodytis[17] and part of Arabia Felix near the Red Sea. He goes on to say that Eophren, perhaps correspond-

---

16. Ronald H. Sack, "Nabonidus," in *ABD* 4:973-76; Paul-Alain Beaulieu, *The Reign of Nabonidus King of Babylon, 556-539 B.C.* (New Haven and London: Yale University Press, 1989), 169-85. On the Arameans on general, see Wayne T. Pitard, "Aram," in *ABD* 1:338-41; Alan R. Millard, "Arameans," in *ABD* 1:345-50.

17. More correctly Trogodytis rather than the land of the troglodytes (cave dwellers), corresponding to the eastern desert region of southern Egypt and northern Sudan.

ing to Ephah or Epher in the Ishmaelite list, occupied Lybia and called it Africa, after his own name. In support, he cites *The History of the Jews* of Cleodemus-Malchus, as transcribed by Alexander Polyhistor, to the effect that a descendant of Keturah called Apher (Apheras) not only gave his name to Africa but joined forces with Heracles in his war against the Lybians. Heracles even married into the Abraham-Keturah family (*Ant.* 1.238-241), which must be considered a strange match indeed.

Ishmael's fame is, however, shared with Hagar, his mother. In these genealogical notices and lists the female ancestors are prominent, and it is about these that the three texts call for interrogation. Milcah, daughter of Haran and wife of Nahor, is the mother of Bethuel and grandmother of Rebekah. According to rabbinic opinion, Keturah was either another name for Hagar or Abraham's third wife, following the death of Sarah. *Jubilees* (19:11-12), on the other hand, states that she was a replacement for Hagar, who predeceased Sarah. Starting out from Abraham's sending Keturah's sons and grandson away to the east (Gen. 25:6), other readers made an ingenious contribution to the exegesis of another problematic text, Num. 12:1, which records Moses' marriage to a Cushite (Ethiopian) woman in apparent violation of the prohibition of exogamous marriage. This unnamed woman is first identified with Zipporah daughter of Jethro, Moses' wife named earlier, whose quick thinking saved his life (Exod. 4:24-26); then it is shown, by an exegetical tour de force, that Jethro was the son of Reuel, Reuel of Dedan, Dedan of Jokshan, and Jokshan of Keturah; ergo, the woman from Cush, wife of Moses, is identified triumphantly as a descendant of Abraham, the taint of intermarriage removed from the great lawgiver, and the complaint of Miriam and Aaron disposed of.[18]

We already know from the basic narrative that Hagar the Egyptian provided an Egyptian wife for her son and an Egyptian daughter-in-law for herself (Gen. 21:21). The wife remained nameless, but we know this would not be for long. One suggestion in *Pirqe de Rabbi Eliezer (The Chapters of Rabbi Eliezer)*, from the eighth century, written probably under Islamic rule, is that Ishmael had two wives named Aisha and Fatima, which happen to be the names of Muhammad's wife and daughter, respectively (*Pirqe R. El.* 30). Rather than coincidence, this could have been a way of em-

---

18. There is no Reuel, son of Dedan, in Gen. 25:1-6. One of the two additional names of Dedan's sons in the LXX is Raguel, which is close but perhaps not close enough. On the contribution to this rescue of Moses' reputation of *Targum Neofiti* and Demetrius the Chronographer, see James L. Kugel, *Traditions of the Bible: A Guide to the Bible as It Was at the Start of the Common Era* (Cambridge: Harvard University Press, 1997), 512-13, 534.

phasizing the close affinity of Islamic peoples with the great prophet and founder. At all events, Ishmael (Isma'il) became the symbol, representative, and patriarch of the Arab peoples in general and, in virtue of his noble descent and Arabian origins, of Islamic peoples. He is Abraham's other beloved son in the Genesis narratives. Throughout the long history of the interpretation of these texts, Ishmael and Isaac have often been presented as bitter rivals — one element in a long history of wasteful interreligious and interethnic polemic — but this conclusion must be tested against a close and careful reading of the Abraham narrative cycle independently of its numerous interpretations. Ishmael is Abraham's other beloved son, and he and Isaac go their separate ways, Ishmael to the wilderness of Paran (Gen. 21:21), Isaac to Beersheba. But at the end of the day, they come together around the grave of their father in the cave of Machpelah (25:9).

9

The Death and Burial of Sarah and Abraham

The End of the Journey

The chronicle reaches its conclusion with the death of Sarah (Gen. 23:1-2), Abraham's purchase of a burial site (23:3-20), and his death and burial alongside his wife (25:7-10). Though clearly belonging together, the records of these events are interrupted by a detailed account of the finding of a wife for Isaac (24:1-67) and the list of Abraham's offspring with another Arabian woman, Keturah (25:1-6). The first of these interpositions was necessary to create the essential link with the next generation. Further to that end, the account of Abraham's death is rounded out with a brief notice about the passing on of the blessing to Isaac, thus assuring continuance (25:11): "After Abraham's death God blessed his son Isaac. Isaac then settled in Beersheba." As for the list of Keturah's descendants, if a place had to be found for Arabian lineages claiming descent from Abraham and Keturah, it had to be before Abraham's death. The central importance of Ishmael in the Abraham story earned him a separate genealogical unit *(toledot),* however brief, between those of Abraham and Isaac (25:12-18), and, in any case, the Abraham descent of the Ishmaelite Arabs had already been established (16:1-3).

There is something close to a critical consensus that, in its main lines, this last section of the Abraham story derives from the Priestly-scribal school (P), for the most part easily recognized by a distinctive style, idiom, vocabulary, and theological orientation. There is also good support for dating this last section of the P narrative core to the late neo-Babylonian or early Persian period, therefore, in the broadest terms, from the mid–sixth century to the mid–fifth century B.C.[1] According to the standard source division as set out conveniently by Otto Eissfeldt and Martin Noth,[2] the basic events recorded in the Priest-scribal version of the Abraham cycle can be summarized as follows: departure of Terah and his family from Ur (11:27, 31-32); Abraham's journey from Harran to Canaan with Sarah and Lot (12:4b-5); Abraham's separation from Lot (13:6, 11b-12); the infertility of Sarah, and Abraham's acceptance of Hagar as a surrogate wife who gives birth to Ishmael (16:1a, 3, 15-16); the promissory covenant and circumcision (17:1-27); the rescue of Lot from the destruction of Sodom (19:29); the birth and circumcision of Isaac (21:1b-5); finally, the death of Sarah, purchase of the burial cave, and death of Abraham (23:1-20; 25:7-10). There are gaps and discontinuities, but on the whole this makes for a reasonably coherent narrative, one to which much will be added from other sources.

This outline includes the principal crises and high points of the cycle, but, needless to say, many questions about individual passages remain, some of which were addressed in previous chapters. In addition, much still remains to be clarified about the basic understanding of the idea of a "Priestly writer" and the general orientation of this foundational Priestly-scribal narrative.[3] If the date proposed for this basic narrative line is correct, its primary goal would have been to provide those who had survived the obliterating disaster of the Babylonian conquest with a religious ba-

---

1. A glance at recent introductions to the Hebrew Bible/Old Testament will confirm this estimate: Otto Eissfeldt, *Einleitung in das Alte Testament,* 2nd ed. (Tübingen: Mohr Siebeck, 1956), 246-47; Eng. *The Old Testament: An Introduction* (Oxford: Blackwell, 1956), 207 (sixth or possibly fifth century B.C.); Georg Fohrer, *Einleitung in das Alte Testament* (Heidelberg: Quelle & Meyer, 1965), 201-2; Eng. *Introduction to the Old Testament* (Nashville and New York: Abingdon, 1968), 185-86 (fifth century B.C.); J. Alberto Soggin, *Introduction to the Old Testament: From Its Origins to the Closing of the Alexandrian Canon* (Philadelphia: Westminster, 1976), 138-44 (close to the time of Ezekiel); Walther Zimmerli, *1. Mose 12-15, Abraham* (Zurich: Theologischer Verlag, 1976), 7-9 (sixth to fifth century B.C.); Bruce Vawter, *On Genesis: A New Reading* (Garden City, N.Y.: Doubleday, 1977), 21 (fifth century B.C.).

2. See the summaries in Eissfeldt, *The Old Testament,* 188-89; Martin Noth, *A History of Pentateuchal Traditions* (Englewood Cliffs, N.Y.: Prentice-Hall, 1972 [1948]), 263-64.

3. It seems to me, for example, that Albert de Pury, "The Priestly Writer's 'Ecumenical' Ancestor," in *Rethinking the Foundations: Historiography in the Ancient World and in the Bible; Essays in Honour of John Van Seters,* ed. S. L. McKenzie and T. C. Römer, BZAW 294 (Berlin: De Gruyter, 2000), 163-81, exaggerates the "ecumenicity" of this narrative strand. The author is by no means xenophobic, quite the contrary, but his broader vision of Abraham's role only comes fully into view when we connect it with the preceding history of the ancient world from the creation to the Terahite family in the tenth generation from the time of the great deluge.

sis on which to rebuild their lives and rediscover a collective identity; to come to terms with life in a wider and vaster world, that of the Persian Empire, which can plausibly be designated the first world empire; and to reconfigure their relationship to a deity who, as creator of the world, had concerns well beyond their own ethnic and national boundaries. In this disconcertingly new situation, the figure of Abraham was intended to provide assurance that, just as a new dispensation and a way into the future was offered to the eight survivors of the deluge (Gen. 9), a similar offer was now being held out to the eight members of Terah's family and their descendants listed under the names of his three sons.

The Death of Sarah

The temple scribes who created the overall chronological schema in the Pentateuch assigned Sarah a life of 127 years (23:1), and Abraham 175 years (25:7). The notice about Sarah's death (23:1-2) follows a familiar pattern: length of life, death, place of death. Throughout the account of her relationship with Abraham, Sarah's age had been pegged to his. She was 10 years younger (17:17), but Abraham outlived her by nearly half a century. She died in Hebron, the earlier name of which was Kiriath-arba, "the City of the Four," perhaps with reference to a tetrapolis, a cluster of four settlements.[4] Use of the original name may have had the purpose of showing the antiquity of the ancestral links with Hebron, especially in view of the situation at the time of writing when Hebron was disputed between Judeans and either Edomites or Qedarite Arabs, if it had not already been lost to Judah.[5] By the time of the Maccabee revolt, Hebron was already a foreign city under attack by Judah Maccabee and his brothers (1 Macc. 5:65).

The narrative has little to say about Sarah in this later period of her life. On the last occasion prior to the death notice, she was driving Hagar

4. Robert G. Boling, *Joshua: A New Translation with Notes and Commentary,* AB 6 (Garden City, N.Y.: Doubleday, 1984), 358. Following a common practice with local lore, Arba became a personal name (cf. Terah, Nahor, and Haran), belonging to the greatest of the Anakim, a population of impressive physique inhabiting the area (in modern Hebrew *ʿănāq* means "giant"), perhaps originally of Hurrian extraction (Josh. 14:15; 15:13).

5. For the same reason, Hebron is regularly said to be "in the land of Canaan" (23:2), hence in Judah. On the gradual restriction of the southern boundary of Judah after the Babylonian conquest, see Oded Lipschits, *The Fall and Rise of Jerusalem* (Winona Lake, Ind.: Eisenbrauns, 2005), 140-41, 146-47, 230-31.

and Hagar's son Ishmael out of the house on a rather dubious pretext, an act in which Abraham felt obliged to acquiesce. This happened during the celebrations for the weaning of Isaac (Gen. 21:8-14) when, according to the master chronology, she would have been ninety-three years old plus or minus a year, and Abraham ten years older. There is in any case a complete gap in our information on Sarah for the last thirty-four years of her life, and she would not have lived to see Isaac, then forty years old (25:20), happily married to Rebekah. We saw earlier that readers have been particularly concerned about Sarah's absence from the great crisis in the life of her one and only child. How could she not have been a participant, in whatever way, at this time of high drama, emotion, and brooding tragedy? Perhaps she knew but could not bear to witness the death of her own son, as Hagar could not bear to look on the anticipated death of Ishmael in the wilderness (21:16). Or, more probably, she had not been told in advance, either because she was not present with Abraham when the command came to sacrifice his, and her, son, or because Abraham chose not to tell her, or, as one midrash has it, because he misled her. A more sinister explanation, inspired by the introductory chapters in the book of Job, linked the Aqedah with Sarah's death. The Satan brought her the false news that Abraham had slaughtered her son, on hearing which she died of shock.[6]

Sarah's nonparticipation in the sacrifice in the land of Moriah reminds us that, following the present order of events in the narrative, she and Abraham appear to have been in different locations at the time of her death. She was in Hebron, where they had settled soon after their arrival in Canaan (13:18; 14:13; 18:1), but Abraham in the meantime had moved into the Negev, eventually settling in Beersheba (21:33-34), also the destination of Hagar and Ishmael after their expulsion (21:14). It was then to Beersheba that he returned after the sacrifice in the land of Moriah (22:19). All this is consistent with the information that Abraham *came* to mourn over Sarah. We are given no further information on Abraham's movements between that point and his death. The silence about Sarah, taken together with Abraham's marriage to Keturah (25:1-6), might suggest to a modern reader versed in contemporary pulp fiction and film a characteristically modern explanation of this situation, but readings of this kind are too speculative to be convincing. The marriage with Keturah is simply a device to associate another group of Arabian lineages with Abraham. In any case, these "sons" of Abraham and Keturah were born in concubinage (25:6), and

---

6. *Pesiqta de Rav Kahana* 26:3.

therefore could have seen the light of day while Sarah was still alive, and could have done so in a way entirely in keeping with the customs of that time and place.[7]

The Purchase of a Burial Site

What is at once noticeable about the account of these hard-nosed but unfailingly courteous negotiations about the sale and purchase of real estate is the insistence on absolute legality, especially from Abraham's side. Abraham is scrupulously observant of the laws and customs of the region in which he is a guest. In this respect, his attitude contrasts sharply with the approach to land ownership of those Judeans who were not deported and who claimed that "Abraham was just one man, yet he got possession of the land; there are a lot of us, so the land is handed over to us as our possession" (Ezek. 33:24). The proceedings (Gen. 23:3-20), described with convincing detail and not without a touch of humor, unfold in three stages. In the first, preliminary stage (23:3-6), after the period of mourning for Sarah has come to an end, Abraham addresses to the indigenous people the request for a burial site in quite general terms, though it will become evident that he had in view a particular location from the outset. He first establishes his credentials as a bona fide purchaser of real estate. He is "a resident alien among you" *(ger wetoshav immakem),* which seems to have been an accepted form of self-identification for a category of nonindigenous residents who had certain rights, including apparently the right to own property, but were barred from full citizenship and therefore from participation in the central ritual acts of the community.[8] He then requests that he be given, that is, be allowed to purchase,[9] a plot to bury his dead

---

7. This interpretation is based on reading *happîlagšîm* (v. 6) as an abstract in the form of a plural with the meaning "concubinage." On the rabbinic opinion, cited earlier, that Keturah was another name for Hagar, see *Gen. Rab.* 61:4 and *Tg. Yer.* on Gen. 25:1.

8. For example, the *tôšāb* was excluded from taking part in Passover (Exod. 12:45) and certain meals involving food offered to the sanctuary (Lev. 22:10). The phrase "among you" or "in your midst" was generally added to this qualification to indicate permanence rather than transience (Lev. 25:23, 35, 47; Num. 35:15). On these matters of status and terminology, see Christiana van Houten, *The Alien in Israelite Law* (Sheffield: JSOT Press, 1991).

9. This usage, with the verb *ntn* (give), used by both parties (vv. 9, 11), refers either to an outright sale or a donation on condition that the beneficiary becomes a client of the vendor subject to the performance of stated services.

wife "out of his sight," probably alluding to the fear of ritual contamination by contact with a corpse, an addition that is to be expected from a priest-scribe. The response of the Hittites is generous and courteous while making use of a little flattery to deflect Abraham from the idea of an outright sale: "Listen to us, sir. You are an awesome lord among us. Bury your dead in the choicest of our burial sites. None of us will deny you his burial plot or hinder you from burying your dead." Reluctance to alienate patrimonial domain by outright sale is understandable and was practically universal; compare Naboth's rejection of a generous tender for his vineyard made by King Ahab: "The Lord forbid that I should surrender to you my ancestral inheritance!" (1 Kgs 21:3).

After this preliminary sparring, the real action begins (Gen. 23:7-9). Abraham bows low, an act indicating respect and deference to those sitting around in the open space at the city gate, probably in a circle, as is common in such situations.[10] Abraham opens the negotiations by addressing a more specific request to the assembled Hittites, the "people of the land," in other words, the local ethnic group that had been in possession for a considerable time, long enough at any rate to claim with some plausibility that they were the indigenous population of the region.

These interlocutors of Abraham are referred to in this episode and later references to it (25:10; 49:32) only as "sons of Heth" *(bene-het)*, a designation exclusive to the Priestly scribe.[11] Hittites feature in the lists of indigenous nations with which the Israelites had to cope, sometimes listed in the first place (Deut. 7:1; 20:17), and sometimes practically interchangeable with Canaanites (e.g., Judg. 1:10), but this usage can be misleading. The Hittite empire in Asia Minor came to an end during the transition from the Late Bronze to the Iron Age (ca. 1200 B.C.). At one time scholars used to argue that this account of a real estate transaction was conducted on the basis of Hittite law, a good part of which has come down to us. The relevant stipulations (§§ 46 and 47 in the Hittite law collection) state that the purchaser of the entire parcel of land on offer rather than just a part of it renders himself subject to certain *corvée* obligations of a quasi-feudal nature. This approach, which cannot be discussed in detail at this point, has now been abandoned for the most part since, leaving aside other problems involved in dating Gen. 23 to the late second millennium B.C., the legal sit-

10. Compare the account of the sale of Naomi's land in Bethlehem in Ruth 4:1-6.
11. There are also "daughters of Heth" *(bĕnôt-hēt),* the "Hittite" wives of Esau who were making life miserable for Rebekah (27:46), from the same source as 23:1-20.

uation envisaged in Gen. 23 appears to be different.[12] Much closer parallels to the proceedings described in Gen. 23 are certain real estate contracts extant from neo-Babylonian and early Achaemenid Mesopotamia. In these "dialogue documents," one party makes an offer to buy or sell ("give") land, the second party agrees ("listens"), an agreement is reached, and the price is paid in silver.[13] This historical connection is further reinforced by the description in neo-Babylonian royal inscriptions of Syria-Palestine as *māt hatti* ("Hatti land," i.e., "Hittite land").[14] These external data are among the strongest indications in favor of dating the basic narrative of the Priestly source to the late neo-Babylonian or early Achaemenid period.

After these preliminaries Abraham addresses an appeal to those present, representative of the property-holding citizens, to lobby on his behalf one of their number, Ephron ben Zohar, to "give" (i.e., sell) him the cave of Machpelah, situated at the extremity of his property, which would serve him as a burial site.[15] It is evident that the consent of "the people of the land," represented by those present, was required for the validity of the transaction even though they remain silent throughout. Abraham tells them the agreement must take place "in your presence," meaning "with your approval," and he wisely approaches an individual property owner through the assembled citizens and elders. They apparently agree to grant

12. The connection with Hittite law was argued by M. R. Lehmann, "Abraham's Purchase of Machpelah and Hittite Law," *BASOR* 129 (1953): 15-18, and criticized by Gene M. Tucker, "The Legal Background of Genesis 23," *JBL* 85 (1966): 77-84, and John Van Seters, *Abraham in History and Tradition* (New Haven: Yale University Press, 1975), 98-100, among others. For the text of the laws see *ANET*, 2nd ed. (1955), 191 (trans. Albrecht Goetze); Martha T. Roth, *Law Collections from Mesopotamia and Asia Minor* (Atlanta: Scholars Press, 1995), 223-24, 244-45, trans. Harry A. Hoffner Jr.

13. J. J. Rabinowitz, "Neo-Babylonian Legal Documents and Jewish Law," *VT* 11 (1961): 56-76; H. Petschow, "Die neubabylonische Zwiegesprächsurkunde und Genesis 23," *JCS* 19 (1965): 103-20; Tucker, "Legal Background of Genesis 23," 74-84; R. Westbrook, "The Purchase of the Cave of Machpelah," *Israel Law Review* 6 (1971): 29-38; Ephraim Sand, "Two Dialogue Documents in the Bible: Genesis Chapter 23:3-18 and 1 Kings Chapter 5:15-25," *Zeitschrift für altorientalische und biblische Rechtsgeschichte* 8 (2002): 88-130.

14. Donald J. Wiseman, *Chronicles of Chaldaean Kings (626-556 B.C.) in the British Museum* (London: Trustees of the British Museum, 1961), 68-75.

15. Machpelah, only here and in later references to the burial site (Gen. 25:9; 49:30; 50:13), may refer to a double cave, from the verbal stem *kpl*, "duplicate," "fold double." On the later history and archaeology of the site, Haram el-Khalil, see LaMoine F. DeVries, "Machpelah," in *ABD* 4:460-61. On the exploration of the underground chambers at the site by Moshe Dayan, see his brief account, "The Cave of Machpelah: The Cave beneath the Mosque," *Qadmoniot* 9 (1976): 129-31.

approval, and in the final phase (vv. 10-16) the parties reconvene in the plaza at the town gate, a traditional venue for legal proceedings, closing deals, and other public activity.

To encourage a positive response, Abraham offers to pay the full price *(kesef male)* for the cave, another technical term that also occurs in the Chronicler's account of the purchase by David of the threshing floor of Ornan the Jebusite (1 Chr. 21:22, 24). In effect, Abraham is saying that he will accept the asking price, forgoing the anticipated dealing and bargaining down. In reply, Ephron insists that the cave cannot be sold separately from the plot of which it is a part. He is willing to sell, and mentions "giving" (i.e., selling) three times in one sentence, but — this no doubt in a voice expressive of sad reluctance — cave and field are one lot. After once again showing his respect for those assembled, Abraham expresses his willingness to purchase plot and cave. He makes this offer in a more urgent plea to Ephron to listen to (i.e., accept) his offer even before a price has been mentioned. Ephron then comes out with the huge sum of 400 silver shekels, presenting it, in a manner familiar to anyone who has shopped in the Old City of Jerusalem, as a mere bagatelle, mere pocket money, not worth haggling over. No doubt to his astonishment, Abraham at once agrees, the silver is weighed out there and then and the sum verified by those present, calculated according to the standard accepted in commercial transactions, in other words, legal tender (Gen. 23:16).[16]

In spite of different values of currency at different times, we can get some idea of the exorbitant price casually proposed by Ephron by comparing it with other examples. David bought the threshing floor of Araunah with a yoke of oxen thrown in for 50 shekels (2 Sam. 24:24). Jeremiah bought a field from his uncle in Anathoth, his own town, for 17 shekels (Jer. 32:9). Omri bought the hill on which Samaria was to be built, a huge investment, for two silver talents, equivalent to 3,000 shekels (1 Kgs. 16:24). Abraham's ability to pay the very large sum of 400 shekels highlights not only the importance of patrimonial domain but also the wealth and relative prosperity of the ancestors referred to more than once in the Abraham story.

This battle of wits over a real estate deal concludes with the em-

16. The technical term *kesep 'ōbēr lassōhēr* indicates silver standard in use among merchants engaged in overland trade, equivalent to the neo-Babylonian *kaspum ittiq*. See Ephraim A. Speiser, *Genesis: Introduction, Translation, and Notes,* AB 1 (Garden City, N.Y.: Doubleday, 1964), 171 n. 16; Victor A. Hurowitz, "*Kaesaep 'ober lassoher* (Genesis 23:16)," *ZAW* 108 (1996): 12-19.

phasis still on legal ownership of an iconic spot. The parcel of land has changed hands in a legally unchallengeable purchase agreement, and, as part of the agreement, there is a detailed inventory, duly witnessed, of the property sold: the field of Ephron with its location duly noted, the cave in the field, the trees planted in every part of it (Gen. 23:17). The only element unrecorded, the drawing up of a legal document recording the sale, may be supplied by reference to the signed and notarized deed of purchase for the parcel of land bought by Jeremiah from his uncle (Jer. 32:9-15) or, closer at hand, the neo-Babylonian "dialogue texts" mentioned earlier. There is now at last patrimonial domain, a first installment of the land of promise, a fixed and inalienable link and conduit between the living and those already "gathered," one that will receive the revered dead (Gen. 23:17-20): "Ephron's plot in Machpelah, which is east of Mamre, the plot with the cave in it and all the trees in the plot in its entire area, passed to Abraham as his legal property in the presence of the Hittites, all those who had come together at the city gate. After this, Abraham buried his wife Sarah in the cave on the plot of land of Machpelah, east of Mamre, which is Hebron. So the plot of land with the cave that is in it passed from the Hittites to Abraham as a burial site." The significance of this defining moment in the history of the ancestors is indicated by the threefold reference to the location, and we find the same quasi-legal, meticulous attention to detail in Jacob's admonition to his sons about the disposal of his body (49:29-32).

The Death of Abraham

Abraham is the first biblical paradigm of the good death. Noah was certainly "full of years," 950 to be exact, but we are simply told that he died (9:29). Abraham breathed his last and died at a great age (literally, "in good gray hair"), old and content, and was gathered to his kin. This is the pattern of the good death that will be reproduced in full with Isaac (35:29), Job (Job 42:17), Gideon (Judg. 8:32), and even David in spite of a life full of lows as well as highs (1 Chr. 29:28). Many others would be gathered to their kin, among them Ishmael, Jacob, Aaron, and Moses. Abraham's death was foretold in the course of "the covenant of the pieces," in the same terms but with one significant addition: Yahweh assured him that he would go to his ancestors, *in peace,* and would be buried at a great age (Gen. 15:15). To be buried "in peace" *(beshalom)* means to be buried in your own earth, the land, the actual soil of your ancestral domain, which gives entry into full aggregation to the great kinship company that has preceded you. The prophetess Huldah predicted that King Josiah would be gathered to his ancestors and to his grave in peace (2 Kgs. 22:20); the prophecy was fulfilled in spite of his tragic death at Megiddo, since he was brought back to Jerusalem and buried in his own tomb (23:30). The same nuance may be present in David's dying injunction to Solomon not to let Joab's gray head go down to Sheol in peace (1 Kgs. 2:6).

Abraham's age at death, corresponding to the year 2121 *anno mundi* according to the overall chronology of the Pentateuch, put the seal on a century of activity in Canaan. These schematic ages inevitably complicate the reader's attempt to follow the narrative sequentially. If Abraham was 100 years old at the birth of Isaac (Gen. 21:5) and 175 at death, while Isaac was 60 at the birth of Esau and Jacob, as recorded after the account of Abraham's death (25:26), Abraham must have lived to see his grandsons grow into teenagers. In this instance, however, the concern of the final redactor was to connect the deaths of the two principals, Sarah and Abraham, with the purchase of a burial plot, and to present this episode as an example of how to conduct oneself in the crucial matter of land ownership. Given the probable time of composition of this episode, it would have been intended for those who, in the decades following the fall of the Babylonian Empire, returned to the Persian province of Yehud (Judah), or aspired to return, or indeed for those who had never left the province, as an example of how to conduct themselves in relation to other indigenous or ethnically diverse populations in the province. Hence Abraham's respectful and courteous attitude to the "Hittites" and his scrupulous insistence on the absolute legality of the real estate transaction at each stage of the negotiations. He was not a carpetbagger coming in from outside to take the land of those already in possession by stealth, skullduggery, or outright theft. This is a characteristic of his behavior throughout the cycle, as we have seen in his deference to Lot in the resolution of a conflict about *Lebensraum* and his even-tempered negotiations with Abimelech about access to water. Furthermore, we hear no complaints about the "abominations" of the local people or their religious practices and no prejudicial comments about their morals. Whatever Abraham may have thought about the morals of the local population, he doesn't comment on them.

The final statement (25:11) about the transfer of the blessing from Abraham to Isaac links with the Isaac-Jacob *toledot* beginning "These are the descendants of Isaac" (25:19). The connection has been interrupted at the setting up of the *toledot* series by the insertion of the brief Ishmaelite *toledot* (25:12-18).

Filling In the Gaps

There seems to be more concern in the midrash to associate Sarah's death with the near sacrifice of Isaac that precedes it than with the purchase of the cave that follows it. In one version Satan is responsible. He disguised himself as an old man and brought the news to Sarah that Abraham had slaughtered her son, which led to her dying there and then, on the spot. According to another version, she survived but, unable to believe the news, went in search of Isaac. In the course of her wanderings she ran into Satan again, still in the same disguise, who admitted he had lied. Assured that Isaac was still alive, she was overcome with emotion and died of the shock. Abraham and Isaac eventually discovered that she had died in Hebron (Kiriath-arba). They mourned over her, and Abraham pronounced a eulogy over her body, still beautiful at the age of 127. The whole country mourned her death, all places of business in Hebron were shut down in her honor, and everyone of note attended her funeral, including Shem, his son Eber, the Philistine ruler Abimelech, and Abraham's Hebronite colleagues Aner, Eshkol, and Mamre.[17]

According to an even more imaginative account from a midrash of unknown provenance, Satan visited Sarah and asked her where her son was. She replied that he had gone with his father to learn about the laws governing sacrifice, but Satan assured her that this was not true; in fact, Isaac himself was to be the sacrifice. Sarah therefore had recourse to the three giants, Ahiman, Sheshai, and Talmai, resident in Hebron (mentioned in Num. 13:22 and elsewhere), and asked them to look into the distance to see if they could see an old man with two youths. They looked, and told her that what they saw was an old man with a knife and one youth bound ready for sacrifice. The shock was so great that her soul left her body.[18] Josephus (*Ant.* 1.237) has a much shorter and more sober account. Sarah died at the age of 127 and was buried in Nebron (i.e., Hebron). The local Canaanites generously made available at public expense a burial plot, but Abraham

---

17. *Pirqe R. El.* 32; *Gen. Rab.* 58.

18. Louis Ginzberg, *The Legends of the Jews,* vol. 5 (Philadelphia: Jewish Publication Society of America, 1955), 256 n. 259.

bought it for 400 shekels from Ephraim (i.e., Ephron). There Abraham and his descendants made their tombs. The same sobriety marks his notice of Abraham's death, to which he adds a brief word of praise for Abraham's great virtue and zeal in the service of God (*Ant.* 1.256). Quite different is the emotionally vivid account in *Jubilees* (23:1-7). Abraham lay dying with his grandson Jacob, a young child, lying on his chest. The child fell asleep, and when he woke up his grandfather was as cold as ice. He called out "Father! Father!" and, receiving no reply, knew his grandfather was dead. He ran and told his mother Rebekah, who told Isaac. Isaac and Ishmael, both apparently living in the same house, and therefore reconciled, buried him in Machpelah beside Sarah, and the whole household, including the sons of Keturah, mourned him for forty days.

The cave of Machpelah, beneath the Ibrahimi mosque in the old city of Hebron, is a holy site for both Jews and Muslims. It has changed hands more than once over the centuries, and has in recent years witnessed scenes of mutual hatred and violence foreign to the spirit and witness of the great ancestor common to Jews and Muslims. The site is also religiously significant for Christians, who claim spiritual descent from Abraham, though it is challenged by the rival Samaritan tradition that reveres Shechem, now Nablus, as a site sanctified by association with Abraham. In the cave at Machpelah, according to tradition, all the ancestors male and female were buried with the sole exception of Rachel, who died in childbirth and was buried near Bethlehem (Gen. 35:16-21). There, in the Ibrahimi mosque, these ancient stories of the great ancestors are memorialized by the monumental tombs covered in damask, red for the men, blue for the women.

The Marriage of Rebekah and Isaac

A First Reading

The story that follows in Gen. 24 tells how Isaac, having survived the sacrificial knife, was provided with a wife. It is situated in the Abraham cycle, though it obviously has much more to do with Isaac than with Abraham, but it is there by rights. It represents the completion of the Abraham narrative, the terminus of the plot about Abraham's legal heir, and the removal of the last obstacle to the fulfillment of the promise. There is then nothing left for Abraham to do but die and be gathered to his kin. According to the schematic chronology, the death of Abraham takes place after the marriage (25:7-11),[1] but we shall see that the provision of a wife for Isaac is his last significant act before his death. At any rate, the present order makes it clear that, in terms of plot and narrative logic, the marriage belongs to the Abraham cycle.

From the literary point of view, the expedition of Abraham's faithful servant in search of a wife for his son has much in common, both in length and in style, with the novella-type storytelling exemplified by the Joseph narrative in Gen. 37–50. The story is built up around two familiar type-scenes: the deathbed commission and the fateful encounter at a well. As for the first, the solemn and urgent wording of the commission presupposes a deathbed scene. Abraham does not expect to be alive when his majordomo returns, and the fact that the latter returns to Isaac rather than to Abraham confirms that the death took place during an absence — given the distance

---

1. He is 100 years old at the birth of Isaac (21:5), Isaac married at age 40 (25:20), and Abraham died aged 175 (25:7), therefore 35 years after the marriage.

involved — of no less than two months. Gunkel understood the servant's anxiety to return to his master as indicating that Abraham was still alive at that point, but in the absence of telegraph, cell phone, or other means of communicating at a distance, how could he have known? This problem notwithstanding, Gunkel emended the final verse of the chapter (24:67) to read that marriage with Rebekah comforted Isaac for his father's death rather than for his mother's death, but this is quite unnecessary.[2] We find a similar situation later in the history. Isaac is old and could die at any minute ("I do not know the day of my death") as he prepares to bestow the death-bed blessing on his elder son, Esau (27:1-4). In this case, however, Isaac surprised everyone, since he was still alive years later when Jacob returned from Mesopotamia, dying at the ripe age of 180 years (27:1-4; 35:27-29).

The type-scene of the fateful meeting at a well is also a familiar feature of traditional narrative. At the village well, the most important site for women to meet and socialize, Jacob meets Rachel, the woman destined to be his wife, and the need to water animals provides the occasion for the two to get to know each other. Like Rebekah, Rachel runs and informs Laban, her father, who invites Jacob into the house, and from that point the rest, as they say, is history (29:1-12). A similar pattern can be traced in the encounter of Moses with Zipporah and her father Reuel at a well, an encounter that also ended in marriage (Exod. 2:15b-22). But unlike these cases, and much more in line with the Joseph story, the encounter of Rebekah with Abraham's faithful envoy is suffused with a strong sense of providence and providential guidance, which pervades the Abraham cycle from beginning to end. Abraham is assured of the success of the mission on the basis of his previous experience of contact with his God (Gen. 24:40). In the same trustful spirit, the majordomo prays to Abraham's God, who has guided him thus far and brought him to his destination (24:12-14, 42-44, 52).

In the ancestor stories in general, with their strong paradigmatic sense, character portrayal is much less in evidence than plot. It is generally left to the reader to draw conclusions about what kind of people the characters are from what they do or say and how they interact with each other. Abraham, by now well known to the reader, appears only at the beginning, and Isaac appears at the end. Sarah is by now dead, and

---

2. Hermann Gunkel, *Genesis* (Macon, Ga.: Mercer University Press, 1997), 244. Claus Westermann, *Genesis 12–36* (Minneapolis: Augsburg, 1985), 385, also maintains that a notice about Abraham's death originally followed 24:9.

Hagar and Ishmael are nowhere in sight. The action is dominated by the majordomo, a man of great integrity, long in Abraham's service, faithful and pious. The father of the host family, Bethuel, is mentioned once (v. 50), but it is evident that the name has been added. The first to be informed by Rebekah of the arrival of the envoy are her mother's household and her brother Laban, which would be unusual if Bethuel had been present. Bethuel, moreover, takes no part in the important negotiations connected with the proposal of marriage, which are left to Laban and the mother (vv. 55-60), and they rather than the father are the beneficiaries of the gift giving customary on such an occasion.[3] Bethuel's wife is unnamed but plays a leading role, together with Laban the brother, in the all-important negotiations concerning a marriage in the family, a point also consistent with Babylonian law.[4] In these scenes, Rebekah's brother Laban appears as a rather avaricious and boorish individual. What first catches his attention is the jewelry with which his sister is bedecked, upon which his guest is at once addressed as "blessed of Yahweh" and invited into the house (vv. 29-31). When, a little later, the precious accessories are once more in view, it provokes the pious avowal that "the thing comes from Yahweh" (v. 50). His conduct in his relations with Jacob at a later stage of the story, and later still his treatment at the hands of rabbinic commentators, as we shall see, does nothing to improve our impression of his character.

The narrative line is not without irregularities, difficult transitions, and the usual crop of textual problems. Practically all commentators have noticed repetitions or duplications that have inevitably prompted the hypothesis of a conflation of two parallel versions: there is a father's house (v. 23) and a mother's house (v. 28); Laban runs to the envoy (v. 29b) and then approaches him (v. 30b); Rebekah is released to the envoy twice (vv. 51, 57-58), and she has a nurse (v. 59) and several maids (v. 61), which to some commentators has seemed somewhat *de trop*. To these we add that the central character, Abraham's house steward or majordomo, is referred to as "the servant" at the beginning and end but as "the man" in the middle section, from the appearance of Rebekah to his long statement during the festive meal (vv. 21-33). Rebekah, too, is at first referred to as a woman and a wife (the same word, *ishah,* in Hebrew), but as a girl *(na'arah)* during the

3. The death of the father would have affected the legal status of the daughter with respect to inheritance, ownership of property, and choice in contracting marriage. This explains why her consent was solicited before the departure (vv. 57-58).

4. Similar instances in the Laws of Hammurapi ##178, 179. Further references in John Van Seters, *Abraham in History and Tradition* (New Haven: Yale University Press, 1975), 77.

encounter at the well.[5] But these small-scale irregularities do not call for appeal to large-scale redactional theories; they do not affect the narrative flow, and even if more than one hand has been at work, the result is perfectly coherent and intelligible.[6] We are therefore entitled to read the story of the commission and its outcome as a narrative that not only makes good sense but also is one of the most lively and absorbing in Genesis.

The Commission

We are given no indication where this opening scene (24:1-9) took place, but the most recent notice of Abraham's location placed him at Beersheba after returning from the land of Moriah (22:19). Since Abraham must have died at some point during the expedition, the servant returned to Isaac, his new master, either at Beersheba or at Beer-lahai-roi, where Isaac had settled (24:62; 25:11).[7] Indications of time are also lacking, and we must bear in mind that incidents recorded in the Abraham cycle are not all from the same hand and not always in chronological order. All we can deduce from the account of the commission and expedition to Aram-naharaim is that it occurred after the death of Sarah (24:67; 23:1-2).[8] The envoy chosen

5. Susanne Gillmayr-Bucher, "The Woman of Their Dreams: The Image of Rebekah in Genesis 24," in *The World of Genesis: Persons, Places, Perspectives,* ed. Philip R. Davies and David J. A. Clines (Sheffield: Sheffield Academic Press, 1998), 90-101, has an impressively learned psycholinguistic analysis of the incidence of these terms referring to Rebekah, that is, woman and girl, together with the personal name.

6. On the hypothesis of two recensions, both under the siglum J, see especially Gunkel, *Genesis,* 241-44, and on the view that, in spite of irregularities, the narrative is basically a literary unity see Gerhard von Rad, *Genesis: A Commentary* (London: SCM, 1961 [1956]), 248-49; Westermann, *Genesis 12–26,* 382-84.

7. The problem is the textual uncertainty of 24:62 ("Isaac meanwhile had moved on as far as Beer-lahai-ro'i and was living in the Negev," REB), on which see John Skinner, *A Critical and Exegetical Commentary on Genesis,* 2nd ed. (Edinburgh: T. & T. Clark, 1930), 347-48; Westermann, *Genesis 12–26,* 255. Since Isaac had settled at Beer-lahai-roi (25:11), it seems more likely that he would have come from there and met the caravan on or shortly before its return. This, of course, raises the further problem of the location of "the well of the Living One who provides." It is said to lie between Kadesh and Bered (16:14), but there may be more than one Kadesh, and the location of Bered is a matter of speculation. For the options see Gary A. Herion, "Bered (Place)," in *ABD* 1:676.

8. The ages of the principals according to the schematic chronological system in the Pentateuch, put in place at a late date, cannot easily be reconciled with the narratives into which they have been inserted. In the present instance, the encounter with Rebekah marked

by Abraham, who is anonymous, is referred to throughout as "the servant," or "Abraham's servant," or simply "the man." Following the midrash, some have identified him with Eliezer, heir to Abraham's household (15:2),[9] but this title does not seem to match "senior servant in his household, in charge of all his possessions" (24:2); in other words, household steward or majordomo.

Abraham puts his emissary under an oath of the most solemn and serious kind, the testamentary statement of a dying man. The oath is sworn in the name of Yahweh as "God of heaven and earth," a title unattested prior to the Persian period (sixth to fourth century B.C.).[10] The practice of swearing an oath while touching the genitals of the one administering the oath is attested in biblical texts only here and at Gen. 47:29-31, in which Jacob has his son Joseph take a solemn oath to bury him with his kin in their own burial plot; both cases have to do with fundamental, life-and-death issues in the kinship network. This archaic practice connected with swearing oaths seems to have been widespread; examples have been cited among Egyptian Bedouin, the indigenous peoples of Australia, and the Kaffirs of southern Africa.[11] In this instance, the oath places the majordomo under the obligation of getting Isaac a wife from Abraham's own country and kindred rather than from among the local Canaanite women. The injunction is dictated not by considerations of ritual self-segregation, as in Ezra-Nehemiah, but in accord with endogamous tribal marriage custom. Within the tribal system, the individual household perpetuated itself by importing women, ideally from within the broader kinship network. Hence the popularity of cross-cousin and uncle-niece marriages in ancient Israelite and comparable societies. All three of the great ancestors — Abraham, Isaac,

---

the end of Isaac's mourning his mother's death (24:67), but at her death Abraham was only 137 years old (23:1-2; cf. 17:17) and still had 38 years to live (25:7). He could not then have died shortly after sending his servant on the mission. He would also have been alive for Isaac's marriage, and since Isaac was 40 years old at that point (25:20) and Abraham 140 (21:5), 35 more years of life remained to him.

9. For example, von Rad, *Genesis,* 249.

10. In a letter of Jewish elders to Tattenai, governor of the trans-Euphrates satrapy, cited in the governor's letter to Darius I, the elders claim to be "servants of the God of heaven and earth" (Ezra 5:11). The claim was worded prudentially since this title would also be compatible with the official cult of Ahura Mazda, the Zoroastrian deity. The shorter form "the God of heaven" at Gen. 24:7 is also found only in Second Temple texts (Jonah 1:9; Ezra 1:2 = 2 Chr. 36:23; Neh. 1:4-5; Ps. 136:26; Dan. 2:18-19; etc.).

11. Noted by some of the older commentators, including August Dillmann, *Die Genesis,* 3rd ed. (Leipzig: S. Hirzel, 1892), 301; Skinner, *Genesis,* 341.

and Jacob, together with many others in that kind of society, married either their cousins or their nieces. Such women, who would be responsible for the education of the children, could be presumed to be familiar with the ethos and religious practices of the household in question, but the choice had other advantages. It made it easier to avoid the alienation of the economic assets of the household, especially the plot of land, the patrimonial domain, on which the very existence of the household depended.

It is apparent from the way Abraham's instructions are formulated, and their practically verbatim repetition by the majordomo before the brother and mother of the bride-designate, from whom consent had to be obtained (24:34-49), that they presuppose practically the entire Abraham cycle, probably in a written form. The command to "go to my country and my kindred" reproduces the command made to Abraham long before to "go from your country and kindred" (12:1, 7).[12] The Abrahamic blessing is recalled (12:1-3), and the promise of land for Abraham's offspring is confirmed by oath — a typical Deuteronomic formulation.[13] In his formal address to Rebekah's kin requesting that she be given in marriage to Isaac, the majordomo adds a brief but detailed inventory of Abraham's wealth to be passed on to Isaac: flocks and herds (cf. 12:16; 13:5-6), camels and donkeys (cf. 12:16), silver and gold (cf. 13:2), male and female slaves (cf. 12:5, 16) — to be confirmed and given substance by the valuable gifts soon to be distributed. In all cultures, marriage is associated with wealth and the bestowing and receiving of material goods. We may be confident that the rather detailed account of the negotiations conducted skillfully by the majordomo reflects quite closely the actual experience of making matrimonial alliances in that culture and, with different modalities, in situations quite different from that culture.[14]

This lively novella was introduced toward the end of the formation of the Abraham cycle, therefore at a rather late date in the Second Temple period. It was no doubt added to round off the plot of the Abraham narrative cycle in a more adequate way than the mere inclusion of Rebekah's name in the Aramean genealogy in Gen. 22:20-24.

---

12. We note once again that Abraham's homeland is in the northern, not the southern, reaches of Mesopotamia, in Aram-naharaim, the headwaters of the two rivers.

13. Deut. 1:8; 6:10, 18, 23; 8:1; etc.

14. An example: the inseparability of wealth and marriage in the utterly different world of the minor aristocracy in nineteenth-century England is brilliantly portrayed in Anthony Trollope's *He Knew He Was Right* (1869) and *The Way We Live Now* (1875).

The Encounter at the Well

Like the other journeys in the ancestral narratives, this journey, which must have taken at least a month, is not described at all, and not much is said about the necessary preparations. For a description of biblical journeys we have to go to Josephus. What Josephus tells us is that Abraham's majordomo assembled ten camels, mindful of the need to transport the prospective bride and her maids on the return journey. The gifts customary on such an occasion, and of a quality calculated to impress the bride's family, also had to be assembled, packed, and loaded on the camels. Several assistants, who would also have acted as guards en route, would have been necessary, though their presence only becomes apparent on arrival (24:32, 54, 59). The destination was the city of Nahor in Aram-naharaim in the region of the upper Euphrates. There was a city of that name near the river Habur (*na-hu-ur* in Old Babylonian and Middle Assyrian inscriptions), but a destination more consonant with the envoy's instructions would be Harran, which was in fact the city of Nahor, Abraham's brother, situated in the country of Abraham's kindred (24:4). Eventually the caravan reached its destination, and one evening the leader called a halt outside the city where there was a well, a spring, and a water trough for the animals.

At this point and in this place the encounter occurs between Abraham's majordomo and the young woman destined to be Isaac's wife (24:10-27). One can think of several reasons why Abraham did not send Isaac himself in search of a suitable wife, as Isaac would send Jacob sometime later (28:1-5). The author may have represented Isaac as still in his minority, or in shock, so soon after the close call with the sacrificial knife, notwithstanding the "schematic" age of forty at the time of the marriage (25:20). Or it may be simply that the uncertainty of the outcome counseled an exploratory investigation before proceeding further.

This defining moment in the story of the ancestors is constructed on the grid of a type-scene frequently encountered in folktales: the fateful meeting at a well or spring of water that has unforeseen consequences but will often lead to a good outcome such as liberation from an evil spell, wealth, or marriage.[15] Comparable biblical examples are the encounters

---

15. An example: the Irish folktale "The Well at the World's End"; for one version of this see Stith Thompson, *One Hundred Favorite Folktales* (Bloomington: Indiana University Press, 1975), 237-40. More familiar is the encounter between Jesus and the Samaritan woman at Jacob's well (John 4:5-26). On the sacred character of wells and springs among Semites,

between Jacob and Rachel in the same region (Gen. 29:1-14) and between Moses and Zipporah in Midian (Exod. 2:15b-22). In both, there are a well and flocks to be watered, a task carried out in the one case by Jacob, in the other by Moses. Rachel reports the encounter to her father Laban; the seven daughters of the Midianite priest likewise report to their father Reuel; both parties then offer hospitality to the guests. And, of course, both encounters end in marriage.[16] In our version the majordomo, having arrived at the moment of decision, prays, and in praying addresses his prayer to the God of Abraham as if praying on behalf of Abraham, perhaps no longer alive. The prayer ends with a request for a sign, a good omen, but one that is almost a wager as to whether Abraham's God will continue to be faithful to his servant and constant interlocutor one more time.

As worded, the proposal sounds very risky. The young woman whom he approaches must not only give the required answer to his request for a drink but also offer to water the camels. The majordomo, gazing with anxious, silent anticipation at the young woman, waits until the camels have drunk their fill and the sign has been fully played out. The request is answered instantaneously. It is noteworthy that wherever Rebekah's name occurs it is followed first by her descent from Milcah wife of Nahor, her grandparents, then from her parents: Bethuel, probably deceased, and an unnamed mother who plays an important part in the proceedings. This is understandable since, from Abraham's point of view, her family history is all-important, indeed, the point of the expedition. Once the prayer has been answered and the outcome is certain, gifts follow, but not yet the bride-price *(mohar),* which will be paid to the bride's family. The gift of a gold nose ring and gold bracelets was more than a generous tip for services graciously rendered, or a hint to the family of an advantageous match in prospect, though it was that also. It was in the first place the majordomo's way of designating Rebekah as the object of the mission, which he now knows will have a successful outcome. Relieved, he offers a prayer of thanksgiving.

---

see W. Robertson Smith, *The Religion of the Semites: The Fundamental Institutions,* 2nd ed. (New York: Schocken Books, 1972 [1894]), 165-85.

16. See the interesting paper of Susanne Bucher-Gillmayr, "Begegnungen am Brunnen," *BN* 75 (1994): 48-66.

The Majordomo Meets the Family

At this point, inevitably, the family appears on the scene (Gen. 24:28-60). The majordomo was so sure of the outcome of his bargain with Abraham's God that he identified the girl as the bride-to-be and gave her expensive gifts before asking her who she was. She told him, and then ran off to tell her mother's household what had happened. This mother's household *(bet 'immah)* is not the alternative to the paternal household *(bet 'av)*, the basic unit of a patrilineal society. In most cases the designation "mother's household" simply indicates the separate living quarters of the unmarried females of the household and, as in this case, its widowed matriarch.[17] The author, more familiar with an urban setting, was no doubt thinking of real buildings rather than tents, like the tent shared by Abraham and Sarah (18:6, 9-10), or Isaac's (deceased) mother's tent into which he brought his bride (24:67), or the situation in the next generation when Jacob, Leah, Rachel, and their maids Bilhah and Zilpah all had their own tents (31:33-35). Having set eyes on the jewelry Rebekah was wearing, Laban foresaw the likelihood of a more prosperous future, and was therefore motivated to extend hospitality, if possible to vie with that of Abraham (18:1-8). Laban will be married with male and female children by the time Jacob has to put up with him (28:2; 31:1; etc.), but if he was unmarried at the time of the majordomo's visit, which seems to be the case, gifts from a wealthy relative, in addition to the bride-price, may have created the only possibility for him to marry, a situation often confronting the unmarried brother of a nubile sister.

Conscious of the importance of the official request for the hand of the woman made by Isaac's surrogate, the author has presented it in full (24:34-49). After introducing himself (v. 34), Abraham's emissary itemizes Abraham's assets, in a list that draws on the entire Abraham cycle. The intent is, of course, to convince Rebekah's relatives that she — and they — are in no danger of ending up destitute. This inventory is rounded off with the information that Abraham has already deeded all of it to Isaac, reproducing

17. Allusions to the mother's house in Canticles (3:4; 8:2) are not of much help on account of the highly sophisticated and recherché language in which relationships are expressed (e.g., lover as brother). In the book of Ruth (1:8), Naomi tells her daughters-in-law to return each to her mother's house, that is, the family of origin where, as widows, they would share the women's quarters. A somewhat different interpretation is in Carol Meyers, "To Her Mother's House: Considering a Counterpart to the Israelite *Bêt 'āb*," in *The Bible and the Politics of Exegesis: Essays in Honor of Norman K. Gottwald on His Sixty-fifth Birthday*, ed. David Jobling et al. (Cleveland: Pilgrim Press, 1991), 39-51, 304-7.

almost verbatim the statement to that effect in the Keturah genealogy. He then repeats, again almost verbatim, his commission from the *paterfamilias* with a view to establishing his authorization for presenting the request (vv. 37-41).[18] There follows a detailed account of how he discharged his commission (vv. 42-47), ending with a prayer of thanksgiving to the God of Abraham (v. 48). All this leads up to the formal request for a positive or negative answer, introduced by the forceful little particle *we'attah* ("and now . . ."), used to indicate that preliminaries are now over and it is time to get down to business: "And now, tell me if you mean to deal in integrity and truth with my master; and if not, tell me so that I may turn to the right or the left" (v. 49).[19] Laban's reply, redolent of pious-sounding and self-interested religiosity, accepts the offer of marriage on behalf of his sister, who will be consulted only at the end of the proceedings, after gifts indicative of the betrothal as a fait accompli have been handed over, and the celebratory meal eaten. We see how, in that kind of society, marriage was too important a transaction to be left to the two individuals most directly concerned. The majordomo was anxious to start out at once, no doubt to find out whether his master was still alive. So, at the very end of a crowded two-day visit, Rebekah's consent, probably required in the absence of the father, is asked for and given. The blessing pronounced on Rebekah, presumably by her mother and brother, is of a familiar kind, often attested.[20] It was rhythmic, and was probably sung or chanted repeatedly with an instrumental accompaniment:

"You are our sister!
May your children be countless in number,[21]
May your offspring possess the gates of your foes!"

The presence of Rebekah's nurse need not be queried. Rebekah, almost certainly in her teens, would have been accompanied by and perhaps in-

---

18. One addition: he borrows from 17:1 the description of Abraham's God as the God "in whose presence I walk" (*'ăšer-hithallaktî lĕpānâw*).

19. Following REB, the expression about turning to the right and the left means simply looking elsewhere. The expression has been retained to show how Laban imitates this contrasting form of speech by declining to say anything either good or bad in reply (v. 50).

20. Ruth 4:14-15; Tob. 7:12-13; 10:11. The form is comparable to the oracles of Jacob (Gen. 49:1-27).

21. Literally "thousands of myriads"; *rĕvāvâ* (myriad) perhaps chosen for assonance with *rivkâ* (Rebekah).

separable from her nurse from infancy. This nurse may be the Deborah who died and was mourned on a later journey (Gen. 35:8). As the Hebrew word for "nurse" (*meneqet*, from the verbal stem *ynq*, "suck") suggests, she would be needed to serve as wet nurse in the event of the marriage producing children. At any rate, Rebekah, the majordomo, and their attendants, cheered by this send-off, mounted their camels and left.

The Return

Like the journey out and all the other journeys in the cycle, the return journey (24:61-67) is passed over in silence. Its destination was the same general area, if not the same precise point, from which the majordomo departed, but now that Abraham was dead, his servant had a new master, and perhaps therefore a new location. In the meantime, in fact, Isaac had moved from a place unnamed to the vicinity of Beer-lahai-roi and was living in the Negev. At this point (24:62) the text is obscure, but in view of what we will soon be told, that after Abraham's death Isaac settled in Beer-lahai-roi (25:11), it seems likely that this was the destination to which the caravan returned and at which the meeting between Isaac and Rebekah occurred.[22] Beer-lahai-roi was the sanctuary near the sacred well at which Hagar, pregnant with Ishmael, encountered the deity who sees and provides for those in need (16:13-14). We have seen that Abraham moved from his place at Mamre-Hebron into the Negev, eventually settling at Beersheba, to which he returned after the sacrifice in the land of Moriah (21:22-24; 22:19). Some locations mentioned throughout the Abraham cycle, especially those in southern Palestine and the Sinai, are practically impossible to identify with any assurance, and there is an as-yet-unexplained connection between Beersheba and Beer-lahai-roi discussed at an earlier point.

Further problems await us in the description of the first encounter between Rebekah and Isaac. We are told that Isaac went out in the evening into the open country, but the purpose of his excursion is unclear on account of the verb employed at this point, which occurs nowhere

---

22. The MT of 24:62, *bā' mibbô' bĕ'ēr-laḥaî-rō'î*, cannot be construed to give a satisfactory meaning as it stands. LXX read the first two words as *bammidbār* (*dia tēs erēmou*, "across the desert"), likewise the Samaritan Pentateuch. Jerome's Vulgate has Isaac walking "on the way that leads to the well of the Living One who sees" (*Viventis et Videntis*), which is Beer-lahai-roi.

else in the Hebrew Bible, and the meaning of which is unknown.[23] In view of Rebekah's question addressed to the majordomo about the identity of the man "walking in the open country to meet us" (24:65), the meaning "to walk" may be the best guess, and the walking may have been in expectation or in hope of Rebekah's arrival. It is a fine point of narrative art that Isaac and Rebekah both look up and see each other for the first time simultaneously. On seeing the man approaching, Rebekah dismounted,[24] and when she was told that the man was Isaac, her destined husband, she took her veil and covered herself. Here, too, there is something to disambiguate. It is generally assumed that she covered her face with a veil, on the grounds that this was considered mandatory for a woman prior to her marriage. But the only other occurrence of the word *saʿif*, usually translated "veil," refers to the covering used by Tamar, daughter-in-law of Judah, to cover her person and disguise herself when posing as a prostitute; in other words, a kind of burka (Gen. 38:14, 19). At this stage, the narrator finishes his story with a few rapid strokes, making no mention of the presumed death of Abraham. The majordomo makes his report to his new master, Isaac escorts Rebekah into her tent,[25] she becomes his wife, and his love for her comforts him for the death of his mother.

Filling In the Gaps

Even a fairly rapid and unsystematic search through the corpus of Jewish midrash on this biblical text will demonstrate the capacity of a good story to generate more narrative. Early Christian interpretation, most of it in the genre of the homily, is of a different kind, for the most part moralistic and allegorical: the well is the fountain of wisdom or a symbol of baptism; the gold earrings are the divine words of Scripture, the bracelets are good works; and Isaac and Rebekah foreshadow the union between

---

23. NRSV and JPS translate *lāśûaḥ* "to walk"; REB has "hoping to meet them"; LXX "to have a chat" *(adoleschēsai),* no doubt with *lāśîaḥ,* "to converse," in mind; Vulgate "to meditate" *(meditare),* and Syriac "to walk," probably with the similar-sounding verb *lāśûṭ* in mind.

24. MT 24:64, "she fell off the camel," is unlikely; read *watēpen,* "she slipped off," "turned to dismount."

25. MT adds *śārâ ʾimmô,* "the tent of Sarah his mother," an addition by a glossator with the purpose of clarifying the feminine suffix in *hāʾōhĕlāh* ("her tent").

Christ and the church.[26] What caught the attention of Jewish interpreters in Abraham's commissioning of the servant, identified as Eliezer,[27] was the absolute exclusion of marriage with Canaanite women. Prohibitions of intermarriage may entail ritual self-segregation, as in Ezra-Nehemiah and *Jubilees*,[28] or the exclusion of unacceptable foreign cults, as in the prohibition in Deuteronomy (7:3-4). Abraham's commission confided to his majordomo does not necessarily exclude such considerations, but read in context, it can be understood more readily in terms of the well-attested practice of endogamous marriage in a tribal setting. The language in which Abraham's command is couched is deliberately reminiscent of the original command to "go from your country and kin" (Gen. 12:1) to found a new lineage in another country. Isaac will address the same injunction to Jacob as Abraham to the servant, but in more specific terms: Jacob is to marry a daughter of Laban his uncle, a typical example of uncle-niece marriage within a tribal endogamous system (28:1-5). Then, after twenty years in Mesopotamia, Jacob will be told in a dream to return to the land of his own kin, traversing the same route as the servant but in the opposite direction (31:13). This strong and anxious need to maintain solidarity within lineages is a feature of much literature inspired by the ancestral narratives; for example, in Tobit's deathbed injunction to Tobias to marry within his own kin (Tob. 4:12-13), or in the admonition of the dying Job to his sons to avoid marriage with strangers in the *Testament of Job* (45:3).

The first of several "improvements" of Josephus, in his presentation of the episode to a public unfamiliar with Jewish customs (*Ant.* 1.242-255), is his explanation that the placing of the hand under the thigh as a way of sealing an agreement is an act performed by both parties. He fills out the journey to Harran, limited to one verse in Genesis, with an account of the difficulties of travel in Mesopotamia — mud in the winter, drought in the summer, and brigands all year round. Perhaps dissatisfied with the explanation of how Rebekah was recognized as the chosen one, Josephus has the servant address the request for a drink of water to the girls in general, who rudely repulse him. Then one of them, who turns out to be Rebekah, rebukes her companions, offers him a drink, and waters the camels (1.246-

---

26. A selection of these texts in Mark Sheridan, *Ancient Christian Commentary on Scripture: Old Testament II; Genesis 12–50* (Downers Grove, Ill.: InterVarsity, 2002), 120-38; Theresia Heither, O.S.B., and Christiana Reemts, O.S.B., *Biblische Gestalten bei den Kirchenvätern. Abraham* (Münster: Aschendorff, 2005), 177-78.

27. *Gen. Rab.* 59:10; *Pirqe R. El.* 16.

28. *Jub.* 20:4; 22:20; 25:1; 30:7-17.

247). He ends with an original and down-to-earth touch in explaining that Isaac was able to marry Rebekah since he had inherited his father's estate after the other sons had left to found colonies out east, borrowing this idea from Gen. 25:6.

A much more baroque and, frankly, more interesting and even amusing account can be put together from different rabbinic sources. The men accompanying Abraham's majordomo are mentioned only incidentally (Gen. 24:32), but in one retelling of the episode the ten camels imply ten men, the number required for a *minyan* (quorum) for the nuptial blessing to follow (*Pirqe R. El.* 16). Since they are said to have arrived in the evening (Gen. 24:11), it must have been the evening of the day of departure, hence the outbound journey lasted only a few hours. This was due to a miraculous and convenient phenomenon known as "the shrinking of the way" *(qefisat hadderek),* by which the road kept coming toward them as they progressed further.[29] For the same reason, the return journey lasted only three hours, from midday to 3 P.M., and they arrived just in time for the *minhah* prayer.[30] There follows the encounter with the uncooperative women at the well, similar to, and perhaps the origin of, the account in Josephus, then the recognition scene, following which Rebekah runs and tells her family.

With the appearance of the family on the scene, things begin to turn nasty very quickly. On seeing the expensive jewelry bestowed on Rebekah, Laban decides to kill Eliezer in order to possess his wealth. He is prevented by miraculous means from doing so, but, nothing daunted, he places poisoned food before the guest at the feast that follows. Unfortunately for his plan, the food is placed by mistake before his father Bethuel. Bethuel eats it and dies on the spot. By this original means the absence, or at least inactivity, of the bride's father is conveniently accounted for.

The midrashic version continues in the same vein. After the celebratory meal, the servant makes his formal request for the hand of Rebekah on behalf of Abraham and Isaac. After he insists on departing as soon as possible, Rebekah agrees to go with him, and her mother and brother pronounce the blessing upon her. Both being impious, however, their blessing is disingenuous, more a curse than a blessing, which is responsible for Rebekah's initial infertility.[31] The return journey is passed over in silence, but

---

29. *Gen. Rab.* 59:11; *b. Sanh.* 95a.
30. *Tg. Yer.* on Gen. 24:61; *Pirqe R. El.* 16.
31. *Gen. Rab.* 59:11-60:13; *Pirqe R. El.* 16; *Ag. Ber.* 45.

the circumstances accompanying it seem nevertheless to have inspired the similar situation of Tobias's quest for the hand of Sarah. In Tobit chapter 10 Tobias, after fourteen days of celebration, insists on leaving since he fears that his father and mother may die before his return. There is an exchange of gifts, but in the opposite direction from the Genesis narrative: Tobias's father-in-law Raguel gives Tobias and Sarah half of his property in the same currency as Abraham's wealth: male and female slaves, oxen, sheep, donkeys and camels, clothing, silver and gold. Raguel and his wife Edna pronounce the wedding blessing, and Tobias ends with praising God that his journey, accompanied by an angel (Raphael), has been successfully completed.

There is a near consensus among rabbinic commentators that what Isaac was doing out in the open country as the caravan was arriving from Harran was praying or meditating.[32] Refusing to have recourse to emendation, one midrashist maintained that Rebekah did indeed fall off her camel and sustained an injury, as may easily happen falling off a camel, after receiving a premonitory revelation from the Holy Spirit that she was destined to be the mother of the impious Esau.[33] All ended well, notwithstanding, especially for Isaac and Rebekah, who loved each other, but also for Abraham's servant, who was given his freedom.[34]

---

32. *b. Ber.* 26b; *b. Avod. Zar.* 7b; *b. Pes.* 88a.

33. On this midrash see Louis Ginzberg, *The Legends of the Jews,* vol. 1 (Philadelphia: Jewish Publication Society of America, 1961), 297; vol. 5 (Philadelphia: Jewish Publication Society of America, 1955), 263 n. 301.

34. *Gen. Rab.* 60:7.

Descent from Abraham in Early Christianity and What It Might Mean for the Christian Today

1

Abraham comes to us as a link in a genealogical chain, as part of the ethnogenesis of a particular people among whom the first traditions about him were either created or transmitted and transcribed. It is understandable that, as adherents of the first of the three Abrahamic religions, Jewish believers would be the first to rightfully claim descent from Abraham. However, in this epilogue to our discursive commentary on the life of Abraham, I do not intend to enter into the conversation on interfaith issues on which so much has been, and continues to be, written. Beginning with the figure of Abraham as presented in the earliest Christian texts, and writing explicitly as a Christian devotee of Abraham, I aim rather to reflect, in a quite preliminary and exploratory way, on what the figure of Abraham might mean for the Christian today.[1]

Pride in descent, and especially descent from Abraham, was a common feature of Jewish self-identity throughout the period of the Second Temple.[2] After the extinction of the Judean state followed by the deportations, genealogical continuity could no longer be taken for granted, and from that time onward the ability to produce written proof of descent became a major issue, especially for persons in the public view. A case in

---

1. In doing so I am reacting to the salutary warning of Jon D. Levenson about the ambiguous use of the designation "Abrahamic religion," which tends to underestimate the different ways in which the figure of Abraham functions in Judaism, Christianity, and Islam. See his *Inheriting Abraham: The Legacy of the Patriarch in Judaism, Christianity, and Islam* (Princeton and Oxford: Princeton University Press, 2012).

2. For example, *Pss. Sol.* 9:9-10; 18:3; 3 Macc. 6:3; Josephus, *Vita* 1-6.

point is the status of those priests who, after their return from the Babylonian diaspora, were excluded from ministry in the temple still to be rebuilt on account of their failure to verify their Israelite descent.[3] Something similar is apparent in early Christianity. Since descent from Abraham implies, in the first place, genealogy, the detailed genealogy of Jesus in the first and third Gospels (Matt. 1:1-17; Luke 3:23-38) would be one of the clearest indications of this tendency. To be a member of the people of Israel is, by definition, to be a descendant of Abraham, and both genealogies make it clear that Jesus satisfied this requirement, even though Luke's version begins not with Abraham but with Adam. Moreover, the emphasis in both genealogies falls more on descent from David than descent from Abraham. Matthew's version is introduced as "the book of the genealogy *(biblos geneseōs)* of Jesus Messiah (i.e., anointed king), son of David, son of Abraham" (Matt. 1:1), and both lists incorporate the shorter Davidic genealogy appended to the book of Ruth, who was an ancestress of David.[4] These genealogies probably originated in those early Christian circles that retained in their religious practices and general orientation a more distinctively Jewish identity. James, brother of Jesus, put to death by the Sanhedrin at the instigation of the high priest Ananus in A.D. 62, was a leading figure in these circles.[5] There are also the *desposynoi,* followers of Jesus the Lord *(despotēs),* who, Eusebius or his source informs us, carefully preserved genealogical records (*Historia ecclesiastica* 1.7.14). Some of these may have been among those who claimed descent from David rather than Abraham and were rounded up and executed by Vespasian after the suppression of the Jewish revolt (*Historia ecclesiastica* 3.12).

From the beginning, this claim of Abrahamic descent had the potential for both expansion and contraction. As a descendant of Noah and his son Shem, Abraham was designated as the agent of a new initiative of God

---

3. Ezra 2:61-63 = Neh. 7:63-65. See also on the importance of genealogical verification, *m. Qidd.* 4:1; *b. Qidd.* 69b. Of interest in this regard is the anxiety of members of the Qumran Damascus sect to establish religious affiliation with the first to return from exile, the *rishonim*, "pioneers," or *shavim*, "returnees," also "penitents" (CD I, 3-11; VI, 2–VII, 6; cf. also 4Q390, frag. 1:4-10).

4. The Matthean genealogy is divided into three sections, each comprising fourteen generations. By gematria, fourteen corresponds to the letters daleth (fourth), vav (sixth), daleth (fourth), hence to the three consonants of the name David (דוד). Davidic descent is therefore encrypted in the genealogy. On the genealogies in the Gospels, see Marshall D. Johnson, *The Purpose of the Biblical Genealogies with Special Reference to the Setting of the Genealogies of Jesus,* 2nd ed. (Oxford: Oxford University Press, 1988).

5. Josephus, *Ant.* 20.200; Eusebius, *Historia ecclesiastica* 2.23.11-25.

on behalf of the damaged postdisaster world, a point emphasized in the commentary. He is proclaimed right from the beginning as the ancestor of many nations (Gen. 17:4, 6) and the one destined to bring blessing to all peoples (12:1-3). In the opposite direction, the claim of descent from Abraham was not immune from challenge from within the Jewish people. Those who had escaped deportation argued that they had inherited the Abrahamic promise of territory to the exclusion of the deportees (Ezek. 11:14-16; 33:23-29). A different and more radical kind of contraction is represented by the self-segregating *bene haggolah* (the diaspora group) associated with Ezra (Ezra 4:1-3; 9:1-4), of diasporic origin. Then, much later, there was the Damascus sect whose writings came to light in the Cairo Geniza fragments and the Qumran texts. According to the discourse prefatory to the laws of this sect, Abraham, Isaac, and Jacob are presented as free from the moral corruption of the Watchers and the Sons of Noah. But beginning with Jacob's sons and the "out of Egypt" generation, religious infidelity set in. This led to the failure of that generation, including Moses, to enter the land and, eventually, to the disaster of the destruction of Jerusalem and its temple. It was then, at that defining point in the providential history recorded in the biblical texts, that God established his covenant with the faithful remnant that returned from exile, the "penitents of Israel" *(shave yisra'el).*[6] For the Damascus sectarians, these pioneers, the first to return, were the founders of their group and the only ones left who could claim to be in the authentic line of descent from Abraham.[7]

The redefinition of descent from Abraham implied in the *Damascus Document* would be of obvious interest to those scholars of early Christianity who detect points of contact between Qumran sectarianism and the beginnings of the Jesus movement, but for anyone interested in Christian origins it invites comparison with the ways in which the issue of the identity of Abraham's children was posed and answered in those first Christian communities. The Gospels according to Matthew and Luke are prefaced

6. Use of the verb *shuv* permitted the double meaning of "penitents" and "those who returned (from exile)."

7. CD I, 3-11; II, 14–III, 20. Philip R. Davies, *The Damascus Document,* JSOTSup 25 (Sheffield: JSOT, 1983); Joseph Blenkinsopp, *Judaism: The First Phase; The Place of Ezra and Nehemiah in the Origins of Judaism* (Grand Rapids: Eerdmans, 2009), 219-22, 225-27. George J. Brooke, *The Dead Sea Scrolls and the New Testament* (Minneapolis: Fortress, 2005), 184, suggests that the fragmentary narrative of Gen. 12–15 in 4Q252 (4Q Commentary on Genesis A) made a similar point, namely, that not all who claim physical descent from Abraham are heirs to the promise made to him.

by genealogies, but they also share the belief that Mary conceived Jesus without the cooperation of her husband Joseph. According to both Evangelists, this came about by the mysterious action of the Holy Spirit (cf. Matt. 1:18-21), and Luke reminds his readers that Joseph was only the putative father of Jesus (Luke 3:23). Belief in the miraculous conception of Jesus emerged with the growing sense that the unique relationship of Jesus to God, acknowledged fully after his resurrection, must have been there from the beginning of his existence. This belief is not in evidence a few decades earlier in the writings of Paul, who, at the beginning of his letter to the Romans, as much a treatise as a letter, announces that the theme of his gospel is God's Son descended from David according to the flesh, that is, on the human level, but proclaimed Son of God by an act of divine power through which he was raised from the dead (Rom. 1:4). But the virgin birth is assumed in the two infancy Gospels, as we have seen, as also in some of the earliest noncanonical Christian writings, conspicuously the letters of Ignatius from the early second century.[8] The emergence of this belief, rejected by Judeo-Christian groups like the Ebionites, would inevitably relativize genealogical descent from Abraham, and this relativization can be seen as a significant aspect of the "parting of the ways" between the early Christian movement and its parent body.

Descent from Abraham is radically relativized, or at least left open for redefinition, in the saying of John the Baptist recorded in the same two Gospels, addressed in Matthew to Pharisees and Sadducees (Matt. 3:9), and in Luke to the crowds who came to be baptized by John (Luke 3:8): "Do not presume to say to yourselves, 'We have Abraham as our father'; I tell you, God is able from these stones to raise up children to Abraham."[9] This disavowal is not unlike the claim made in the Admonition of the *Damascus Document,* with the difference that it expresses a broader and more radical sense of the sovereign will of God with respect to ethnic ties, descent rules, and human conventions in general. It is particularly significant in view of the close relations between John and Jesus. Jesus was baptized by John (Matt. 3:13-17); in one version Jesus recruited his first disciples from among John's disciples (John 1:35-42); he began his public ministry after John was arrested and removed from the scene (Matt. 4:10); after

---

8. *To the Ephesians* 7.2; 18.2; 20.2; *To the Smyrnaeans* 1.1-2.

9. The saying reveals an elegant little pun when retro-translated into Hebrew, perhaps the original language of Matthew's Gospel: *bānîm,* "children, sons," *'ăbānîm,* "stones"; perhaps also *'āb-bānîm,* "father-sons."

the execution of the Baptist, he was regarded as a reincarnation of John or John *redivivus;* and only after that point did he begin to speak of his own impending death (Matt. 14:1-12; 16:21-23).

This programmatic statement of John the Baptist is, moreover, consistent with the marked tendency of the teaching of Jesus to challenge privileged social status based on lineage, ethnicity, or wealth. Examples are not lacking. The healing of a Roman centurion in Capernaum (Matt. 8:5-13; also Luke 7:1-10), or perhaps Cana (John 4:46-53), provided the occasion for the statement of Jesus that "many will come from east and west and be invited in the end-time to the banquet[10] with Abraham, Isaac, and Jacob in the kingdom of heaven, while those who had first claim on the kingdom ('the sons of the kingdom') will be ejected into the darkness outside where there will be weeping and grinding of teeth." Those who come from afar are Gentiles who make no claim to descent from Abraham, and yet may have a share in the life to come presented in the prophetic figure of the eschatological banquet presided over by Abraham (e.g., Isa. 25:6-8). A similar conclusion is drawn in Luke 13:22-30 in answer to the question addressed to Jesus whether only few will be saved. In this instance the contrast is between those who claim privilege on the basis of having heard Jesus' teaching, or even having shared a meal with him, and those who come from all points of the compass looking for salvation, who will be invited to the banquet with Abraham and the other ancestors. Even more extreme is the contrast between the fate of the conspicuously wealthy man and Lazarus, the sick and destitute beggar lying at his gate (Luke 16:19-23). The poor man died and was carried away by angels to be with Abraham.[11] The rich man also died, was buried, and was consigned to the torments of hades. His conversation with Abraham across a great abyss typifies the inefficacy of the genealogical bond to which he could have laid claim, for even in hades he addresses Abraham as "father" and Abraham addresses him as "son" (Luke 16:24-25). The chilling feature of this little parable is that the wealthy individual did not have to do anything to end up in hades except dress in grand style, eat expensively, and enjoy the good life while ignoring the presence of one sick and destitute person. These and other

---

10. The more common translation "recline" (verb *anaklinō*) is meant to represent the posture adopted at banquets in Greek and Roman antiquity.

11. Literally, "he was carried away by angels into Abraham's bosom" *(eis ton kolpon Abraam)*. Here, too, the image is of the banquet where guests reclined and a favored guest, or the guest of honor, would recline in close proximity to the host; compare John 13:23, the Beloved Disciple at the Last Supper.

paradigmatic stories (parables) in the Gospels instruct us as to what it means to be a true descendant of Abraham.

The disjuncture between discipleship of Jesus and the claim to salvation through membership by descent in the household of Abraham is starkly in evidence in the dispute recorded in the Fourth Gospel between Jesus and some of his contemporaries who, after joining the ranks of his disciples, had turned against him (John 8:31-59). To their claim to be Abraham's children, Jesus replied that the claim is negated by their failure to imitate Abraham's conduct and to discern the divine source of the message now proclaimed by Jesus. The dispute becomes even more acrimonious when Jesus accuses them of planning to kill him and they repeat their claim that Abraham is their father while insinuating that Jesus himself is illegitimate. This counteraccusation elicits the shocking response from Jesus that, far from being children of Abraham, their descent is from the devil, a murderer and liar from the beginning. The allusion seems to be to the midrash on Gen. 4:1 ("The man knew Eve his wife"), according to which what the man (Adam) knew was that his wife had been seduced by Satan, in the guise of the serpent, who was therefore the father of Cain, her first son, murderer of his brother.[12] The passage seems to reflect controversy between the Johannine community and a community of Judeo-Christians who were attempting, or had attempted in the past, to reconcile their own ideas of Christian discipleship with a strong conviction of the religious efficacy of descent from Abraham.

2

At an earlier stage in the evolving self-understanding of Christian communities, Paul set about redefining descent from Abraham in light of the life, death, and resurrection of Jesus, and he did so while affirming and even boasting about his own Abrahamic descent: "Are they descendants of Abraham? So am I!"[13] He sets out his argument in the first chapters of the Epistle to the Romans, which is as much a treatise as an epistle. The first stage is to establish the universality of sin understood as alienation from God, in order to explain the universal need for *dikaiosunē*,

---

12. *Tg. Ps.-J.* on Gen. 4:1; *Pirqe R. El.* 21. Cf. 1 John 3:11-12.

13. 2 Cor. 11:22; Rom. 11:1. In one of his discourses in Acts of the Apostles, Paul addresses his Jewish audience as descendants of Abraham (Acts 13:26).

usually translated "justification" but more appropriately, in this context, "acceptance by God" (1:18–3:20).[14] Since he is writing to Jewish communities in Rome, he divides humanity according to the familiar classification of Jew and Gentile, or Jew and Greek, or circumcised and uncircumcised, or those under a written law over against those subject to the law of nature.[15] The conclusion is clear and categoric: "There is no distinction. . . . Do you suppose that God is the God of the Jews alone? Is he not the God of Gentiles also? Certainly, of Gentiles also" (3:22-29). Here especially Paul is most faithfully Abrahamic in the scope of his language about the God who had revealed himself to him as he had in times past to Abraham.

The key text for Paul, which he cites in the Septuagint translation at Rom. 4:3 and Gal. 3:6, is Gen. 15:6: "Abram believed God, and he reckoned it to him as righteousness." To be righteous for Paul is to be acceptable to God, and this came about for Abraham, and comes about for the children of Abraham, by faith and trust in God. This affirmation is confirmed by the kind of exegetical argument familiar from the Jewish midrashic tradition. It was Abraham's faith and trust in God that brought him acceptance *(dikaiosunē)* while still uncircumcised, in fact fourteen years prior to his self-circumcision (Gen. 16:5; 17:24).[16] This chronological argument is extended further in writing to the Galatian Christians who were under pressure to practice major aspects of the Jewish law including circumcision. In writing an at-times-angry letter to them, Paul argues that once a will has been ratified it cannot be annulled or modified; hence the law given at Sinai does not annul the promissory covenant given to Abraham on behalf of his descendants 430 years earlier. Abraham was therefore rendered ac-

---

14. "All alike have sinned and are deprived of the divine glory" (Rom. 3:23). "Justification" allows for too much ambiguity; we are not usually at our best in justifying ourselves. It also puts too much emphasis on the legal field of discourse and metaphor. In the tightly worded conclusion to the argument in Rom. 3:21-26, in which the ambivalent term *dikaiosunē* occurs four times, language associated with sacrifice is more in evidence than forensic terminology: *apolutrōsis, hilastērion, en tō autou haimati* ("redemption, propitiation, in his own blood").

15. Rom. 1:27, 33; 2:9-10, 12-16, 17-18, 25-29; 3:19-20, 27-31.

16. The key text, Gen. 15:6, reads "He believed the LORD; and the LORD reckoned it to him as righteousness" (NRSV) or "Abram put his faith in the Lord, who reckoned it to him as righteousness" (REB). At that time Abraham's "schematic" age was 85 (Gen. 16:3, 16), 14 years prior to his self-circumcision (Gen. 17:24). *A fortiori*, Abraham achieved acceptance by God 400 years (Gen. 15:13; cf. Acts 7:6), or 430 years (Gal. 3:17), before the giving of the Law (Gal. 3:15-18).

ceptable to God ("justified") by faith in God's word and not by observance of a law that at that time did not exist (Gal. 3:15-22).[17]

Abrahamic inclusivity is stated by Paul in a more comprehensive, irenical, and radical way in writing to the Galatian Christians (Gal. 3:28-29): "There is no longer Jew and Greek, there is no longer slave and free, there is no longer male and female, for you are all one in Christ Jesus. So if you belong to Christ you are Abraham's issue, heirs by virtue of the promise." From Paul's perspective, these are the most fundamental divisions of humanity: the order of divine providence in history (Jew, Greek), the order of custom and convention in a sinful world (slave, free), and the order of nature (male, female). On principle, therefore, viewed from the perspective of the universality of a sinful condition and the possibility of becoming acceptable to God through faith in Jesus Christ, even these basic divisions can be overcome.

We can therefore take away from our reading of these major Pauline texts two interpretations of the life story of Abraham. The first takes serious account of the context of that story in the damaged and still sinful world inhabited by those that survived the near extinction of the deluge and their descendants, the universality of the need for a new initiative from God and the extension of that initiative, of which Abraham is to be the agent, to "all the families of the earth" (Gen. 12:3). This is the point Paul stresses at the beginning of Romans: the universality of sin and therefore of need (Rom. 1:18–3:20). The second is the conviction that Jesus represents a new initiative of God calling for a response in faith similar to Abraham's prompt obedience to the voice that sent him on a long journey of faith. The connection with Abraham is apparent, since it is the same God as the God who summoned Abraham who has now, at this later juncture of providential history, given glory and the highest honor to his servant Jesus by raising him from the dead (Acts 3:13). This is the point at which, in spite of so much held in common with his Jewish and Islamic interlocutors, the

---

17. The 430 years is the time Israel spent in Egypt (Exod. 12:40), with the alternative duration of 400 years in Genesis, repeated in Stephen's discourse (Gen. 15:13; Acts 7:6). Paul's exegesis contains two peculiarities. He uses the term *diathēkē* to stand for a covenant in the biblical sense and a last will and testament; Jesus is identified as Abraham's offspring at the cost of ignoring the collective meaning of *zera'* ("offspring," literally: seed). It is tempting to think that the rabbinic tradition, that Abraham fulfilled all the prescriptions of the law in advance of its promulgation, an argument based on Gen. 26:5 ("Abraham kept my charge, my commandments, statutes and laws"), may have been in response to Paul's argument (*m. Qidd.* 4:14; *m. Ned.* 3:11).

Christian interpretation of Abraham in the context of a providential history must go its own way.

3

The same issues are discussed eloquently and without polemic by the author of the Epistle to the Hebrews, which begins with a statement about initiatives of God throughout history to the present (Heb. 1:1-2): "Long ago God spoke to our ancestors in many and various ways by the prophets; but in these last days he has spoken to us by a Son whom he appointed heir of all things." All these divine interventions or initiatives are for the benefit of the children of Abraham (2:16). Toward the end of the epistle, the anonymous author gives greater depth and scope to the concept of faith *(pistis)* by linking it with hope, the virtue or quality that enables us to go on living and facing the many unknowns of our lives and of the future with a trustful attitude. The author defines faith as "the assurance of things hoped for, the conviction of things not seen" (11:1 NRSV) or, less literally, "that which gives substance to our hopes and convinces us of realities we do not see" (REB). Of this trustful acceptance of a future guaranteed only by a voice heard for the first time, Abraham also is the leading example. The author presents a summary of biblical history marked by the faith of chosen individuals at important turning points, a faith that underpins the hope that kept their relationship to God alive, as it does with us. We hear how Abraham, in faith, set out on a long journey to an unknown destination, without question and without hesitation — unlike Moses, who, when given the charge to lead his people out of slavery in Egypt to freedom in the Promised Land, made one objection after another until God lost patience with him: I am just too insignificant; maybe they won't believe me, and, in any case, I don't even know your name; I am not good at public speaking, so please send someone else on this mission (Exod. 3:7–4:17). Abraham heard the voice, which must have had some self-authenticating quality that led him to obey without demur. On arrival, he settled as an alien in an unfamiliar land, underwent numerous trials, and was even told to offer his son as a sacrifice, the son on whom the future rested. We hear also how the infertile Sarah conceived a child well past the age of childbearing; and how both Abraham and Sarah died with the promises unfulfilled, faithful to the end (Heb. 11:8-19). Reading the story of Abraham's life may, we hope, open up something of the depths implicit in our own Christian faith.

4

At the time when these retellings of the Abraham story were being put together, there were no Christians and no Muslims. We owe the preservation and transmission of the Abraham story to the industry and piety of Jewish scribes during that long-distant past. In following its course in our commentary, we have noted how, while affirming a particular ethnogenesis, the story of Abraham also transcends it. The outcome of the labors of these learned scribes, which we have followed chapter by chapter, serves as a model and paradigm for the Jew, the Christian, and the Muslim certainly, each in his or her own way. For each, there is a core commitment of faith that is not communicable and cannot be shared. We should listen and try to understand these other commitments, while accepting and exploiting the many things that the three so-called Abrahamic faiths share. But beyond all this, the life story we have narrated will also serve for anyone seeking a model for a religiously serious life, a life lived, like that of Abraham, in the presence of God.

Index of Subjects

Aaron, death of, 182

Abimelech (in Genesis), 22, 86, 90, 90n18, 162, 163n2; the nonaggression pact between Abimelech and Abraham, 86; and Rebekah, 49, 86; and Sarah, 48-51

Abimelech (in Judges), 38, 39

Abiram, 28

Abraham: Abraham in Egypt as a preview of Jacob and his sons going to Egypt during a famine in Palestine, 38; the Abraham story as an attempt to respond to the aftermath of the Babylonian conquest in 286 B.C., 21-24; Abraham's building of altars, 39, 149; Abraham's endangering of the life and honor of Sarah when in Egypt, 44-51; Abraham's family, 27-30; Abraham's name change, 99, 107-8, 108n25, 109-10; as Abram, 1n1; ages of in the Abraham cycle, 80n4; as the antithesis to Nimrod, 19, 105; the Aramean derivation of Abraham's name, 28; attachment of to Hagar, 164; attachment of to Ishmael, 89, 90, 92, 104, 164; in the book of Ezekiel, 8-9; in the book of Genesis, 15-19; in the book of Hebrews, 155; and the ceremony involving dismembered animals and Abraham's nocturnal

trance experience *(tardemah)*, 69-75, 70n8; circumcision of, 84, 97, 103, 108; as a culture hero in the Hellenistic period, 25; death of, 186; death of at the age of 175, 27, 183; death of in Josephus, 185; death of in *Jubilees*, 185; death of "in peace," 74, 74n15, 182-84; in Deutero-Isaiah, 9-11; the exclusion of Abraham's proposed surrogate heir *(ben-mešeq)* after the exclusion of Lot, 67-69, 68n6; in extrabiblical ancient texts, 24-26; extrabiblical ancient texts on Abraham and God's dialogue over the fate of Sodom, 138-39; extrabiblical ancient texts on Abraham's death, 185; extrabiblical ancient texts on Abraham's entertaining of the three guests, 136-37; extrabiblical ancient texts on Abraham's faithfulness, 75-76; extrabiblical ancient texts on Abraham's vision, 77; the first revelation of God to Abraham, 32-36; as "friend," 9; God's covenant with, 18, 24, 104-8; as a Hebrew *(ivri)*, 56; in the historical books, 1-4; in Islam, 39, 41; laughter of, 109, 109n27, 110-11; the narrative traditions about Abraham as a later extension backward in time, 4, 14, 20-21, 64-65, 70-71; the nonaggres-

Index of Modern Authors

Index of Biblical and Other Ancient Texts